A Theory of ISIS

A Theory of ISIS

Political Violence and the
Transformation of the Global Order

Mohammad-Mahmoud Ould Mohamedou

PLUTO PRESS

First published 2018 by Pluto Press
345 Archway Road, London N6 5AA

www.plutobooks.com

British Library Cataloguing in Publication Data
A catalogue record for this book is available from the British Library

ISBN 978 0 7453 9911 9   Hardback
ISBN 978 0 7453 9909 6   Paperback
ISBN 978 1 7868 0169 2   PDF eBook
ISBN 978 1 7868 0171 5   Kindle eBook
ISBN 978 1 7868 0170 8   EPUB eBook

This book is printed on paper suitable for recycling and made from fully
managed and sustained forest sources. Logging, pulping and manufacturing
processes are expected to conform to the environmental standards of the
country of origin.

Typeset by Stanford DTP Services, Northampton, England

Simultaneously printed in the United Kingdom and United States of America

Contents

List of Figures

List of Tables

List of Abbreviations

9/11	Al Qaeda's attacks on the United States, 11 September 2001
AQAP	Al Qaeda in the Arabian Peninsula
AQI	Al Qaeda in Iraq
AQIM	Al Qaeda in the Islamic Maghreb
CIA	Central Intelligence Agency
FBI	Federal Bureau of Investigation
GWOT	Global War on Terror
ICRC	International Committee of the Red Cross
IS	Islamic State
ISI	Islamic State in Iraq
ISIL	Islamic State in Iraq and the Levant
ISIS	Islamic State in Iraq and Syria
PFLP	Popular Front for the Liberation of Palestine
UN	United Nations
UNSC	United Nations Security Council

Acknowledgements

This work closes a series of three books on the transformation of political violence in the late twentieth and early twenty-first century, which I embarked on in September 2001. This transnational trilogy has been concerned with the nature and meaning of the groups Al Qaeda and the Islamic State, and the wider contemporary radical Islamist movement they belong to. The first volume, *Contre-Croisade: Le 11 Septembre et le Retournement du Monde* (the original edition is subtitled *Origines et Conséquences du 11 Septembre*) was written in French (an Arabic version was released in 2010 but it remains untranslated in English) and published in 2004 as I was in the process of moving from Geneva to Boston in the aftermath of the 11 September 2001 attacks (having previously lived for ten years in New York). That work sought to document in as much details as possible the 9/11 attacks and inquire as to their significance in the longer-term history of relations between the Islamic and Western worlds. The second volume sought to expand the investigation from the attacks to the group behind them, widening both the scope and lens of the issues at hand. Researched during a second stay at Harvard University (the first one was in 1996–7 at the Centre for Middle Eastern Studies) at the Programme on Humanitarian Policy and Conflict Research, of which I was the associate director in 2004–8, and where I led an international research project on Transnational and Non-State Armed Groups (TAGs), *Understanding Al Qaeda: The Transformation of War* came out in 2006 (an expanded second edition was released in 2011 and a coda was added in 2013 as a chapter in the book *An International History of Terrorism* co-edited by Jussi Hanhimaki and Bernhard Blumenau). *Understanding Al Qaeda* positioned itself against the overemphasis on Al Qaeda's religiosity, proposing an alternative reading anchored in three concepts it sought to introduce, namely Al Qaeda's 'militarisation of Islamism', 'transnationalisation of terrorism' and 'democratisation of responsibility' (concepts discussed afresh in Chapter 1 in this volume). That work dealt, secondarily, with an unpacking of the *modus operandi* of Al Qaeda (the so-called regional franchises and their meaning) and the 'non-linear' nature of the group's war. Overall, the book was an argument about the transformative, not merely innovative, nature of Al Qaeda's materialisation and Osama Bin Laden's project.

The present volume began in August 2014 with a policy paper – 'ISIS and the Deceptive Rebooting of Al Qaeda', researched and written at the Geneva Centre for Security Policy, of which I was the deputy director and academic dean from 2014 to 2017 – and an invitation by the students of the Middle East Initiative at the Graduate Institute of International and Development Studies in Geneva, Azra Avdagic and Olivia Mathys. The lecture I delivered before the students in September 2014, 'Understanding ISIS: The Islamic State, Al Qaeda and Post-Modern Globalised Violence', is the basis of this book. Earlier versions of some of the arguments were published in various forms in *The Muslim World*, *Project Syndicate*, *Open Democracy*, *The Conversation*, *Les Clefs du Moyen-Orient*, *Le Temps* and *Al Monitor*. The ideas contained here were also aired in a number of venues over the years since the 2014 policy paper and lecture, at conferences and colloquia where I benefited greatly from the thoughtful comments and searching questions from audiences at the Fletcher School in Boston, the University of Exeter, Sciences Po Paris, Sciences Po Grenoble, the University of Saint-Joseph in Beirut, the University of St Andrews, the City University of New York, the London School of Economics and Political Science, the Overseas Development Institute in London, the Institute for Human Sciences in Vienna, the Africa Studies Centre in Leiden, the New School in New York and the Rockefeller Centre in Bellagio, the University of Milan, the University of Geneva, the George C. Marshall Centre for Security Studies, the Egmont Institute in Brussels and the United Nations University in Tokyo. I warmly thank my hosts at these institutions, respectively, Nadim Shehadi, Klejda Mulaj, Bertrand Badie, Jihane Melhouf, Karim Bitar, Bernhard Blumenau, Thomas Weiss, Sara Pantuliano, Shalini Randeria, the late Stephen Ellis and Benjamin Soares, Erin McCandless, Mariele Merlati, Matthias Schulz and Ozcan Yilmaz, Joerg Kuntze, Sebastian Einsiedel, Marta Cali and David Malone for their invitations, hospitality and conversation.

I am particularly indebted to the Graduate Institute in Geneva, where I found a rich and congenial intellectual home in the International History Department. I thank my colleagues at the Institute for the rich exchanges I had with them, notably Philippe Burrin, Davide Rodogno, Gopalan Balachandran, Jussi Hanhimaki, Riccardo Bocco, Alessandro

Monsutti, Keith Krause, André Liebich, Andrea Bianchi, Carolyn Biltoft, Andrew Clapham, Jean-François Bayart, Paola Gaeta, Gilles Carbonnier and Isabelle Schulte-Tenckoff. Debates with the students at the Graduate Institute in my classes on political violence and on state-building and war-making were invariably inspiring and I thank them all for their intelligent and refreshing engagement, and I extend my appreciation to the staff at the library of the Graduate Institute for their valuable and efficient assistance in locating key works. Cherished conversational partners I had on these issues included Ahmad Khalidi, François Burgat, Bertrand Badie, Melissa Finn, Adam Shatz, Christophe Bourseiller, Nadia Marzouki, Eric Degila, Maha Yahya and Anthony Samrani. Other friends and colleagues who supported me with their encouragement or by sharing ideas include Oliver Jütersonke, Dominic Eggel, Victor Santos Rodriguez, Adrien and Nathaniel Burkhalter, Gyula Csurgai, Katia Papagianni, Bruce Fudge and Christophe Rime, and I thank them for their intellectual camaraderie. For his confidence in and support of this book, I extend my full gratitude to my editor at Pluto Press, David Shulman, a true gentleman. Finally, Matthew Bamber, a brilliant young scholar working on the state-building aspects of the Islamic State, provided valuable research assistance and expertly shepherded the chronology of events, and I thank him for his excellent collaboration.

My most inexpressible debt is to my father and mother, and to my family whose unconditional support was always the single most precious source of sustenance. I dedicate this work to them, the balms of my soul, my beloved wife Shainese, and my cherished children Bahiya, Kemal and Zaynab, with all my love.

Mohammad-Mahmoud Ould Mohamedou
27 July 2017

Introduction
The Islamic State and Political Violence in the Early Twenty-First Century

Madam, your imperial Majesty gives me life back by killing Turks.

Voltaire, Letter to Catherine II of Russia,
Ferney, France, 30 October 1769

Little babies in make-up terrorise the Western world.

Prince, 'Crystal Ball' (1986)

What is the Islamic State (IS)? What lies behind this name? From whence did it originate and what is its function? What meaning has been given to it, and for what purposes? What does the manifestation of this phenomenon reveal? What do the narratives built around it say about the evolution of international relations in the early twentieth century, and not merely about security affairs or counter-terrorism? How is it that within a mere three-month period – the summer of 2014 – a previously nondescript acronym, ISIS (Islamic State in Iraq and Syria), became, so rapidly and so globally, an instantly recognisable brand name, at once carrying threat for millions of people and appeal for thousands? Where did this entity come from and where is it heading?

This book attempts to answer these questions through an examination of the place IS occupies in contemporary international history and politics. The critical interpretation offered here is a departure from the dominant existing literature, which portrays the group primarily as an apocalyptic religious entity bent solely on destroying the West. Considering the organisation's declarative religious identity as one of adornment, and secondary to its more consequential social and political nature, this analysis argues instead that a conceptual geology of IS holds the key to its understanding, and is to be found in three related dimensions: a continuation of the earlier armed radical Islamist group Al Qaeda and that entity's deeper upstream regional context; degenerated political developments in Iraq in the aftermath of the American invasion of that country in March 2003 and later in Syria in 2011; and the wider rise of an original type of political violence linked to both the unfinished and resurgent practices of the colonial era and more recent problematic military interventionism. In reconstructing this complex and interwoven genealogy of the group, the analysis similarly situates IS in three different and interrelated contexts, constitutive, it is argued, of a transformation moment of violence-production in the early twentieth century: post-colonialism, post-globalisation and post-modernity. As such, the work traces the emergence and evolution of the organisation and identifies its nature, highlighting an understanding whereby *periodisation* and *spatialisation* of IS warrant further qualitative expansion, beyond the available narrative of mad-terrorist-group-bent-on-destroying-the-West-and-establishing-a-Caliphate, if they are to be meaningfully accounted for historically.

Since its emergence, IS has been studied overwhelmingly under a reductionist and sensationalist mainstream journalistic approach and through policy-oriented security expertise – the same twofold perspective that had been used previously for analysis of Al Qaeda in the aftermath of the 11 September 2001 (9/11) attacks on the United States. Focus on the group's extreme violence and its alienating discourse has prevented deeper examination of the political and social conditions behind its rise. In contradistinction, the present study discusses the IS group from a historical and social science perspective, unpacking its dynamics not merely in terms of the group's terrorist nature and its religious rhetoric, but with a view to arguing for a reconceptualisation of the production of violence by IS – a group this analysis locates at the dawn of a novel form of globally privatised, transnationalised, interweaved and hybrid insurgent political violence. It is submitted that the cultural mixity and multilayered nature of IS inaugurated a revealing moment in both the nature and direction of contemporary political violence, while echoing its deeper colonial underpinnings. Once expressed only domestically or internationally, the new violence now travels back and forth, at once impacting periphery and metropolis with equal acuity and consequential unpredictability, as the full spectrum of the interaction space is occupied rather than a single point. 'Return to sender' is in effect the motto of the violence counter-produced, remixed and shipped back by IS to the imperial centres, but also to the group's immediate domestic and regional contexts of states it seeks to reconfigure. In turn further deepening the vicious circle, defensive reaction to that beamed violence has led to a renewal of authoritarianism in the Middle East anᴇ faltering of democracy in the West, as seen in the rampant, all-purpose securitisation and unrestrained Islamophobia rising in the United States and Europe.

Close to two decades after the 9/11 attacks conducted in New York and Washington by the transnational non-state armed group Al Qaeda, and several years into IS's own saga, the patterns of a transforming form of globalised political violence are cementing, and the longer-term impact of the Al Qaeda/IS story is vividly perceptible beyond the latest episodic 'crisis', 'attack' or 'terror'. Although the deeper questions about ISIS abound by virtue of the novelty the group carries, they have not been asked fully and unpacked scientifically. Captive to a self-imposed normative cul-de-sac on the issue of radical Islamism generally, and Al Qaeda and IS specifically, social sciences have so far failed to initiate a historically contextualised, global (not merely Western or Westernised) and nuanced discussion on the phenomena at hand. Such persistent lack of deeper analysis is consequential, as a ritual of contorted commentary on the international situation ushered in by the two groups has solidified in spite of being unconvincing to many. Anchored in the matrix developed in the autumn of 2001 following the 9/11 attacks on New York and Washington, this zeitgeist-seeking, catastrophising sequence is at the heart of both the conceptual misunderstanding of IS and the policy impasse, leading to the replay of violence in recent years. For every time a new radical Islamism-related attack takes place in New York, Washington, London, Paris, Brussels or Berlin, a ritual of denial of the deeper political issues plays out in an increasingly familiar fashion. The sequence is performed thus: shock gives way to fear followed by anger; security experts step up hurriedly in television studios and on social media to denounce the lack of preparation by the authorities; specialists in radical Islamism (or simply Islam) follow, declaring that IS (previously Al Qaeda) has been weakened, is on its way to be defeated and is merely lashing out with desperate attacks; Muslim communities in Western countries are called out and racist and violent attacks against them sometimes take place (hours after the March 2016 attacks in Brussels a #stopislam movement started trending, revealing the depth of the bias that had come to overtake sectors of the Western world, readily associating Islam and terrorism); sympathy movements for the victims or city where the attack took place are set up (*Je suis Charlie*, I am Brussels, etc.); calls for tougher legislation (surveillance mechanisms, 'ions, nationality measures, immigration procedures, dress codes, access to pools, prayer sites, etc.) are ... arrests are made in neighbourhoods where Muslim ...are known to reside and bombing is redoubled in Iraq, Syria, ...ghanistan, Yemen or Libya.

In such a context, where ethos becomes pathos, and as was the case for Al Qaeda in the 2000s, IS became in the 2010s the bogeyman of international security – *naturally named* as a *natural* threat. Yet as Salman Sayyid remarks, 'the act of naming is an exercise in history-making … A name is not just a label that can simply be attached to something that is already there: it is the means by which heterogeneous elements are marshalled together to become the intrinsic features of the named entity.'[1] That marshalling was the unexamined mainstay of what IS heralded for the world, for the Middle East and for the West in particular. Above and beyond IS itself, its extremism and violence, such evocation has deeper problematic roots. In the contemporary political geography, terrorism has been not-so-subtly placed in the middle of a canvas that has been painted in the vivid green and black colours of Islam. As a result, the notion of terrorism is now in a state of conceptual deformation, whereby the elasticity it has been given in recent years allows it to serve almost exclusively the purpose of identifying threats against Western states and societies as coming primarily from Islam and faceless Muslim attackers. To be certain, terrorism suffered by other regions is reported regularly, and is portrayed equally as an ill of our times to be dealt with urgently. Indeed, according to the Global Terrorism Index released annually by the Institute of Economics and Peace, the first casualties of terrorism in this period were Iraqis, Afghans and Nigerians. However, the core representation of terrorism per se in the well-embroidered media and policy drapery is centrally the menace it represents to the West. An illustration of this – only partially coded – reality is the inconsistent use of the term 'terrorism' by mainstream media, at once resorting to it reflexively when attacks have Muslims associated with them, and opting for another terminology ('attack', 'shooting', 'security incident', 'assault', 'situation', etc.) when events of a similar nature have different types of perpetrators involved. Hours after a gunman had performed terroristically in Munich, Germany, on 22 July 2016 – killing eight civilians, mostly children and teenagers, in a mall – authorities were 'still considering whether this was a terrorist event' and the main international media outlets (CNN, BBC) were refraining from using the word when video had already surfaced of the masked attacker boasting about his murderous actions. In an obvious attempt to link the ongoing event to the question of migration from the Middle East which has engulfed German and European politics since 2014, the first question put by journalists to the Munich chief of police at the press briefing that evening was an inquiry as to how long the perpetrator had lived in Germany. When, in February 2017, US President Donald Trump provided a list of 78 recent terrorist attacks (from September 2014 to December 2016), which he claimed misleadingly had not been reported by the media, he revealingly overlooked an anti-Muslim terrorist attack that had taken place a few days earlier in Canada, which a Republican congressman who supported his policies justified. Defending Trump's stance, US Representative Sean Duffy declared to CNN that 'there is a difference' between terror acts by white people and those committed by Muslims.[2] When, on 19 June 2017, Darren Osborn drove a van into a crowd near the Finsbury Park Mosque in London, re-enacting a terrorist *modus operandi* seen earlier in London, Berlin and Nice, the BBC and CNN refrained from using the term terrorism for several hours, initially depicting the attack as a 'collision'.

The primary subtext of the IS discussion is that terrorism is today largely serving the purpose of naming Islam as an enemy without actually naming it. The Global War on Terror (GWOT) that was declared in September 2001 by the George W. Bush administration has almost exclusively targeted radical Islamist groups; initially Al Qaeda, then its franchises and affiliates, and eventually IS. The power of a hegemonic discursive conflict of the sort the GWOT represented was in effect to attain *a victory of interpretation*, ensuring that a particular viewpoint triumphed,[3] which played out precisely in this fashion. Two logics emanating from the Global South itself enabled the furthering and perpetuation of this state of affairs. The first was a similar, all-purpose delegitimising and criminalising use of the 'T' term by authoritarian regimes such as Abdel Fattah al Sisi's in Egypt and Bashar al Assad's in Syria against their political opponents (regardless of the actual use of violence by those opponents). The second was the consequential propping-up of these authoritarian-clientelist systems by their partners in the North, even in the wake of the 2011 Arab Spring, in the name of fighting terrorism and under a logic of needed 'security partners' (as had long been the case with Hosni Mubarak's regime in Egypt or Zein al Abidine Ben Ali's in Tunisia, among others). Consequentially, and again regardless of the actual terrorism performed by the radical groups, a diffuse, intangible, unfathomable 'terrorism' endowed with a free-floating, independent existence is presented as having taken over the world parasitically. Omnipresent, the threat is defined almost only in relation to the presence of Islam in its vicinity and of ISIS ostentatiously.

Regularly replayed and patterned in such depoliticised and culturalised ways, the contemporary presentation of political violence has not evolved significantly beyond this static dimension. The public commentary context in which the representation of IS was initiated in earnest in mid-2014, when the group emerged publicly, illustrated that powerfully. Just as Al Qaeda had been called a formula system, a venture capitalist firm, a commissioning editor, a newspaper, a television production, a publishing house, a wealthy university, a financial godfather, a transnational corporation, a franchise outfit and a multinational holding company, IS conjured up a variety of similarly eclectic names: revolutionary chameleon, cult, super-gang, proto-state, network, state of mind and online Caliphate. Beyond the groups' objective complexities, the proliferation of appellations is indicative of a discomfort in the presence of the type of intricate actors that both Al Qaeda and IS represent. Indeed, the very action of naming the new group ('an exercise in history-making') became itself an issue: ISIS, ISIL or Daesh?[4] As in the Zapruder film, the disconnects between what was seen and what was unseen, hidden or imagined, interpreted or reinterpreted, became legion.

Misunderstanding IS

This book examines the history and the historiography of the organisation of IS. It argues that the IS phenomenon takes place as neo-colonialism continued lastingly to define the setting in which the group appeared in Iraq; as globalisation[5] deepened worldwide, offering further opportunities for the organisation to beam its violence internationally; and as modernity accelerated, bringing North and South into an ever-closer interface, with individual actors on both sides experiencing related, but not similar, radical insurgent and violent rebellious urges. It is proposed that, above and beyond the important domestic and regional story of the evolution of radical Islamism, IS is more importantly the manifestation of the persistent dystrophies that have long been playing out politically between the West and the Middle East (and, beyond, the Islamic world). Furthermore, the book argues that the path embarked on in facing up to the group in the name of the defence of democracy has paradoxically fuelled authoritarian patterns in the West itself, as the effect of lingering colonial strategies and more recent interventionist outlooks used to control distant lands are echoed corruptively in the heart of the Western metropolis. These nascent but possibly lasting dimensions are playing out in largely unexamined ways, as relates to the discussion of IS. However, for the majority of commentators the problematique has remained one of 'terrorism and counter-terrorism', 'them against us', 'Middle East strife' (a region given only in terms of 'unreadability', 'enigma' and 'riddle') and 'Islam and its problem'.[6] The actual political archaeology of the group has been sidelined,[7] displaced by a Pravda-like focus on religion[8] and rah-rah presentism that is emptying the historical context of its crucial backdrop and pinpointable consequences. The radical Islamist group – as the titles of most books devoted to it denote in their echoing of the policy phraseology – is apprehended as a 'phoenix' 'cult' of 'strangers' that has 'madness and methodology' in an 'empire of fear', setting a 'trap', with a 'doomsday vision' whose 'brutal' 'rise' is a 'new threat' that 'can't be ignored' and must be 'defeated' in this 'great war of our time'. The larger setting of this call-and-response is the absence of a dispassionate, intelligent framework to understanding the question of contemporary terrorism and its permutations away from a unilateral, state-centric and depoliticised stance.[9] Such work has had a direct relationship with the contemporary practice of power and the projection of force in increasingly culturalised and long-skewed international relations. In effect, the uncritical and unreflective mobilisation of prestidigitator expertise on terror is today a *political* process featuring officialdom, journalism and their networks. However problematic this may be, it is nonetheless of lesser concern here, as it remains a matter or prerogative (including in the case of the media per editorial choices). What matters more to an academic analysis seeking to conceptualise IS is that such practice has resulted in an un-nuanced under-theorisation of one of the most important developments of our times. As a result, academia has remained captive to a simplified twofold narrative about apocalyptic terrorism and theology readings. That horizon-closing narrative has not so much found its ways into institutions of higher learning as it has stunned them into emollience, since it has not yet been debunked – and also because its power derives from the fact that it is the product of a mostly Western-based uncritical understanding of societies that are not Western but which are beholden to that reading. (For example, Malian newspapers circa 2012 reflexively calling Paris-based terrorism experts to seek enlightenment on what was happening up north *in their own country* with Al Qaeda in the Islamic Maghreb (AQIM) was a tell-tale sign of such withdrawal from self-representation and intellectual dependence on the former colonial power.)

The wider discussion that has not been tapped into, and was indeed kept at bay when it comes to understanding the origins of the contemporary transnational violence of IS (and before it Al Qaeda), concerns two important ongoing phenomena of our times that have been termed respectively the 'decolonisation of international relations' and the 'decolonising of war'.[10] As concerns the new breed of non-state armed groups, these ongoing shifts primarily imply, I argue here, a transnational repositioning of violence – precisely what Al Qaeda introduced in the 1990s and 2000s (see Chapter 2), and what IS deepened in the 2010s (see Chapters 3 and 4). Grammatically, colonial war was *inter*national. Postcolonial conflict is, for its part, eminently *trans*national. Both connect in the martial nature of that encounter between actors, times and spaces, and if, as Isabel Hull summed it up, imperialism was war,[11] then so too are Al Qaeda's and IS's actions essentially military. Despite the military studies and philosophical works at both ends of the spectrum, the revolutionary cross-pollination of these strands has not been researched with a view to deciphering the situation in relation to its historically intertwined *dual* Muslim and Western context. Instead, starting in autumn 2014, the emergence of IS led to the publication of a number of works on the group *telling* its *inside* story in isolation from those histories and contexts.[12] As the (self-standing) 'problem of ISIS' took shape thus: the military-academic network was expanded to the military-academic-terrorism-expert on this issue and, just as had been the case a decade earlier with Al Qaeda, the discussion remained explicitly about mapping the defeat of a repellent entity bent on annihilation of the West. When present in the analysis, the entanglement of domestic and foreign was confined to matters of 'failed policies' (in Washington or in Baghdad) or of dangers of the spillover of these actors (coming to attack Fortress West or returning as 'foreign fighters'). Commentators in Western mainstream media oscillated between the appearance of objectivity and the knowingness of the corporate-driven culture of sensationalism, and moved ever closely to giving voice solely to the sentiments of an irate and frightened public rather than offering sober and contextualised analysis, while all the time stressing the religion of the assailants. In time the problem emerged thus: to understand Western terrorists of the 1970s such as the German Red Army Faction or the Italian Red Brigades, one is invited to examine the societal conditions of post-war Germany and Italy, the ambient malaise in these countries 25 years after Nazism and fascism, and their relationship with their rebellious youth; to make sense of Al Qaeda or IS, one is asked to read the Qur'an.

Such voluntary matriculating in a school for the blind, as Tennessee Williams once put it poetically, is arresting and deserves emphasis as it is in effect a component of the problem at the root of the question of contemporary political violence. The public deployment of tokenism expertise on IS is itself a symptom of this lost analysis with at least four trends dominating the discourse on IS: impatient journalistic accounts, one-dimensional security expertise, ethereal Islamism exegesis and short-term think tank analysis. To varying degrees, these approaches share the following: the evidence used for the analysis is taken unquestionably from often unverifiable governmental statements; boastful statements by IS itself or 'found' documents are accepted at face value (one can only be amazed at the proclivity of these non-documenting-inclined groups to produce compulsively and lose regularly such materials, and indeed at the luck of the counter-terrorists in systematically recovering readable self-explanatory materials[13]); emotionalism is worn on the sleeve by analysts who are expected to be detached; sensationalism is the mode of communication; and analysis knows only two directions, that of rise or fall, victory or defeat, new or old. Who's-up-and-who's-down scorekeeping accounts of the rise of IS are, however, not sufficient to make sense of the incubating, asynchronous and dysrhythmic transformation of terrorism taking place at the hands of this group. Such 'rise' talk also locates explanations of violence in the stance of the Western observer who, atop the hill, scans the landscape for threats to his dominion. Can the subaltern restrategise his or her violence? If he or she actually does, and visits it upon the Westerner's living room, as IS did in the extreme, then surely that larger shift in meaning is happening factually. Yet, time and again, willy-nilly, analysts and experts take us down the self-satisfied road of elevation of religious theatrics or demonisation of identity, with the ways of the *homo islamicus* observed with a magnifying glass, from Raqqa to the French suburbs. What matters is solely the materialisation of a religion- and identity-driven problem that needs to be seen as disappearing as soon as possible. The more this story proceeded monotonically, the more its intellectual contradictions became visible as a matter of political violence dealt with minimally and peripherally by historians, political scientists and sociologists. In effect, media vigilantism, terrorism expert pronouncements and condescending interrogations of Islam and its long-awaited *aggiornamento* have joined hands to produce a non-history of one of the dominant forms of contemporary non-state violence.

Locating uncritically, the violence of IS in the religious mantle of the movement was the first and often only choice made by many observers. No matter how many facts piled up to demonstrate the political nature of the violence and the relevance of wider contexts (colonialism, post-colonialism, interventionism, authoritarianism, rebellion, armed conflicts), Muslim studies, or rather studies of Muslims, invariably remained the preferred locus of alleged explanation. This rising Muslimology (often with roots in works such as Raphael Patai's racist 1973 book *The Arab Mind*) took Orientalism to new dimensions. Beyond the imagined Muslim and the extrapolated ins and outs of Islamist jurisprudence (what Irfan Ahmad calls 'an over-legalisation of Islam and Shari'a'[14]) came two new categories: the reformed Muslim and the faux Muslim (and so inevitably too the Uncle Tom Muslim). Stunned in this way, or allowing themselves to be, international scholars were made to understand that thinking on Al Qaeda and IS should be limited to those exercises of dutifully, one-dimensionally compiling information and data demonstrating the group's violence, irrationality and dangerousness. Any effort to map the groups' historical significance beyond those confines ran the risk of being depicted as an exercise in *political* thinking – a peculiar value-judgement, we should note, seldom applied to work on other questions of international affairs. Engagement with the issue beyond these given narratives is often near-unrecognisable to many mainstream journalists (who need to translate it in the by-now-familiar vernacular of reporting on these entities as variably 'on the rise', 'on the retreat', 'adopting new tactics', 'developing new ways to finance themselves', 'kidnapping sexual slaves', 'using human shields', 'expanding foothold', etc.) and stigmatised intellectually or deemed controversial. Soon enough coloured as 'angry' (particularly if it is voiced from the South), critical analyses are next asked to offer solutions, lest their usefulness be lessened. Skip the diagnosis (we know it) – solutions please.[15] Indeed, if formulated – justice, state-building, international reciprocity – these are dismissed as unrealistic; the religion of pragmatism overtaking the discussion. Yet such side-stepping pronouncements are precisely the reproduction of a controlled process emptying the violence of its meaning and therefore enabling its circularity. Evidently ethnocentric and a sleight of hand, such disciplining of terrorism and of Muslims is spread paradigmatically, as a world religion then becomes regarded as being held by predicaments;[16] trapped, it has to reconcile so as to exit its violence and backwardness, or so goes the reading. The narrative next becomes a self-fulfilling reality, and watching stories about Muslims and their 'inclination to terrorism' unpacked by talk-show hosts (such as Bill Maher[17]), citizens start taking matters into their vigilante-like hands and ordering flight attendants to de-board individuals deemed 'suspicious', or because they feel 'ill at ease' sitting next to them. As these dispositions are ultimately endorsed in official and private business regulations, as they were with the Donald Trump administration's 2017 Muslim ban, the international system drifts into irrationality, perpetuating injustice and fuelling the very violence it seeks to end. In that context, work on IS is expected to be solely of the niche technocratic terrorism expertise kind. Such disciplining of political violence away from its political anchoring and into terrorism per se has, as noted, produced a form of anti-knowledge.[18] Consequently, any political militancy or social dissidence that turns violent runs the risk of earning the label 'terrorism';[19] becoming an open-and-shut matter of delegitimation, as the assignment of that term ensures the non-discussion of the issues raised by the given group.

The literature on IS is thus dominated by the following recurring phraseology: abhorrent, barbaric, threatening, chaoplexic, brutal, savage and apocalyptic. Introduced forcefully post-9/11, the terms became part of a repertoire dusted off regularly post-Paris, post-Brussels, post-Berlin and post-Manchester with each new attack. Foundationally, President George W. Bush spoke of the 9/11 attackers as 'heirs of the murderous ideologies of the twentieth century … fascism, Nazism and totalitarianism'. Such terminology is indulged without the audience learning anything fundamentally new or specific about groups depicted as atavistic evil; a species that warrants extermination. These narratives have in effect dehistoricised what IS and Al Qaeda represent. Instead, the perspectives unpack the nature of the Islamist extremist groups in ways that exceptionalise their violence as unique and uniquely evil. The criminal sexual exploitation and rape of women captured by IS is, for instance, called by one author a specific 'theology of rape'.[20] The crime of rape is not sufficient as a category of depiction and must be elevated to an additional actor-specific Islamist dimension. Such productions are unscientific, as they are formulaic and seek to allay public fears and accompany policy formulation artefactually. The pantomime of stylised rituals and storytelling about IS partakes, more importantly, of the making of a neo-imperial culture that ascribes irrational barbarity to political extreme violence so as to avoid addressing the reasons for that violence's recurrence. With each new attack, the same set of arguments is restated tirelessly to establish authoritatively the apocalyptic nature of the actor. Arguing that we are missing the point if we delve too much into history, such instantly catchy analyses decouple the actors from their context to endow them with a maximal dangerousness underwritten by an unshakeably evil character displayed by these super-predators. The result is not so much advancement of knowledge but emotional release and ethical pronouncement.

The narratives are also provided with grounding through repeated references to alleged documents exposing the groups' cult-like demonic ways that would have been produced and read dutifully by all these violent actors around the world. In the 2000s, that influence was attributed to the Syrian radical Islamist ideologue Mustapha bin Abd al Qadir Setmariam Nasar, known as Abu Mus'ab al Suri, who had authored the book *Da'wat al Muqawama al Islamiya al 'Alamiya* (*The Global Islamic Resistance Call*). A decade later, another book, *Idarat al Tawahoush: Akhtar Marhala satamour biha al Umma* (*The Management of Savagery: The Most Dangerous Phase the Umma will go Through*), written by the Al Qaeda senior operator Mohammed Khalil al Hukayma, known as Abu Bakr Naji, was alleged to be the primary inspiration for the violent ways of IS. Besides the fact that such actors would, in effect (in the latter case), be referring to themselves as 'savages' (*wuhush*), or contradictorily praising savagery while claiming 'noble' religious aims, such non-demonstrated alleged inspiration proceeds very much from a *Mein Kampf*-influenced, Western-centric perspective, locating agency in a discrete document/actor/ideology whose evil nature can then be referred to as a stand-alone reason for the violence observed, and thereby excise the political and historical components out of that equation. This approach also ends up presenting IS in terms of a homogeneity impacted by a single ideology, when again there is no evidence to that effect. Indeed, it is arguably quite the opposite, with IS fielding a system of continuities and ruptures under a dominant trait of hybridity. This is because IS dwells continuously in fluidity: emerging from a mutated scene (the emergence of self-empowering militarised Islamism in the 1980s and 1990s) it has gone into a further transformed one (the global expansion and atomisation of the transnational groups in the 2000s and 2010s). The under-theorisation of IS is then the continuation of the under-conceptualisation of Al Qaeda, and treating IS as an already-settled question has led to unsatisfactory responses to the group's bewildering actions. The cementing of that pattern is also indicative of given narratives, which in classical Orientalising fashion claim to know and represent the actor better than himself. A canon of Al Qaeda- and IS-customised terrorology is now available and can be consulted by students seeking to study these groups. To this can be added a latter-day 'jihadology' built primarily by a younger group tweeting insight (responses to the group on that front have ranged from declaring digital war on it to satirising it, as does *The Bigh Daddy Show* – a series of short cartoon videos launched online in July 2016). There is, overall, a distinct and by now recognisable one-dimensionalisation of the issues that is present in all these works that study 'ISIS', merely as an object of curiosity, a zoo-located thing that is at once exciting to observe and dangerous to touch.

One route to remedying those shortcomings is to upgrade the presence of alternative histories, and reintroduce a thoroughgoing political history perspective on the question of violence. As noted, thinking about IS itself has been led by security-driven Western-centric approaches and derivative paradigms gone global (as many think tanks and security experts in the South faithfully reproduce those perspectives on their own societies). Specifically, what is missed by such readings is the central notion that IS functions inherently at multiple levels, and that therefore the security lens can only inform on one aspect. At a first level, IS is but the continuation of the Al Qaeda saga; formed in its womb, once part of its fold and in time seeking to replace it, it does not escape echoing in its midst the self-capacitating militarised radical Islamism logic that presided over the birth of Al Qaeda and its 1995–2005 heyday. At a second level, IS is the result of the societal degeneration of Iraq following the 2003 US invasion and the large-scale and unceasing brutality that overtook that country. Under that same dimension, the group is the result of the situation in Syria after 2011, with leaders of IS capitalising on the civil war in that neighbouring country to reboot their Al Qaeda in Iraq (AQI) franchise of Al Qaeda into a new, battle-hardened entity also made up of the remnants of Saddam Hussein's military and secular Ba'ath party, able to move on two territories and fold them into a larger and more ambitious strategy. Finally, at a third level, IS is a global phenomenon whereby some 25,000 to 30,000 individuals (including teenage girls and whole families) have flocked to the territory the group controlled in the Levant to join this project. The sum total of this construction yields a group that must be understood first and foremost in relation to different levels and to its epoch. This transformation reveals a matrix of the new groups around the world that increasingly behave in such a mode – now local, now transnational, all the time repositioning and adapting to dynamics of post-globalisation. The absence of a clinical analysis of these actors is also an indication of a consequential normative dissociation. The removing of the political is a prelude to the acceptability of the forceful response, with management techniques rather than knowledge and scientific inquiry as a sheet-anchor. This has produced a demand for quick solutions, the search for a single response in the face of complexity and the constant staging of dichotomous thought applied to anything labelled terrorism. From CNN's *Crossfire* in the 1990s to RT's *Crosstalk* in the 2010s, by way of Al Jazeera's *Al Itijah al Mu'akiss* in the 2000s and the totality of Fox News' style of reporting, the simplification of current affairs to essentialised viewpoints has become a problematic trademark that migrated logically to the discussion on IS once the group appeared. In effect, IS could not be understood any differently once the Al Qaeda demo had been circulated successfully. As a result of such international affairs' socialisation-in-the-making, many policymakers and students increasingly approach foreign matters with impatience for history and for multilayered and ambiguous phenomena. Instead, they readily search 'quick fixes', 'overarching concepts', 'lead factors', 'so-what's-the-answers', 'cut-to-the-chases' and 'bottom lines'. Shortcuts of this type can hardly provide helpful – much less valid – responses to the arresting mutation of violence playing in the late twentieth and early twenty-first century. 'They may have known the plot and salient details of Joseph Conrad's *Heart of Darkness*, but they were unable to tell you why the story was important', as Chris Hedges remarked about the examination of imperial darkness being lost on contemporary students. This is arguably because, as Philip Roth noted, 'when everything is requisitioned for the cause, there is no room for ... history or science ... that is seriously undertaken'.[21]

Why then did terrorism become war? Why was that war declared 'global', and then 'long'? The 'intrinsic endlessness'[22] of the GWOT, redubbed the 'Long War' since 2006, was indeed an indication of its downloaded nature as a power exercise, and the pre-determinacy of these answers allowing pertinent questions to be avoided. *The neglected dimension of the IS discussion is the political one and the historical one.* As Des Freedman writes:

> It's worth asking what the point is of 24/7 reporting of terror attacks. Is it to provide blanket coverage of despair and horror, which is what the attackers are said to want? Is it to construct a 'national sentiment', to lay the basis for further securitisation? Or should it be to provide explanation – or at least some degree of context – to help people understand the political circumstances in which terror thrives? This last is the approach that is largely missing from the deluge of coverage, and is often dismissed as somehow apologising for acts of terror. But without a recognition of geopolitical dynamics and recent Western military intervention overseas terror attacks come to be seen as entirely mysterious, spectral events.[23]

The straight-jacketing of the terrorism discussion evidences a larger problem of the paternalism, chauvinism and Orientalism that sit atop security discussions of issues playing out in the Middle East and North Africa, and the wider Muslim world and sub-Saharan Africa. It is not yet fathomable to many that, beyond the threat conceptualisation, a development outside of the West may be able to transform the nature of international order, wrestling agency of these matters away from the 'centre' and to the 'periphery' (concepts that are themselves problematic).[24] The result of the dominant cultural cantonisation of terrorism is that, at a point, it is no longer necessary even to describe or establish the Islamist groups' alleged relationship to a given terrorist event – simply stating it does the trick performatively and ubiquitously.[25] As Michael Bathia remarks about the terrorism phraseology, 'once assigned, the power of a name is such that the process by which the name was selected generally disappears and a series of normative associations, motives and characteristics are attached to the named'.[26] This has been perfected with IS and before that with Al Qaeda. Isolated, terrorism is boxed-in reflexively and solely with radical Islamism. Such objectification is then unpacked as regards a single leading (Islamist) terrorism actor. Discussion of IS takes place in that context per an exceptionalising of the 'barbaric' violence that plays out in such 'perennially troubled' spots such as the Middle East. Yet, many who are shocked today at the trouble, violence, vengeance, revenge on women and children, physical destruction, chaos, thirst for blood and ethnic cleansing forget that these are precisely the ills that, for instance, played out in the heart of Europe a few decades ago in the aftermath of World War II.[27] Properly reading IS is not, however, solely about de-Westernising its construct or reminding ourselves of forgotten histories of violence elsewhere. Local representations of IS have been equally problematic. There, the overall problem is at least twofold. On the one hand, as noted, authoritarian states play the terrorism card very well, gaming fragility and modulating assistance requests to keep Washington, London and Paris constantly in need of their guardianship of these *troubled* spots from where *danger* brews and swarms against the Western fortress. On the other hand, Arab and Muslim conspiracy-minded analysts constantly seek answers to the self-serving and misleading questions 'Who created IS?' and 'Who created Al Qaeda?', invariably pointing to the US Central Intelligence Agency (CIA), and in so doing stripping non-state actors in their midst of violent agency and contradictorily handing the keys of their own history to those imperialists or former colonialists they readily denounce. (A revealing moment in the unrestrained instrumentalisation of the meaning of IS took place in August 2016, when the leader of the Lebanese group Hezbollah, Hassan Nasrallah, echoed US presidential candidate Donald Trump's words that US President Barack Obama was 'the leader of IS'.)

Following Edward Said, the literature on Al Qaeda and IS of the past 20 years can today already be assessed as mostly neo-Orientalist, for just as the original nineteenth-century Orientalism was not merely an *ex post facto* rationalisation of colonialism but worked to justify it in parallel, the current wave of commentary about 'Al Qaeda/IS' serves to normalise the acceptance of a narrative that depicts these groups as enemies of humanity beyond the pale, foes who need only be exterminated because of who they are culturally and religiously, eschewing or minimising larger political dynamics and context. The silences in the terrorism text *are*, however, the text – a culturalist, inconsistent and exceptionalist one. What has to be left behind at this end-of-the-2010s stage is what has played out problematically in the first quarter of the twenty-first century, and which Hamid Dabashi captures crisply:

The recodification of racism ... whereby the Jew became the Muslim and the Black the brown (or Arab, in a colour-coded register) was predicated on a fundamental logical flaw, whereby the criminal acts of a band of militant Muslim adventurers was ... identified as definitive to a world religion and called 'Islamic Terrorism'. Islam is a world religion; terrorism is a political act, indiscriminately targeting civilian populations – examples of which in modern history include the Irgun in Palestine, the Khmer Rouge in Cambodia, the Janjaweed in Darfur. The events of 9/11 and other similar incidents are sporadic criminal acts – conditioned, of course, by wanton American imperialism around the globe.[28]

The building up of IS as an all-purpose jack-in-the-box and jack of all trades allows the disappearance of the political question. It is time to, in turn, decouple the respective yet related history of IS and of Al Qaeda from the security and securitisation narrative they have been captive to. Relocating those histories in a context beyond these tested confines is no easy task, so entrenched has that narrative become. Such intellectually disobedient rupture can help establish a richer genealogy of the non-state armed groups currently projecting themselves beyond states, borders and societies. The pluriversal, forward-moving radical project of IS as a twenty-first century tech-savvy producer of post-modern globalised violence cannot be accounted for by zombie explanations that proceed from the hermetic sheet-anchors of Orientalism and securitisation. The obvious extreme violence of the group has been used as an easy bulwark against asking the larger and pertinent questions regarding why such violence has been used and what attempted legitimacy is being pursued.[29] These questions start against an invisible background.

The issue of IS – and that of Al Qaeda before it – is located in the context of a riverbed of long-racialised international relations and a larger issue of understudied, non-Western insecurities. By the time the discussion of 'anarchy' and 'intervention' had gathered steam in the 1990s and was then followed in the 2000s by the emergence of the neo-imperial security state, discourse about terrorism had already began settling down immutably in its negation of the political nature of the questions at the source of the manifested violence.[30] To open the Pandora's box of the political nature of terrorism instead of dutifully implementing the discourse about identity and religion is therefore, by now, to disturb a cemented power sequence. As the issues played out towards the 2020s horizon, they were then both the culmination of a pre-existing sequence morphing into its crucial next stage, and the enabling of a revisionist examination of colonial domination whereby that experience was now presented with aplomb as benign and orderly – and therefore, in new ways, they irrevocably needed to halt things such as Al Qaeda and IS.[31] As the two groups emerged amid that dissociation, there has been no genuine erosion of the earlier colonial mindset that had presided over the setting up of international relations in the early twentieth century.[32] Accordingly, the rising groups were looked upon logically as evil in the same manner that rebels had been under the colonial configuration. Facilitated by the groups' resort to extreme violence, that delegitimation conveys larger dimensions that take us back to both the colonial era and the birth of international relations as we have come to know them, study and teach them, practice them and all along accept their skewed, incestuous framework fatalistically and uncritically.

The (important) study of what IS is must be wrestled from the hijacking it has suffered at the hands of reductionist, a-historical and culturally chauvinist[33] accounts. Tellingly, 'security', 'the international community' and 'terrorism' are, in this context, too often coded words for an asymmetrical architecture of interaction among nations, terms whose nature escapes fundamental questioning and, for now, the possibility of redefinition. Security for whom? Threat by whom? Who is included empirically in that international community led arbitrarily by a group of five self-appointed countries at the outcome of a conflict in Europe 70 years ago? What is considered terrorism in a context that in effect does not acknowledge state terrorism, except when performed by 'rogue' nations? As it paradoxically hardens under each new assault, this obsolete stucco construction (which gives more formal power to France than Germany, Brazil, India or Indonesia) evades the fundamental questions about the nature of the order. At the heart of this praxis and discourse, however, stands the gnawing question of conflict and political violence, which we can also subsume under the generic term of 'war'. Yet the very nature of what *that* war is (not the one on terrorism), a form of counter-violence emerging reactively from the South, has equally been hijacked. As Tarak Barkawi notes: 'The problem is *not* that the Global South and its conflicts are ignored. It is that European histories of war provide the (provincial) basis for the putatively universal concepts and definitions with which we study war in *both* the Global South and North.'[34] The question of IS clearly raises wider questions about the current configuration of international affairs, which, as noted, in turn highlight the issue of their genesis. Specifically, two problems arise: one grammatical, the other behavioural. First, international relations have been structured around the pre-eminence of the state and of Western discourse about statehood and the nation state. State-initiated, state-defined, state-owned, state-monitored, state-centric and state-led, international relations as they emerged a century or so ago moved to negate all action in the international sphere of that which is not the state, or that which is not somehow derivative from that construct. To the extent that the then-largely colonised countries of the Global South were still undergoing a process of nation formation and state-building, these sectors of the world were therefore *de facto* and *de jure* excluded from this determination, except as objects of that power (e.g. the scramble for Africa, the Sykes–Picot treaty). The second difficulty proceeds from the fact that, contrary to the narrative given in the now-dominant international relations, the previous direct control by major Western powers of most of the world was in effect not disappeared after World War II but merely reconfigured. The crucial 1940s–1970s period can then be read as one in which the different but combined challenge of now-restless colonies – in parallel discontent with systemically segregated communities in the North, such as African Americans in the US – led to political concessions known as decolonisation, which in turn paved the way, 30 years later, for global norms such as human rights, global governance and human security. At the heart of this sequence, and its unexamined impact on the genesis of our mapping of contemporary terrorism, stand the twin pillars of racism and dispossession – underwritten by a invisibilised practice and sidelined discourse on these issues.[35] In *The Silent War* (1998), Frank Furedi addressed the place of race in international relations, arguing that the silencing of Western direct colonial control practices was in effect tactical and reactive. Racism, which is eminently about control, is then among the unspoken elements of the current discussion of that political violence known as terrorism and of the groups such as IS that manifested it much later on – as seen in the nature of the acts performed to counter it, and which often took the form of a dehumanisation that correlated with those earlier colonial cultural constructs (see Chapter 2). The over-elaboration of the terrorism concept in recent years in terrorology, or its hollowing out in security studies, are but related ways of escaping its primary political driver, namely the stealth racialisation of terrorism throughout the past decades, and specifically as regards Islam and the Al Qaeda and IS episodes.

To be certain, the discussion of IS sits amid a larger discussion where scholarship on issues of national security is complex if one is to pursue objective, empirically verifiable truth.[36] However, racism itself sits – unquestioned – at the heart of that discussion on IS, with the violence beamed at Europeans and Americans considered exceptionally unacceptable and particularly heinous; elevated to a stand-alone dangerousness, not because of what it is but because of whom it dares target. As Philip Lawrence writes: 'A central element in the *real* culture of modern societies has been racism, and in warfare racism has been crucial to generating images of the enemy which justify acute forms of violence ... [T]his fact is one that is still found to be discomforting and shocking. The real racist and imperialist history of Western countries is inconvenient to current forms of self-satisfaction.'[37] Against that background, the type of war that has been practiced since the Napoleonic Wars has worked on two standards. The distant killing of the savage was decoupled from liberal war reserved for the players in the same club, and made subject to international humanitarian law. With violence now shipped back to the metropolis courtesy of IS's avatars, the understanding of that violence of the savage has become boxed into a discussion on terrorism that strips it of its political nature and moves to discuss anthropologically the Muslim, Arab, Brown, Black or Southern perpetrator and the scriptures of their nominal religion.

The reification of IS in this racialised manner is linked to the long practice of a specific (colonially informed) tradition of power by (Western) states and their understanding of external and internal dominion. When codified, new war was tilted towards states, particularly powerful ones. Indeed, the rules introducing humanity into warfare in the late nineteenth century through the early treaties on the laws of war had consistently served the already-stronger party of an invading state in unequal wars.[38] This – indeed any – discourse on terrorism 'carries power ... and strategically orients a broad set of practices – inflicting punishment, disciplining, surveilling'.[39] Therefore, *bringing colonialism back into the terrorism discussion* allows for a historicised reconnecting of geopolitics and domestic politics. That connection was there in the 1970s (see Chapter 4), and it came back with acuity and innovation in the 2010s. Having been brushed off, their relevance in the security discussion dismissed, the 'C' and 'T' words tend, however, to be generally received with a sense of fatigue, as both colonialism and imperialism are widely considered to be things of the past. The 'serious' policy reader disconnects the moment these words are uttered. However, 'the colonial empires have come to an end, all regions of the world have been thoroughly integrated into a global economy and a veritable cornucopia of institutions and organisations is now dedicated to upholding a dazzling array of human rights. Yet, while some things have changed, certain fundamental parameters remain in place, and the unpleasant past described by Conrad continues to haunt the present.'[40] One of the signs of this important continuity is the systematic delegitimising of the counter-violence of the savage that is always shown to be solely destructive (and therefore only in need of destruction in turn). IS operators, like those of Al Qaeda earlier, are presented as being 'more interested in the spectacle of destruction, in violence for its own sake'.[41] Though it played out in more complex ways than such one-dimensional assessments (see Chapter 2), the opposition between the two sides is then presented in a Manichean way as that of rationality vs. irrationality, calm vs. hysteria, reason vs. emotion and civilisation vs. savagery. 'Fatally interconnected, war and racism fuel each other. Racism feeds war's atrocities, offering us a perverse permission to punish demonised others not so much for their actions as for their difference. War, in turn, support's racism's most dangerous assumptions about that difference, urging that our best hope for security lies in eradicating it in any of its guises ... thus we generate the very hatred we most resent.'[42] Ultimately, as Julian Saurin remarks on the larger question connected here to terrorism: '[T]he problem of decolonising [international relations] will not be resolved by ever-greater sensitivity to the multiple histories that are demanded by the postcolonial turn in historical and cultural studies – though one can never be too intrigued by the varieties of experience and representation. Instead, it requires *a re-engagement with method*, philosophy of science and history on the one hand and a political economy of knowledge on the other.'[43] Such historicised methodological re-engagement with international relations calls for a refocus on the question of racism and how it impacts the current politics of violence.

While I want to insist that IS is a radical Islamist group that takes its religious project seriously (more so, for instance, than the Sahelian entity AQIM or the West African group Boko Haram, or even the East African organisation Al Shabaab), I suggest that (i) such *mise-en-scène* religious self-representation is not sufficient analytically, and that (ii) writing on IS against the background of a deeper history that escapes the extreme Islamism frame and in the context of open-ended political and societal developments in both the Global South and the West allows us to answer more fully the larger contemporary questions posed by the movement. Al Qaeda reconnected the history of terrorism with the nineteenth-century Anarchists. Both were modernity-ushering entities, but IS moves beyond that by pointing to the limits of the state, and it does so not by sitting at the periphery of world politics but by acting precisely at its centre. Indeed, the new group sought actively to locate itself at that core by attacking Paris, London and Brussels, not by remaining concerned solely with its management of the cities it had gained control of in Iraq and Syria, notably Mosul and Raqqa. IS was also aloof with regard to its domestic community, with the so-called enabling environment arguably not key as it visited massive violence on those populations it dominated in Iraq and Syria. The threatening nature of IS lies, then, not so much in its violence (terroristic and obvious) but in the nature of the counter-order it is claiming to uphold. The post-modernity it is representing lies at once in that aspect, as well as in the pursuit of a state-building logic combined with a disseminated appeal to empowered individuals (through both personal authority and community roles). The disruption it is introducing in the system comes from the symmetrical relationship between the certainty of its aims and the uncertainty it reveals on the part of its state enemies (with the intelligibility of its political aims more often than not clear to its state enemies who nonetheless disingenuously paint them publicly as elusive). Ultimately, however, the theoretical underpinnings of the non-mapping of IS, and its dominant representation as an apocalyptic movement devoid of any political logic that is only meant to be addressed through eradication, have their roots in a continuing imperial sequence which started in the nineteenth century. Whether on the liberal or conservative wings of the political spectrum, many producers and influencers of ideas about terrorism have developed a stance whereby the larger production of violence in the South is depicted relatedly as impenetrable.

Genealogies of New Violence

If racialist articulations of international relations continued apace, normalised and naturalised throughout the modern era (with liberalism playing a foundational part in this process),[44] the recodification of violence at the hands of IS constitutes in and of itself a sea change in the history of political violence. Since the early days of modern terrorism, we have been accustomed to thinking about the phenomenon in terms of sub-state agents. Today, the commodification of the means of syncopated warfare by privatised actors on to a global scene and for local purposes, constitutes the projection of a new entrepreneurship of independent politics and violence. At the dawn of this transformation, we find the movements of the 1970s, which were the first to move towards violently infiltrating untapped spaces of contestation beyond the underground logic of nineteenth-century Anarchists and Nihilists. In that sense, IS's story is influenced less by the declamatory religious aims of its leaders, but more so by the operational wherewithal and rerouted violence dynamics introduced by movements such as the Palestinian *fedayeen* (themselves non-religious, indeed mostly secular) during the pivotal years of 1967–75. The increased power of those synergistic non-state agents, their expansion into and navigation of worldwide revolutionary networks, the counter-terrorism techniques they inspired and their impact on the post-Cold War global security architecture[45] preside over what, behaviourally, both Al Qaeda and IS would later engage in. This evolution also partakes of a historical trajectory that warrants open-ended examination. Of this Ayşe Zarakol writes: 'Increasingly, the international system as a whole becomes the subject of revolutionary ire. This is why, with each subsequent wave of terrorism since the nineteenth century (and with each expansion of the international society), system-threatening variants of terrorism have made a stronger comeback, each time less willing to compromise with principles of Westphalian legitimacy.'[46]

In this context what, then, is the genealogy of the violence embarked on by Osama Bin Laden in 1989 and pursued by Abu Bakr al Baghdadi in 2009? In a nutshell, their brand of post-globalised violence can be depicted as having emerged from the more distant colonial experience and the subsequent post-colonial one. Those experiences stand at the heart of the modern world the radical groups inhabit. From this perspective, decolonisation in particular was but a *moment*, and the violence it dealt with was never settled. In this unstable architecture are to be found large segments of what drives the subsequent violence visited upon societies in the North and in the South by these new armed groups. Whereas decolonisation is usually understood as a site-specific event that, in fixity and resolution, gave rise to the norm-regulated contemporary international system, one can read it differently – particularly as it relates to the now-shifting locus of violence. In the pages that follow, we will examine the origins and development of IS, starting with its mother organisation, Al Qaeda. We will also, more importantly, seek to engage with a so-far-absent theory of transnational political violence and invite a different type of debate on IS. Ultimately, the recounting of the IS-specific story is but a chapter in that ongoing story-in-the-making of a new/old type of violence which, it is argued here, is redrawing the boundaries of what international politics will increasingly come to mean in the twenty-first century. In that sense, the transnational violence introduced by Al Qaeda and IS is not merely a set of disruptive challenges to an international system that would have somehow to weather them.⁴⁷ That is no longer possible. The cementing of those pseudo-randomised patterns is already beginning to usher in an international system that is a collage of old patterns of colonial control projected imperially, and new promiscuous encounters at the heart of the post-modern metropolis, which are delocalising threats from the distant (and controllable and colonisable) to the internal (and unmanageable and colonising). Such embryonic organic repatriation of force is currently not visible to many in the West, who read terrorism primarily in terms of culturally, ethnically and religiously informed violence from specific alien communities threatening them. Will the fundamentals of the international system change as a result of this new interaction? Not necessarily. Authority, legality and coercion remain for the time being with the five permanent members of the United Nations (UN). However, the *fluidity* and *release* of the disseminated IS violence are not merely destabilising and chaos-inducing; they are also transformative *de facto*. More importantly, these characteristics spring from a continued reappropriation of the vectors of imperial power. As such, their violence is increasingly less derivative and more intrinsic to the empire itself. Two ideas of this entrepreneurship also need to be addressed. The first is that the IS brand of asymmetry is not defensive but offensive. It is not the classical emaciated asymmetry of the weak, but rather of the one-seeking-to-rise-to-prominence and endowing himself with the extreme ways to do so. Second, IS is, if anything, martial and political. Its violence is calculatedly and opportunistically transgressive. It beheads (to scare and pressure) just as a state chooses to drop an atomic bomb (to intimidate and inhibit).

In the closing years of the twentieth century and the inception of this current century, a critical international security challenge was thrown to Western powers. The reaction of those states created the conditions of a renewed martiality in international affairs, as explicit calls for colonialism in response to terrorism were formulated.⁴⁸ This founding to and fro in turn reinforced the non-state challengers in their belief that their violence project was viable, which they then pursued with newfound vigour and dramatically augmented lethality. With no real evidence to that effect, these insurgent actors became increasingly confident in their ability to secure results and effect change. From hopeful to impactful, as they portrayed themselves assertively, the self-empowerment of these irregulars was nonetheless *de facto* ascendant, striking the minds of thousands of so-called foreign fighters around the world and, as such, benefited greatly from its era's fetishisation of individual achievement. The imagology and connectography of IS places the three dimensions of post-colonialism, post-globalisation and post-modernity into a seamless narrative with the political discourse and violent actions of IS, which is ever-moving on these three planes. If the backstory of IS is Al Qaeda, and its frontstory Iraq and Syria, its sidestory is post-colonialism and post-modernity. In the post-colonial phase, war conducted by Western powers was recodified, and it increasingly invisibilised the actions conducted by the major powers. The 'secret wars' of the 1980s gave way to the 'dirty wars' of the 2010s, both invisible and all the time playing out far away from the metropolis.[49] In response, the new armed groups developed precisely the opposite, namely an über-visible type of war that would be conducted completely in the open and at the heart of the Western capital. Modernity was to be disseminated further by the non-state in such a fashion (in that sense, IS's post-modernism should not be mistaken for a defence of modernity but could rather also be *anti-modern*, as a *modern* alternative mode of organisation and contestation). We then witnessed the reappropriation of war as it was wrestled from the West – initially by Al Qaeda from Arab and Muslim governments, and then by IS. After 9/11, it was argued that 'everything had changed', including the very concept of international law and the recourse to force. With the emergence of IS, the same argument was made anew.[50] The post-9/11 narrative was, however, anchored in a double exercise of denial. On the one hand, it rested on a refusal to examine the historical roots of the political violence performed by the radical Islamist groups beyond their religious identity. On the other, the narrative built a self-sustaining forward momentum, refusing to establish the links between the policies and reaction to that violence and its continuing nature. As a result, the perspective ended up witnessing the rise of a second-generation Al Qaeda, namely IS. That new group firmed up what Bin Laden did, writing the mythology of the future Iraqi and Syrian (and also Libyan) states and taking us into a *post*-post-colonial era, where the question of control is reopened but in a different, loosened dominion.

One of the most powerful myths of the twentieth century was the notion that the elimination of colonial administrations amounted to the actual decolonisation of the world. This led to the myth of a *post*-colonial world.[51] We might ask today, as we link this construct to a discussion of IS, whether post-colonialism is still warranted as a category. Has it not been surpassed by a more determinant combination of recolonialism and counter-colonialism? The very nature of the post-modern condition is based in a circular, violent empowerment of that sort. It is in this sense that we can inquire: how is it possible to see in post-modernity a challenge to modernity's intellectual, moral and cultural mastery, while also seeing it as a means of exercising that mastery?[52] The normalisation, banalisation and trivialisation of one-dimensional religious terrorism enabled a faulty casting away from these issues, precisely when upgraded scholarship was needed. We are therefore possibly at the dawn of a *transcendence* of the binaries centre/periphery, colonised/coloniser and dominated/dominator in international relations when it comes to political violence – and this, I argue, is seen in the nature and performance of IS violence that is at once born and performed in the South and in the West. The overarching and fundamental link between terrorism and history is demonstrated by the peak of terrorism at the inception of the modern era and its return today – all, again, in the context of empire.[53] Often described as being opposed to modernity,[54] IS operators are in point of fact eminently modern. Their post-modernity (which, as noted, can also be anti-modern) is expressed through decentring and through fragmentation; specifically the collapse of categories and resistive politics. And yet their referentials are of long ago (*al khilafa*) and their trigger colonial. Hence, the issues are located squarely in the post-colonial moment, whereby post-colony is understood, in Achille Mbembe's terms, as a given historical trajectory – that of societies recently emerging from the experience of colonisation and the violence which the colonial relationship, *par excellence*, involves. The institutionalisation of derivative representations, and as Mbembe notes 'a particular way of fabricating simulacra or re-forming stereotypes',[55] led in time to a nascent shift embodied by the brethren IS. With the group's violence featuring brotherhood prominently – actual (the Tsarnaevs in Boston, the Kouachis and the Abdeslams in Paris, the Bakraouis in Brussels, the Abedis in Manchester), forged or imagined – the links foster a promise of community on the basis of that trust that is often absent in the impersonal, *Blade Runner*-esque post-modern society.

The post-modernity of IS – ambivalent, impersonal and ambiguous – lies indeed in its self-generated ability to produce and reproduce the razzmatazz of its own grand community narrative, an artefact that is also the product of manifold micro-narratives about individual stories. Inspiration is packaged and the spectacle is cinematic, beamed continuously at the individual level of consumption and delivered in daily doses of video.

The staging of these transgressions is therefore linked by the group to the nature of the times and places its soldiery inhabits. Inasmuch as, by the measure of its market-driven demands, modernity is violence-driven, with the productive process requiring that a form of soft violence be done continuously to segments of society (expelled, rejected, marginalised, violated, remaining at the gates), the group connects forcefully with a narrative of resistance to such an intimately alienating process. The intensification of that sequence since the late twentieth century has led to more violent societies ushering the rise of what has been termed a savage century – a process IS stands squarely at the centre of today. In the context of the IS-dominated world representation, the purging of violence becomes a necessity; abroad, through increased new/old-style imperial conquest and at home through institutionally channelled, securitised and corporate-themed violence. In time, these two distant/local trends meet, as it is argued here. To be certain, the largely ethnic underclass lurking, zombie-like, in the recesses of the urban Western metropolis was always there, but it was envisioned to come out during end-of-the-world-type disasters; as expressed in paranoid ways in fictions such as the films *The Omega Man* (1971) or *Escape from New York* (1981). By contrast, the 2013 film *The Purge* now imagines a not-so-distant future in America in which, once a year, during a twelve-hour period, any crime is legalised, including murder. The revealing success of the film led to two sequels in quick succession: *The Purge: Anarchy* (2014) and *The Purge: Election Year* (2015). '[W]hat is happening today, and developmentally, increases the possibility for violent discourse. It provides new venues for storytelling, myth-making and logical projections. It speaks to *the collectivisation of individual risk* and the creation of symbolic capital among those for whom economic capital is hard to come by. It *revalidates ethnicity, religion, race, language* and doctrinal, as ways of redeeming projects, discourses and their communities.'[56]

The classical post-colonial practice of force was not, however, fully modern. Bent on addressing the violence of the coloniser, it was backward-looking and had adopted a historical purview on the Global South starting and often ending with the colonial era as its sole definer. In that sense, it could not be modern as it borrowed its identity and located its object of address-redress in the past and in another actor's agency. The violence ushered in by Al Qaeda marked a first rupture with that mode of thinking, projecting itself forward and on to the West. With IS, the dynamic becomes fully post-modern, and indeed pivotally more *post*-post-colonial. As noted, we are now in the early stages of the longer-term effects of this activity on international affairs. However, it is already clear that the rerouting of armed-group violence by Al Qaeda on to the international scene in the 1990s, that violence's embedding into transnational patterns of (electronic, cultural, commercial, financial, military) exchange during the 2000s and its relocation at the heart of the Western metropolis by IS during the 2010s, have impacted profoundly on the ways in which political violence will play out from now on.

Theorising IS

Against the above considerations, this book critically interrogates the dominant representation of the organisation of IS and lays out an alternative argument about its deeper history, labyrinthine identity and multifaceted nature. A central concern of the work is the nature of the discussion on terrorism, the place IS (and before it Al Qaeda) occupies in that debate and the significance of these constructions for the larger international order. Specifically, the analysis advances the idea that, in the second decade of the twenty-first century, political violence evolved as a result of the cumulative revolutionary (as opposed to merely evolutionary) ways of Al Qaeda and IS. Diasporised, deregulated and dispersed in time and space, this process is visibly on its way towards having a lasting impact on the organisation and performance of violence in contemporary international affairs – not solely on the geopolitics of the regions in which the groups are active, the conflicts playing there or the generic security considerations as they relate to the rest of the world.

Tracing the ancestry of IS, Chapter 1 describes how, under the leadership of Osama Bin Laden and Ayman al Dhawahiri,[57] the organisation known as Al Qaeda was set up in the late 1980s to launch a new type of war against the US, a country the group held responsible for the trouble in the Islamic world and the Middle East specifically. Forged in the cruible of the Afghan-Soviet War, this first group holds the key to the DNA of IS, as it introduced a particular type of transnational projection which IS subsequently amplified. In 1991, after the Gulf War, the battle between the US and Al Qaeda began to develop, accelerating in 1998 in Afghanistan following Al Qaeda's attacks on the US embassies in Kenya and Tanzania, and emerging fully in 2001 after the 9/11 events, leading to a militarisation of the world amid which IS would be born. Similarly, as in the second phase of its history, Al Qaeda shifted to taking the form of a decentralised entity, giving birth to so-called franchises – one of these offshoots, AQI, became the actual precursor to IS. Parcelling out its action, Al Qaeda retreated into Afghanistan and Pakistan ('Afpak'), opening the door to a successor in Syria and Iraq ('Syraq') which would come from its own womb, AQI. The discussion highlights the fact that IS is the result of a project embarked on long ago by Bin Laden, dry-docked and soon enough displaced by IS while remaining lastingly coterminous with it in important ways.

Chapter 2 deepens the previous discussion by delving into the specifics of the key post-9/11 period in which the US's forays in Afghanistan in 2001 and especially in Iraq in 2003, following Al Qaeda's 'raid on Manhattan' (as Al Qaeda depicts those terrorist attacks in its communication), opened the way for the further transformation of Al Qaeda and the maturation of its project, laying the ground to the actual emergence of IS after the death of AQI's leader, Abu Mus'ab al Zarqawi. It demonstrates that, if Al Qaeda's birth-cry served as an initial propulsive force, IS is, second, in significant but neglected ways the product of the US's policies in the Middle East and specifically the invasion of Iraq in 2003, and the subsequent brutal neo-colonial occupation of that country.

Chapter 3 analyses the manner in which IS came to surpass its begetter, Al Qaeda, in ambition and in practice. Examining how AQI, led by Abu Bakr al Baghdadi, went on to design a two-pronged strategy to re-establish its power in Iraq, following the American withdrawal, and to expand in Syria in the wake of the 2011 Arab Spring and subsequent civil war in that country, the chapter argues that, thirdly, IS is the product of the conflict in Syria. Attention is paid to the ways in which IS diversified and transformed Al Qaeda's project. As such, it is maintained that IS could have been a previous offering or a mere reissue of Al Qaeda. It was not, and its rebooting was, in that regard, deceptive. Bending the latter's internal logic towards a focus on punishment, it also dramatically expanded the realm of its violence, taking it beyond Bin Laden's *democratisation of responsibility* to a sort of *indictment of innocence* (domestically and internationally) as seen in the patterns of its distinctive personalised violence. The chapter also discusses another important change of perspective introduced by IS, namely the pursuit of state-building and involvement in regions beyond the Levant.

Finally, Chapter 4 dissects the cognitively enhanced, trenchantly cadenced and intricately professionalised communication of IS, and the group's incubus-generating relationship with the Western metropolis.

Tracing the colonial and post-colonial underpinnings of the unresolved violence going back and forth between periphery and centre, and incorporating elements of popular culture as manifest influences expanding contestation,[58] it discusses the importing of nominally distant violence into the heart of Europe and the United States by do-it-yourself terrorists – in a sort of counter-crusade – and, similarly, the exporting of worsening Western societal questions to the theatres of armed conflict in the Levant and other Muslim lands. Examining the matrimony between these two related yet different experiences, Chapter 4 argues that the IS terrorist context also echoes, albeit in far more violent ways, earlier domestic rebellion and tension in the West, notably in the 1970s, and considers the fact that the current terrorism challenge has generated intolerant and undemocratic policy and societal responses.

A concluding chapter synthesises the major themes and analysis from the previous chapters and offers an overarching thesis about the meaning of contemporary violence as violence *shipped back* to its exporter. The *boomerang effect* of such violence has led further to the militarisation of Western societies, primarily the United States,[59] with France, the UK and Germany following on. Al Qaeda, IS and their avatars-in-the-making emerge, therefore, as symptoms of a larger post-colonial dynamic which has been transformed by the patterns offered by globalisation; specifically the normalisation of densified and intensified patterns of exchange, the routinised expectation regarding global coverage of events, the simultaneity of exchanges and the constant circulation and recirculation of ideas and actions. In the final analysis, the aesthetics of IS invite an infinite number of borrowings and appropriations (from the group Boko Haram in Nigeria modelling itself on it, to the likes of Omar Mateen claiming affiliation with it after his shooting of club-goers in Orlando in June 2015). The theatrical and concise Al Qaeda was replaced by the industrial and intricate IS. Both were effective and angular in their distortion of classical violence, which they subjected to a journeying crossover. As the study of terrorism and political violence increasingly calls for differentiation, and points out to the need to apply greater conceptual scrutiny beyond the specifics of this or that group,[60] efforts at conceptualising IS need to link themselves to the wider set of historical contexts in which the group is inserted and the actual consequences of those connections. The most important of those is that the group's violence has transformed the global order. How did international affairs land on such shores? Where does the story start? We turn to these questions in Chapter 1.

1

Al Qaeda's Matrix

In the emergency, it occurred to me that perhaps the virtue of irregulars
lay in depth, not in face.

T. E. Lawrence, *The Evolution of a Revolt* (1920)

I woke up
And sensed the new condition
They won
Storms raged
Things changed forever.

Steely Dan, 'Mary Shut the Garden Door' (2006)

IS cannot be made sense of without properly tracing its lineage to Al
Qaeda's saga, spanning some 20-plus years from the late 1980s to the late
2000s and into the 2010s. Al Qaeda introduced dynamics and established
patterns which stand at the core of what IS came to be and what it did.
However, although Al Qaeda is a primary referent for IS, it is more
than that. Al Qaeda is arguably the most important group so far in the
history of terrorism. Specifically, three key innovations on the part of Al
Qaeda – the *steadied transnational broadcast of non-state violence*, the
militarisation of radical Islamism and the *professionalisation of terrorist
operations*, combined with the dissemination of operational centres of
gravity and a deft use of information technology – have cumulatively
set the stage for IS to emerge lethally in the way it has in the wake of
Al Qaeda's foundational actions. IS's subsequent strength resided not
merely in its behavioural dimensions and its own industrious strategy
and operations, but equally and fundamentally in the important legacy
of the violence matrix set by Al Qaeda.

In the longer term, the history of IS is part of that of Al Qaeda, a
group that underwent a sequence of emergence, expansion, abatement
and indirect reassertion. The hegemonic maturity of Al Qaeda came
from internal transcendence, which in time set the stage for a second

age occupied by IS. The impact of Al Qaeda on global politics is then an affair of long standing. Its inception reaches back decades to the contemporary transformation of a non-state armed group, which has sought to create unprecedented regional and international dynamics anchored in a privatised usage of force for a political purpose. Beyond solely triggering domestic or foreign crises, this organisation has aimed, in particular, to adapt, achieve and prosper open-endedly as it pursued such a novel strategy. It is in that sense that the metamorphosis of Al Qaeda can be assessed to have been moving forward all along. From the beginning, and arising from its own actions, this evolution was an almost inevitable way for the group to ensure its perennation, and set it apart from previous (local) and subsequent (regionalised) Islamist factions. IS is both a continuation and a departure from the entity that enabled such emancipation.

Unleashing Transnational Violence

Up until Al Qaeda, all terrorism was local. Regardless of their ideology or context, previous waves of terrorism had all focused on visiting violence on a local authority (usually the state, colonial or national) with a view to advancing a political perspective that was linked immediately and directly to a domestic scene. In the contemporary modern history of terrorism, this was the case in Tsarist Russia with the Nihilist groups of the 1870s, across Western Europe in the 1890s and 1900s during the Anarchist wave and, later, in the first half of the twentieth century throughout the decolonisation era, notably in Palestine, Cyprus and Algeria. From the late 1960s to the mid-1980s (roughly in the years 1968 to 1986), a number of Palestinian (Black September, the Popular Front for the Liberation of Palestine, PFLP), German (Red Army Fraction/Baader-Meinhof Group), Italian (Red Brigades), Japanese (Japanese Red Brigades), French (Action Directe), Belgian (Communist Combatant Cells) and Armenian (Armenian Secret Army for the Liberation of Armenia, Justice Commandos of the Armenian Genocide) groups expanded their realm, seeking to establish connections beyond their immediate respective societal theatres more clearly. At times, some of these groups – Palestinians of Black September and Germans of the Red Army Faction, for instance – came together in joint operations or provided support to each other, and individual operators such as the Venezuelan Ilyich Ramírez Sánchez (known as Carlos the Jackal) or the Nicaraguan Patrick Argüello enjoyed links with a number of different groups from different regions over the years (in the case of the Venezuelan, from Western Europe to the Middle East to Africa to Eastern Europe). Embryonic transnational influences were also present – a small German left-wing group, whose core members would later form the Second June Movement and the Red Army Faction, had named itself initially the Tupamaros West Berlin after the 1967–72 Uruguayan urban guerrilla movement; the Japanese Red Army was both influenced by the German Red Army Faction and Palestinian groups, as it later renamed itself Arabu Sekigun (Arab Red Army) – but they did not alter the inherently local anchoring of these movements. The driving logic behind each of these organisations remained domestically oriented. Making an impact, putting pressure or indeed obtaining concessions from the (state) actors of their place of origin, remained, as it had been with earlier generations, the primary motivation for them. Palestinians kidnapping Israeli athletes in Munich in September 1972 were doing so to highlight the plight of their people in occupied Palestine. Germans training for operations in Jordan in 1970 were making a point about the societal malaise across Germany a generation after the Holocaust. In the United States, several radical left-wing, African-American and Latino groups were in effect exclusively domestic (Weatherman, Black Liberation Army, Symbionese Liberation Army, The Family and the United Freedom Front).

The 1970s featured a measure of early transnationalism, but this was minimal.[1] If more generally the international environment was witnessing the opening of spaces for 'transnational' dynamics,[2] that environment was still essentially a bipolar era dominated by intergovernmental patterns of exchange. An important shift came with the PFLP (and even more so with its offshoot, the PFLP-General Command), which sought actively to develop an international presence. As a result, patterns of this sort of violence increased, notably in Europe.[3] If such an early form of transnational terrorism materialised during the heyday of 1970s terrorism, it was limited, performative and derivative, facilitated to a large extent by the greater ease of international air travel starting in the mid-1960s. The local focus was not, however, merely operational; it defined the manner in which the terrorist groups conceived of the meaning and direction of their violence. Arguably, the 1970s were the pinnacle of what 'terrorism' could, up until then, manifest historically in its pursuit of destabilisation in a given society; mobilisation, spectacular rupture with the rest of society, choreography of defiance, hatred for the state and its symbols, and hopes and dreams of a cleansing rebirth by way of violence. Over a period of a hundred years, Russian Nihilists at one end, and American and European radicals at the other, in effect book-ended the story of terrorism as we had come to know it. The permutations all remained true to the original animating factors causing consternation and unremittingly promoting discord, locally.

A decade and a half later, terrorism would experience a revolution, and an Islamist group, Al Qaeda, would introduce a consequential innovation in the form of *transnational* terrorism. Why did Al Qaeda make that move and why was it able to? What process inspired Osama Bin Laden and his associates to pursue such a qualitatively different project? Most scholarly work on Al Qaeda in particular, and terrorist groups in general, has focused on causes belonging to a single level of analysis.[4] In contradistinction, one possible response to these initial questions is that Al Qaeda rode a threefold storm: the manifestation of a dead end of the decade-long radical Islamist militancy in Arab countries, leading inevitably to such geographical transcendence through exile; the materialisation of a conflict in Afghanistan that provided the emerging group with a staging ground for its violence; and the take-off of globalisation, in which the organisation ensconced itself opportunistically and naturally, adopting it at once. This three-tiered DNA of Al Qaeda is what would, 20 years later, enable its IS heir-cum-offshoot to modulate its own hybridity without full contradiction, and indeed a measure of continuity.

The first dimension behind the reorienting of terrorism as introduced by Al Qaeda reaches deep, and is concerned with the failed history of state-building in the Middle East and North Africa. As the Ottoman Empire collapsed in the 1910s in the Middle East, and French rule in North Africa also started fissuring, the primary vehicle for rebellion on both the Mashreq and Maghreb fronts was nationalism, with the first part of the twentieth century witnessing a nationalistic struggle for independence playing out across the region. In that context, the main driver behind these social and political awakenings was pan-Arabism. Politically, the roots of the rising movements went back to the time when, in the wake of the Young Turks' 1908 revolution in favour of Turkification, Arabs throughout the Ottoman Empire began agitating for liberation, distinctly using the identity mode. *Wataniya* (patriotism), *qutriya* (regionalism), *ba'ath* (renaissance), *nahda* (awakening), *qawma* (rising), *'uruba* (Arabhood) and *thawra* (revolution) were prominent in Arab minds during these decades, and would remain so for most of the twentieth century. Islamism was present, but as a runner-up to the dominant nationalist mode of political expression. At times, the two strands met and indeed enjoyed mutual and uneasy support, as they shared a common goal of emancipating the colonised Arab and Muslim lands, but their driving logic remained different. In Arabia, in 1916–18 the Hashemites blended their religious legitimacy as direct heirs of the Prophet Mohammad with a British-inspired regional pan-Arab political ambition to establish an 'Arab kingdom' linking the Gulf with the Levant – one that would eventually be thwarted by other simultaneous contradictory British commitments (the secret Sykes–Picot agreement of May 1916 to divide the Levant between Britain and France, and the Balfour Declaration of November 1917 promising to set up a Jewish homeland in Palestine). In Libya, Qur'anic school teacher Omar al Mukhtar led a nationwide movement against the brutal Italian occupation for 20 years, from 1911 until his death in 1931. (Libyan leader Muammar Gaddafi would later partly finance the film *Lion of the Desert*, directed by Hollywood filmmaker Mustapha al Akkad in 1981, depicting that struggle.) In Algeria, Muslim scholar Abdelhamid Ben Badis founded the Jamiyat al 'Ulama (Association of the Ulama), which throughout the 1930s laid the groundwork for the national liberation movement that would emerge more formally the following decade and the war for independence that lasted until 1962.

Decolonisation turned to be anticlimactic. Everywhere across the region, the new states, imbued with nationalism and led forcefully by young army officers promising modernisation and sovereignty, squandered in no time their popular mandate and betrayed their nations' hopes for independence by settling for authoritarianism. In effect replaying the colonial sequence of dispossession and arbitrariness, the leadership of these self-described 'revolutionary councils' and 'national commands' – also speaking similarly a narrative of 'progress' and 'advancement', as the British and French had – took note immediately of the threat that political Islam would come to represent to their regimes. Such a trajectory was best illustrated by the evolution of the relationship between the Egyptian Free Officers – who, led by Gamal Abdel Nasser, conducted the nationalistic 1952 coup against the corrupt, British-supported monarchy of King Farouk – and the Muslim Brotherhood, which initially went along with the army's project under a logic of alliance, before being cast aside by Nasser and his colleagues. By the mid to late 1960s, political Islam had become the nemesis of the post-colonial Arab state. As the regimes in Iraq, Syria, Algeria, Egypt, Tunisia, Libya and Jordan adopted varying degrees of military-led rule, with paramilitary intelligence services (*mukhabarat*) and police investigative units (*istikhbarat*) swelling, and as repression, introduced as a lasting dissent-control mechanism, increased, resistance to authoritarianism lodged itself naturally within those sectors of society that had once been contenders to lead the struggle for independence. Without much difficulty, Islamism found a dual justification for its existence: battling the corrupt and corrupting state and offering a promise of genuine independence to Arab societies under a perspective now stressing not so much identity but faith. 'That in which you believe' rather than 'that which you are' was the Islamist promise. The more the Arab states illustrated their failure – military in the face of Israel, economic in not engineering modernisation and geostrategic in remaining subservient to major powers – the more the formula *al Islam houa al hal* (Islam is the solution) grasped minds and gathered momentum and appeal. Gradually, the different Islamist-inclined student associations, community organisations, trade unions and political parties (often banned) came to see the limits of their action on their societies, as the regimes, younger and tougher then, unleashed their might and violence against these groups – many of which had started resorting to violence themselves in the early 1970s. Throughout the Arab world – in Egypt, Algeria, Iraq and Syria – prisons filled up with Islamists. By the end of that decade – with civil war playing out in Lebanon, and American support to Israel increasing in the aftermath of its incursions in southern Lebanon in 1978 and 1982 – the Islamists had in effect lost the domestic battle to ruthless regimes unconcerned with the effect of their brutalisation of their societies and determined to show that the Shi'a Islamic revolution that had taken place in Iran in 1979 would not be replicated in their Sunni countries. The spectacular (particularly because it was public and filmed) assassination of Egyptian President Anwar al Sadat during a parade in October 1981 by the group Al Jihad al Islami al Masri (Egyptian Islamic Jihad), which had infiltrated the lower ranks of the Egyptian military, indicated paradoxically that the regimes' repression campaigns were hurting the movements; as would, in Syria four months later, the massacre of thousands of Islamists in the city of Hama, besieged for 27 days by the army of Hafez al Assad, and indeed later, in October 1988, the brutal clamping down by the authorities on demonstrators in Algeria, with some 500 killed in Martyrs' Square in Algiers during those three-day riots.

Abdallah Yusuf al 'Azzam, Ayman al Dhawahiri and Osama Bin Laden lived through these years, respectively in Palestine, Egypt and Saudi Arabia (as school teacher, surgeon and millionaire), experiencing a sense of powerlessness. Gradually, these radical militants started reading their domestic scenes as closed ones, and their ability to reform them (through underground social militancy, religious proselytising by way of audiotapes circulated underground and, in time, violence) limited. The link to the external reasons for their domestic conditions became more pronounced, and resentment started being displaced from the local authorities to their perceived Western backers. Years later, Bin Laden, sending a message to the American people and expressing surprise – as he saw it – as to their reluctance to fathom the reasons for his campaign against their country, would explain that what led him on a path of violent opposition to the United States was that country's support for Israeli crimes in Lebanon in 1982:

I am amazed at you. Even though we are in the fourth year after the events of 11 September, [US President George W.] Bush is still engaged in distortion, deception and hiding from you the real causes. And thus, the reasons are still there for a repeat of what occurred. So I shall talk to you about the story behind those [11 September 2001] events and shall tell you truthfully about the moments in which the decision was taken, for you to consider. I say to you, God knows that it had never occurred to us to strike the [Twin] Towers. But after it became unbearable and we witnessed the oppression and tyranny of the American-Israeli coalition against our people in Palestine and Lebanon, the idea came to my mind. The events that affected my soul in a direct way started in 1982 when America permitted the Israelis to invade Lebanon and the American Sixth Fleet helped them in that. This bombardment began and many were killed and injured and others were terrorised and displaced. I could not forget those moving scenes, blood and severed limbs, women and children sprawled everywhere. Houses destroyed along with their occupants and high-rises demolished over their residents, rockets raining down on our home without mercy ... In those difficult moments, many hard-to-describe ideas bubbled in my soul but in the end they produced an intense feeling of rejection of tyranny, and gave birth to a strong resolve to punish the oppressors. And as I looked at those demolished towers in Lebanon, it entered my mind that we should punish the oppressor in kind and that we should destroy towers in America in order that they taste some of what we tasted and so that they be deterred from killing our women and children. And that day, it was confirmed to me that oppression and the intentional killing of innocent women and children is a deliberate American policy. Destruction is [depicted as] freedom and democracy, while resistance is [presented as] terrorism and intolerance.[5]

Unable to reform or take over domestic systems from the inside, reifying their experience of political powerlessness in this way and motivated by radical revenge, Bin Laden and his cohort chose to make a break with their local scene and developed a form of exile militancy – 'radical rebellion as export', as it were – which was ripe for launching when the Soviet Union invaded Afghanistan on 24 December 1979. In that sense, Al Qaeda's action was something akin to a statement that there is nothing inevitable about the vulnerabilities of the Arab and Muslim states; that their governance conditions were but products of a specific colonial and post-colonial history and as such could be remedied similarly, and, more revolutionarily, that violence itself – including offensive international force – was not solely a state prerogative but could be hijacked by a non-state actor beyond moments of terrorist attacks. Thus, by usurping authority which traditionally accrued to the state, and by offering a prescriptive agenda unacceptable internationally, Al Qaeda was from the very beginning immune to statist deterrence, and in so doing laid the foundations of IS's alternative state-building project.

Whereas the start of the war between Iraq and Iran on 22 September 1980 had generated little impact among Islamists in the Arab world, who read that conflict as a geopolitical contest between two regimes which in their respective ways could not muster any support on the part of Sunni Islamists, Moscow's ill-fated crossing into Afghanistan in 1979 was immediately regarded by Islamists across the Muslim world as a *casus belli* and therefore ground for *jihad* (religious struggle). The first layer of the Al Qaeda tapestry was therefore a complex combination of resignation, resolve and pragmatism in the face of gnawing militancy conditions domestically, and the opportunity provided by the Soviet decision. The ten-year period between 24 December 1979 and 15 February 1989, when the Soviet withdrawal from Afghanistan was completed (it had started in May 1988) constituted the formative years of the transnational radical Islamist movement. As early as 1980, radical Islamist militants started moving from different Arab countries (from the Gulf, the Levant and the

Maghreb), converging on Afghanistan to support the Afghan resistance to the Soviet invasion. By 1981, different waves of these actors, soon to be known collectively as 'Arab Afghans', had become substantial and regular enough that the Palestinian former school teacher, 'Azzam, took the initiative to set up a liaison office to welcome and facilitate their travels to Afghanistan. Located in Peshawar, Pakistan, and dubbed Maktab al Khadamat lil Mujahideen (office of work for the combatants) or Maktab al Diyafa (office of hospitality), this unit or way station was in effect the first physical and conceptual incarnation of what Al Qaeda would become later on; literally a base (*qaeda*), headquarters or replenishing centre for combat.

The first-generation Arab Afghans, mostly from the Gulf, was composed of seasoned militants who had already gained experience in battling their respective Arab governments and, in some cases, been imprisoned. The frustrations they brought along as a result of the domestic stalemate combined with religious fervour, which they linked with the Afghan national liberation cause (redefined religiously as *jihad*). The rapidly materialising asymmetrical warfare quagmire the Soviets fell into spelled a series of early victories for the irregulars, which earned the Arabs both the admiration and trust of the Afghan armed groups' leaders and inspired a second wave of fighters coming from North Africa. In effect initiating the radical Islamist movement's investment in communication technology, 'Azzam capitalised on such momentum and launched a publication, *Al Bunyan al Marsous* (the *Solid Edifice*, published in Arabic and in Urdu), and recorded a series of audiotapes in which he called for such backup in the form of military migration as *fard 'ayn* (personal obligation). He declared that: 'Whoever can, from among the Arabs, fight *jihad* in Palestine, then he must start there. And, if he is not capable, then he must set out for Afghanistan.'[6] Osama Bin Laden was among the individuals who heeded that call and travelled to Afghanistan, arriving there sometime in the mid-1980s. As Bin Laden – who brought along important sums of money he had inherited as one of the 24 sons of the successful Saudi (of Yemeni origin) entrepreneur Mohammed Awad Bin Laden – started making local connections in Afghanistan and established himself as a key mover, he came to constitute, with 'Azzam and al Dhawahiri, a *de facto* troika leading the Arab Afghan component of the fight against the Soviets. By 1987, the conflict had turned in favour of the insurgency and the Soviet invasion's failure was a foregone conclusion. As they found themselves managing the political benefits of that impending victory, being careful not to step on the local groups' sensitivities, and supervising their contingent which had swelled anew following the inclusion of new militants from the Balkans and a handful of individuals from Western Europe and the United States, Bin Laden and his associates began reflecting on how to perpetuate their movement. If one superpower could be defeated, couldn't the other one, and wasn't it more involved in the trouble in the Islamic part of the world? Around this time, in the key 1988–9 period, these radical Islamists' 'chatter' (as Western counter-terrorism agencies would later call such loose talk among terrorists) started focusing on the creation of a dedicated, larger organisation that would go beyond the operational purpose of the Maktab al Khadamat, and indeed beyond the confines of the Afghan-Soviet conflict itself.

Enter Al Qaeda. Referred to in early documents as Al Jaish al Islami (the Islamic Army), Sijil al Qaeda (the base's registry) or Al Qaeda al 'Askariya (the military base), Al Qaeda was born in Khost, Afghanistan on 11 August 1988. In the ten years during which it had emerged, in slow motion but insistently, almost inevitably, the entity was already becoming a potentially formidable force.[7] Forged in combat (rather than underground political meetings or social uprising), rewarded doggedly with victory over a military superpower (rather than a regional state) and to an extent already internationalised (with Asians and Europeans in addition to the core Arab component), the new organisation could also field three different profiles. Whereas the first group brought commitment and energy in 1981, and the second added numbers and dedication in the mid-1980s, a third group injected renewal and focus at a crucial phase in 1988–9. As the 'Azzam–Bin Laden–al Dhawahiri troika turned bicephalous, with Bin Laden and al Dhawahiri in the driving seat following the assassination of 'Azzam on 24 November 1989, the concept and purpose of the armed group was refined further. Al Qaeda would pursue a new type of objective, redirecting its oppositional priorities 'from the near enemy to the far enemy' (*min al 'adou al qareeb ila al 'adou al ba'eed*) – with one main objective in mind: to attack that mightiest of far enemies, the United States, in an unprecedented transnational way. Importantly, this configuration was the first full-fledged incarnation of a militarised form of transnational terrorism. In ushering in such a transformation, Al Qaeda was also ahead of state militaries who would in effect be sucked into extra-territorial operations much later – precisely ten years later – with the first such response ordered by US President Bill Clinton in August 1998 authorising the bombing of Al Qaeda's camps in Afghanistan, following the group's attacks on US embassies in Kenya and Tanzania earlier that month. In so doing, the United States, and later many other states, were forced to adapt and improvise in the face of an unexpected challenge to their historical construction of legitimate violence in warfare.[8] Whereas traditional Islamist groups began establishing themselves historically through a combination of religious preaching, political discourse and networks of domestic social services, Al Qaeda's first embodiment was to serve as a welfare service provider originating in the rentier state Arabian Gulf, but one whose action was oriented outwardly and militarily with the *jihad* campaign against the Soviet Union in the 1980s and with little emphasis on religion per se. In a 2014 interview, the son-in-law of 'Azzam, Abdulla Anas, who had taken part in the fight in Afghanistan, noted in that regard that 'Osama [Bin Laden] never thought he was a religious sheikh … [He] never led prayers or gave sermons.'[9] In sum, in such a context of failed Arab and Islamic state-building, Al Qaeda sprang forth as a politico-religious project foregrounding the relocation of authority, the circumventing of the state and the militaristic empowerment of a non-state actor.

The revolutionary newness of Al Qaeda lay in these key aspects, but it was its argumentative force that stood out as an overpowering and purposive mythology. The group did not consider struggle against the local dictators as a rite of passage or a goal, and sought to mark a rupture, not so much from resistance but towards conquest. As Bin Laden and al Dhawahiri saw it, the 'perversity' they were battling was only partly local. In the group *'asabiya* (solidarity) they developed, local militancy was portrayed as ultimately zero sum, and derivative problematically from the state's actions, whereas foreign conquest was more pragmatic and original, also allowing for unexpected initiative. The predicament of the underground rebel held little appeal for the well-off revolutionary that Bin Laden was, and indeed later on the man would not waste much time on instilling a sense of *asala* (authenticity) and community in his organisation, something that partly explains his kindred spirit al Dhawahiri's difficulties in keeping the organisation cohesive once Bin Laden disappeared. Was it clear to Bin Laden, however, that upon landing in Afghanistan he would start such a global movement? Hardly. The symphonic disorder he would orchestrate during the next two decades developed arguably through a slow observation of the Afghan atonal concerto he had initially become involved in. However improvised *in situ*, Al Qaeda's stance owed much to what Bin Laden and al Dhawahiri brought with them in terms of divorce from local militantism. Despite all his speeches denouncing its leadership, Bin Laden had not, for instance, been in maximal opposition to the House of Saud initially. What he sought was the empowering nature of a full-fledged struggle, not the limiting confines of insurrection – and the invasion of Afghanistan by the Soviets provided him with that opportunity. The man could in effect buy a state, or rent portions of it as he did in Afghanistan, so why seek merely to unseat a group of already faltering regimes in the Middle East? The only time one of these regimes appealed to him, Saddam Hussein's Iraq circa 1991, was when that country's conflict with the United States offered him a chance to join the battle with that world power.[10] Beyond defiance and on to reprisal, Bin Laden's ambition was always to elevate himself to an autonomous position of punishing decision-maker. That stance is what would, much later, enable Abu Bakr al Baghdadi to deliver his iconic sermon as a statesman-like figure in 2014 announcing IS's Caliphate, but only after Bin Laden had initiated that divorce process. Al Qaeda then turned upside down what, referring to contemporary states, Bertrand Badie termed 'the powerlessness of power'.[11] In *empowering weakness*, the armed group had in effect broken the mould. For all this innovation, Bin Laden's 2001 attacks on the United States are presented in the classical terrorology canon as a gross miscalculation, when the operation provided strategic dividends beyond what Al Qaeda probably calculated itself. Overnight Al Qaeda became the global actor of international insecurity, making the jump over those regional states it had sought to discredit and sideline. Previously, Arab and Islamist terrorism had been hopeful, almost desperate in the enactment of its strategy, and in effect, as Bin Laden saw it, lacking the conviction that would give it impact and results.

Ultimately, Bin Laden's Al Qaeda project was the result of several strands, but one in which the 1990–1 Gulf War was a key moment. When, on 7 August 1990, the United States decided to move militarily into the Middle East, following Iraq's invasion of Kuwait five days earlier, things changed. As the former assistant secretary of state for politico-military affairs during the George W. Bush administration, Richard A. Clarke, remarked 25 years later:

> The rise of Al Qaeda in the 1990s, the [2001] US invasion of Afghanistan, the second US war with Iraq [2003], the rise of ISIS, all followed that August 1990 decision to deploy large US forces to the Gulf. There were many social and political pressures that contributed

to the upheaval in the Arab and Islamic world, but the continued US military presence in the region and the way those US forces were used, were major contributors. This chain of events also contributed to the Arab Spring and the creation of failed states in Iraq, Yemen, Libya and Syria. Taken together, these events caused the deaths of hundreds of thousands, turned millions of people into refugees and cost trillions of dollars.[12]

In effect, the then-derided and since then commercially repackaged phrase that Iraqi President Saddam Hussein uttered days ahead of the conflict with the United States depicting the clash as 'the mother of all battles' (*um al màarek*) was accurate, as the conflicts that materialised subsequently in the region all derived in important ways from that first military engagement between the United States and an Arab country.

The defining feature of Al Qaeda was then its transnational nature, and this became a marked feature of *fin de siècle* terrorism, whereby terrorist movements increasingly demonstrated a 'purer form of transnational interaction in the relationship they form with each other',[13] and in time this became one of the dominant traits of contemporary terroristic violence. Equally, however, the simultaneity of Bin Laden's project with the larger technological, social-cultural and socio-economic transformation playing out internationally, namely globalisation, was just as important for the structure and patterns of the new group. Though he may have been motivated primarily by regional dynamics, the fact is that Bin Laden benefited both from the end of the Cold War and the materialisation of globalisation. It is in this dual context that the acuity of his displacement project must be understood. James Rosenau captured the initial context of global fragmentation which sheds light on this phenomenon: 'The combination of internal and external dynamics at work in all societies generates simultaneous tendencies towards globalisation and localisation, towards more extensive integration across national boundaries and more pervasive fragmentation within national boundaries, towards a relocation of authority "outward" to transnational entities and "inward" to subnational groups.'[14] Bin Laden independently conceptualised such a disobedient and illegitimate *relocation of authority*, but could only do so because globalisation allowed him to make it a reality beyond his design, and because the Cold War was in any event passing away, thus objectively opening a new phase. The singular identity of domestic opposition (local radical Islamists of old) was shed, boundaries were redrawn (the

Caliphate became a notional reference) and the emancipatory logic of the group's agenda ended up respatialising its violence beyond the confines of the Arab or Muslim region. Aspirational Caliphate references notwithstanding, the a-territoriality of Bin Laden's project was indicative of the fact that his construct was intrinsically *contra* the state – his was expanded war, temporally and spatially, through which he sought to mobilise soldiery and gather resources (political and operational). Through this interaction between state and non-state emerged a new order built on offensive asymmetry, as the *response to* became the *essence of*. The centrality of warfare in this method, which Al Qaeda pioneered and IS perpetuated, cannot be underestimated.

Osama Bin Laden was a 'dreamer of the day', in the sense T. E. Lawrence spoke of regarding the dangerousness of such men who are able to act their dreams with open eyes.[15] He regarded himself as a warrior, in the traditional historical sense given to that status in Arab tribal mythology. As he displayed that aspect of the leadership he sought to bring to Al Qaeda – explicitly orchestrating his terrorism that way and benefitting from globalisation – Bin Laden made use of the lingering impasse of the Arab state system. With Al Qaeda rising in the 1990s, the question of the legitimate monopoly of force had still not been solved by the Arab states several decades into national independence. As noted, the struggle for decolonisation had provided a platform for two competing movements – nationalists vs. Islamists – who contended for power, without, in either case, giving much thought to resilient and accountable state-building, one in which the question of force would be normalised under legitimate institutions. Winning the first couple of rounds of that bout, the nationalists regarded authoritarianism, repressive military and coup d'états as natural outcomes of the defence of the *dawla* (state) and their *nidham* (regime). As Islamism next rose to unseat them, it played that game on their very terms and turf; moving underground, conspiring in secret societies, remaining unreadable to the citizenry and in effect performing as a self-appointed revolutionary vanguard. Importantly, the radical Islamist challenge demonstrated that, well into the 1980s, and for all its bombast and repertoire of repression, the Arab state could more often than not appear as but one contender among other local powers wielding force. The supposedly mighty Algerian army, which had ruled Algeria with an iron fist since 1962, was thus shaken to its inner core by an impromptu street riot that played out for a few days in October 1988, leading in short order to the rapid rise of an Islamic Salvation Front, which proceeded to win the first round of parliamentary elections in December 1991 – a democratic contest that was interrupted abruptly by the Algerian military state for fear of losing it. Such dead ends for authority would be reached more fully by 2011 with the Arab Spring, but in 1988 it was already perceptible as such:

> Middle Eastern state-makers have been burdened with certain problems which their Western European counterparts did not have to confront at a similar stage in their political development. One of these is the need for state-makers in the Middle East to attempt to consolidate their power through the development of political institutions while simultaneously attempting to justify the existence of their various states and regimes to populations for whom the very idea of the territorial nation-state, the specific boundaries of existing states and the concept of secular authority lack legitimacy.[16]

Al Qaeda reconnected with a third site of power in the Arab Islamic tradition that had remained untapped by insurgents during most of the twentieth century: the warrior rebellion. As the early twentieth century witnessed a lot of uncertainty and repositioning of identities in the region, the portrayed parables of (Arab) nationalism and (Islamic) religion played out alongside other types of tribal and warrior mobilisation, both with equally deep roots in the region's longer history. In that respect, the type of Al Qaeda-inherited leadership provided by IS years later is defined not so much by the group's discursive pronouncements about evocative plans for a Caliphate, but more by its raw, blunt and gut-level ability to act out its design in a way that convincingly portrayed to the average Islamist militant an image of order that does not doubt its legitimacy (in the sense that it does not see the state as one to be 'toppled', but as an inherently illegitimate and ineffectual entity that merely needs to be disposed of, so as to focus on the fundamentals of war as represented by the group). To be certain, the agency of non-state actors in the deployment of coercive force is not inconsistent with the classical tradition of *jihad* (which locates the decision of offensive war with the ruler),[17] and historically there has often been delegation of operations to mid-level leaders that later rose to significant political prominence (Khaled Ibn al Walid and Salah al Din, most iconically), but the issue of leadership itself has remained central. Indeed, the Great Arab Revolt of 1916 was thus sanctioned formally by Sharif Hussein Bin Ali of Mecca and Medina, but led by a combination of his sons and lieutenants allied with different tribes from the *jazeera* and with Britain. Around the same time, a first important militarisation of Islamist movements took place with the Ikhwan movement (1908–30) which, in the 1920s, enabled the expansion of the Saudi state beyond the central Arabian region of Najd, helping it topple the Hashemites and reaching into Transjordan, before rebelling against it. Never fully tamed, and its remnants in effect subsequently integrated into the Saudi National Guard (al Harass al Watani) in 1955,[18] the Ikhwan left an important imprint on the socio-genesis and paradigm of Al Qaeda. These actors remained present in Saudi society – and, beyond, in radical Islamists circles – as an undercurrent of *avant la lettre* dormant insurgency, which was linked organically to the establishment of the monarchy itself. Though they did not emerge visibly beyond underground militancy, sporadic local disobedience or the nationwide circulation of audiotaped sermons critical of the authorities, their importance was revealed by one significant episode in 1979. On 20 November that year (five weeks before the Soviet invasion of Afghanistan), several hundred militants led by a Saudi preacher from the Najd region, Juhayman al Otaybi, invaded the Great Mosque in Mecca and occupied it, trapping thousands of worshipers, until 4 December when the Saudi Arabian army (assisted by French and Pakistani special forces) stormed the compound to reclaim it. Al Otaybi's grandfather and other members of his family had been members of the Ikhwan.[19]

In launching Al Qaeda in 1988, Bin Laden was starting an original project but also reactivating a tradition of elite, aristocratic engagement in violence present in Arab and Muslim history.[20] The seventh-century Muslim conquests had been led by the nobility among the Arabs of the *jazeera*, and most episodes told (and reimagined) about victory feature fiercely independent warriors whose feats would owe as much to their prowess on the field as to their going against the system. Bin Laden was a contemporary offshoot of that tradition and that imaginary, combining ascetic, monastic and violent ideals. Away from the underground, almost Marxist-like Islamist militant phraseology of the 1970s – prevalent among Egyptian Islamists and at times detectable in Ayman al Dhawahiri's messages in post-Bin Laden Al Qaeda – the Saudi businessman's language highlighted instead the role of the *shurafa* (noblemen). The warrior type, fighting unselfishly for the *umma* (community), had long constituted one of the most important social-communal expressions of the Muslim martial ethic. Seen as characterised by the temporal bravery and sacrifice of a *mujahid* (fighter) or *munadhil* (combatant) proceeding on a sacred path (*salab*), that actor's behaviour was not historically regarded as naked violence (*'unf*) but rather a way (*tareeq*) into transformation. As he started reintroducing such discourse in October 2001, the tone adopted by Bin Laden in his communication to the West and to his soldiery highlights a break with the previous militancy. The romanticising idiom began to persist and display influence (on 11 September 2003, at the occasion of the second anniversary of the attacks, a Britain-based group calling itself Al Muhajiroun organised a conference on 'The Magnificent 19' to commemorate the actions of the 19 perpetrators of the 9/11 attacks). This approach also represented a further element for dismissal of the state, as the notion of *al qaed al badeel* (the substitute leader) becomes an element of central authority and an option as regards the use of violence above and beyond the formal state. The logic of 'substitution in warfare',[21] as it would also be normalised under IS, sprang from this specific warrior lineage. Whereas the Palestinian *fedai* was a figure depicted more on a platoon soldier level, giving way later to the logic of *kataeb* (brigades), this different theological warrior discourse stresses a dimension of journey, which by virtue of being personal, elevating and communal connects more powerfully with the *jihad* concept as elaborated on by 'Azzam and his followers. In time, it looked to the Al Qaeda militants that a figure like Bin Laden could 'legitimately' build up an army. In a 'the stories are true' kind of self-mythologising process – which also occurred in the early days of the anti-colonial struggle, as in the case of Abdelhamid Ben Badis in Algeria or Omar al Mukhtar in Libya – military-political force in the service of faith is a tradition that among radical Islamists transcends modern statehood. In its claim on the monopoly of violence, Bin Laden's Al Qaeda was also novel in this way, and this allowed for a logic whereby the militants could see the possibility of not merely serving a larger cause (e.g. Palestine) as a good soldier would, but entertained the writing of their own saga, carving a personal space in the larger mythology of the Islamist warrior. The profiles of militants – many of whom were coming from Europe or the United States – that IS would feature in its glossy magazines (see Chapter 4) a quarter of century later were derived from this construct.

What such Saladinisation of Islamist violence indicates is that there was always more to the war of Al Qaeda than simply its immediate terroristic outcome. The new mythology was framed around the contemporary actions of these '*murabitoun ulama* warriors', as Ayman al Dhawahiri referred to them in a 2007 speech (e.g. Abdallah 'Azzam, Abd al Rashid al Ghazi, Mullah Daddulah, Abu Omar al Sayf, Abdallahi al Rashood, Hamoud Al 'Uqla, himself implicitly and, of course, Osama Bin Laden). What was, we might then ask, Al Qaeda ultimately 'the base' for, in that regard? A platform for better, more efficient, transnationalised, against-the-far-enemy warfare (Al Qaeda al Askariya and Al Jaish al Islami were its first names), or a stage from which to redefine the meaning and practice of statehood in the Muslim polity by linking it to an earlier era where leadership was defined by individual achievements in the name of the *umma*? Bin Laden, the terror-advocating warrior aristocrat, would in time be supplanted by commoners from within his own ranks, best embodied successively in ruffian Abu Mus'ab al Zarqawi and roughneck Abu Bakr al Baghdadi (see Chapter 3). Indeed, the story of IS is in many regards one of Bin Laden successfully establishing a pattern which al Zarqawi furthered and al Baghdadi sought imperfectly to replicate but modernised successfully by clothing it in street toughness and unrestrained maximised violence. What IS 1.0 (that is, Al Qaeda) achieved through Bin Laden's influential and consensual authority, Al Qaeda 2.0 (that is, IS) won through force and armed quelling of dissent. Old warrior representation notwithstanding, Arabhood must not be seen in the context of supplanting the wider Muslim dimension of Islamism. Indeed, there has often been an Arab imperial, and at times racist, extension of that ethnic aspect which, besides alienating other Muslims, confuses the picture as to what drove an Islamist organisation such as IS. As Mahmood Mamdani notes: 'Like the history of Western civilisation, the history of Arabs is linked to particular agendas. At times, such a history doubles as a history of "Islam," just as the history of "the West," often doubles as the history of "Christianity." Here, too, the tendency is for cultural identities to get politicised and to take on identities defined by the law.'[22] In effect, for all his personal Arab tribal warrior lineage, Bin Laden sought to shape the new *Muslim* way of war more than the Arab one, and this was taking place at a time when his own Arab identity and culture were being reaffirmed. With some difficulty, IS would deal with this dual and unsettled aspect.

It may appear peculiar that Bin Laden built a bridge into modernity through a harkening back to the long-gone, quaint days of Islamic history. It is, however, the pursuit of a 'purer' form of a warrior spirit, 'untouched' by the corrupt nature of the post-colonial Arab state, that gave him both self-sustaining strength of conviction and appeal in the eyes of all those radical Islamist militants looking for a new 'base' from which to launch their struggle. Such skipping, indeed dismissing of the preceding nationalist historical phase, functioned to create a forward-looking momentum, which precisely matched the modernity of the new generation, embodied later on by the Al Qaeda franchises and by IS.

> As the examples of Bin Laden, Al Qaeda and the 11 September terrorists demonstrate, Islamism is not a cry of distress from 'the wretched of the earth'. It is an implacable summons to war, issued by globetrotting middle-class Muslims, many of them extremely wealthy and most of them sufficiently well-versed in Western civilisation and its benefits to be able to exploit the modern world to the full. These Muslims are the product of the globalising process, and Western civilisation has so amplified their message that it travels with them around the world.[23]

Such transcendence and amplification were possible because in effect – as opposed to IS – Bin Laden, the 'civilisational revolutionary',[24] was interested in neither replacement nor punishment of the Arab and Muslim states. This point needs to be underscored – 'what is noteworthy about Al Qaeda is that as an organisation it is not interested in replacing any *particular* regime in any one *particular* country, even if it supports its local affiliates in such quests'[25] – as the lasting appeal of Al Qaeda in Islamist circles and as its influence on IS attest.

Revenge of the 'Agitated Muslims'

A second component of the matrix introduced by Al Qaeda that can help us inform IS's history is captured in the actual battle plan set in motion by Osama Bin Laden and Ayman al Dhawahiri in 1989, immediately after the end of the Afghanistan war and the Soviet Union's withdrawal. In setting up their organisation, the two men were in effect making a statement akin to 'we defeated one superpower; let us take on another – more important – one'. If the militarisation and professionalisation that Al Qaeda had been pursuing since the early 1990s saw its culmination eleven years later in the 9/11 operation (rehearsed in different configurations since 1996), and if the leader of those commandos, Mohamed Atta, and his team performed like 'perfect soldiers',[26] it is because this militarised perspective was introduced as a long-term approach that was meant to last and to empower a generation of 'warriors', not merely to conduct short-lived moments of attack (as was the case with 1970s and 1980s terrorism). It is also surprising that Bin Laden did not seek to expand his dominion over local Afghan actors. His money and leadership aura combined with their internecine division could have allowed him to seek a position of arbiter, which his Meccan lineage would always forcefully legitimise. Rather, Bin Laden was pragmatic regarding the limits of what the Arab Afghans could do locally. The first international *jihad* was over, fought and won. As the Taliban became occupied and preoccupied with local politics,[27] he struck a deal with them that in effect provided him with a 'rented' part of their territory from which he would develop, build, train and unleash an army to, as he had promised himself a decade earlier, 'punish the oppressor in kind'. In that sense, conceptually, Bin Laden introduced and enacted in his terroristic violence what I have observed elsewhere as the 'democratisation of responsibility', namely the conscious erasing of the lines of responsibility that separate the Western executive political decision-maker from the Western-ruled civilian, whom Bin Laden regarded as an active accomplice of the violence visited upon Muslims by his or her government by virtue of passively tolerating or merely electing such decision-makers and allowing them to persist with such policies.

The issue at the core of the relationship between the state and the materialisation of (any) political violence is, objectively, indeed intimately, bound up with the manner in which governments and citizens carry out their respective and distinct responsibilities towards one another as regards the licence to kill (extended only to the representatives of the state).[28] Under that generic rubric, the singular counter-proposition that Al Qaeda developed came to be adapted shrewdly for the purposes of its brand of terrorism, particularly in terms of its appeal for radical Islamist militants seeking violent non-state agency at both local and global levels.[29] Although this reinterpretation of the production and direction of violence is where an important part of Al Qaeda's influence lies, that aspect was not recognised by many analysts of Al Qaeda, who often carried self-referentialism and paternalistic overtones that blinded their analyses by constantly linking them to Western definitions of the terms of exchange. Analyses in this vein often start thus: 'The problem with Al Qaeda/ISIS is that ... ', with the reader given a single, all-explaining key with which to make sense of the group in the mode of a shortcoming linked to the radicals' stance vis-à-vis others. Slavoj Žižek, for instance, writes that

> *the problem* with terrorist fundamentalists is not that we consider them inferior to us, but, rather, that they themselves secretly consider

themselves inferior. This is why our condescending, political correct assurances that we feel no superiority towards them only makes them more furious and feeds their resentment. *The problem* is not cultural difference (their effort to preserve their identity), but the opposite fact that they have already internalised our standards and measure themselves by them.[30]

Documentarily, Al Qaeda did precisely the opposite of what Žižek assesses. Everything in Bin Laden's actions and speeches, and subsequently with IS, evidences an explicitly conceptualised, agency-wrestling and consciously acted radical rupture, whereby the new groups were independently advocating radical violence, claiming ownership of their narrative of rupture and 'judging' their own regional governments as well as the West, dismissing the irrelevance of the first and pursuing the latter's 'punishment' through extreme terrorism.

Illustrating the policy-academe impasse on these issues, such a logic of dismissal is not surprising, as it has deep roots. In a 16 December 1998 interview with French magazine *Le Nouvel Observateur*, in which he discussed the controversial covert US support of insurgents in Afghanistan opposed to the pro-Soviet Afghan government, former US National Security Advisor Zbigniew Brzezinski had remarked: '[What] is most important to the history of the world? The Taliban or the collapse of the Soviet Empire? Some agitated Muslims or the liberation of Central Europe and the end of the Cold War.'[31] Setting aside the Western-centric nature of such a perspective on *global* security, it emerged that within three years of that statement, these 'agitated Muslims' had led a military-style commando operation on the defence ministry of the most powerful state in the world, simultaneously killing close to 3,000 people in its economic capital. A few years later, their organisation would be regarded as the number one international security threat to that country – as noted in the 2002 and 2006 editions of the White House-issued National Security Strategy of the United States. Fifteen years after that strategically blind statement, an offshoot of that dismissed group of disquieted actors would take that level of dangerousness a step higher.

The initial terrorist campaign by Al Qaeda had taken the form of two strands of action which were always constitutive of a dual approach; on the one hand attracting local operators who would be trained as members of this new army and, on the other, developing leads and forays to prepare the penetration of Western centres (thus setting up the logic of secret cells). These two tracks would remain a legacy that IS would come to replay years later. Possibly the opening salvo of this dual-layered campaign was the 1993 attack on the CIA. On the morning of 25 January that year, Quetta-born Pakistani national Aimal Khan Kansi (also known as Mir Aimal Kansi) shot and killed two CIA employees at the entrance of the CIA headquarters in Langley, Virginia. Kansi, who had entered the United States in 1991, managed to escape. He was later apprehended in 1997 by a Federal Bureau of Investigation (FBI) team in coordination with Pakistani authorities in the Punjab region, transferred to the United States, and executed in 2002. Although he had once attended a meeting led by Bin Laden in Kandahar and met with him, it is not clear whether Kansi had had actual operational links with Al Qaeda in preparing that specific attack on the CIA, or whether he had simply been influenced by the declarations that Bin Laden had begun issuing around that time. However, the gunman's subsequent statement that he 'was real angry with the policy of the US government in the Middle East, particularly toward the Palestinian people'[32] echoed the political messages the group, and Bin Laden himself had made explicit in reference to US foreign policy in the Middle East. Indeed, a month after that shooting, on 26 February, a first attempt at attacking the World Trade Centre took place, killing six individuals. The principal perpetrator, Ramzi Youssef, had been trained in an Al Qaeda camp in Afghanistan, and his uncle, Khaled Sheikh Mohammed, was the first to have proposed the 9/11 operation to Bin Laden.

As the outsized influence of Bin Laden began gaining authority and appeal among Islamist networks internationally, Al Qaeda refined these first attempts and sought to introduce a more sophisticated, professional type of operator, eventually best embodied in the Egyptian national Mohamed Atta, leader of the Hamburg Cell: well educated, technology-savvy[33] and cosmopolitan. An important harbinger of this trajectory was, earlier, another Egyptian operator, Ali Mohamed (whose full name is Ali Abdul Saoud Mohamed). Connected to Al Jihad al Islami al Masri (the Egyptian Islamic Jihad), a group active in Egypt since the 1970s that would fold itself into Al Qaeda in 2002, Mohamed, a first-generation Arab Afghan who had been active in training the fighters, had developed links with Ayman al Dhawahiri in Afghanistan, and then during the latter's visit to the United States in 1995, where Bin Laden's deputy had raised funds in several religious centres across California (in Santa Clara, Stockton and Sacramento). In close coordination with Bin

Laden since 1988, and under the influence of al Dhawahiri, for whom he served as translator during that visit to the US, Mohamed had become a US citizen in 1989 (after being admitted into the United States in 1985 under a special visa programme controlled by the CIA's clandestine service, following a first posting in Hamburg, Germany), and joined the US Army as a drill instructor and support sergeant. He then acted as a triple agent, pretending to gather intelligence about terrorist cells in Afghanistan for the CIA and serving as a US Army sergeant, all the while helping Al Qaeda's senior management conceive and unleash its first batch of high-profile operations against the United States. Mohamed played an important role in the development of Al Qaeda's strategic infrastructure and, revealingly, this was done as he occupied an eminently transnational position and in effect belonged deeply to two worlds. In addition to providing physical training to Bin Laden's new generation of fighters gathered in the Afghan camps, he helped the group increase its understanding of intelligence warfare techniques and communication cipher technologies through data he had privileged access to in the United States, notably at the John F. Kennedy Special Warfare Centre and School in Fort Bragg, North Carolina. Most importantly, he demoed, in Somalia, Tanzania and Kenya, the cell structure that would be used to prepare attacks, preparing the ground for the subsequent franchise model. In effect, courtesy of Mohamed, US Army maps and training manuals were used to develop Al Qaeda's training guide. His by-the-book, duty-driven, transnational criss-crossing between Europe, the US, Asia and Africa came to a halt when, in the aftermath of the August 1998 bombings in Kenya and Tanzania, he came under suspicion and his apartment was searched by FBI agents, who uncovered materials linked to Al Qaeda that led to his arrest. A plea bargain deal was struck between Mohamed and the United States in 2000, and he subsequently assisted the United States in its efforts against Al Qaeda.[34]

As its soldiery was assembled in such a transnational fashion round the world and at a dozen or so camps throughout Afghanistan, supported by a guild of senior operators (led by Abu Ubaida al Banshiri, Abu Hafs al Masri and Abu Zubayda), Al Qaeda put in motion in the mid-1990s its battle plan. Over the next ten years, its new form of terrorism would impact the generation being born in an indelible way. Although the larger strategy of Al Qaeda is commonly understood as having been expanded in the writings of Ayman al Dhawahiri and Abu Mus'ab al Suri in the mid-2000s,[35] it is arguably the earlier period, in which the military actions of Al Qaeda were engineered by the likes of Ali Mohamed, that gives rise to its larger plan and influence. Unbeknown to most observers, including Middle Eastern and Western intelligence services, Al Qaeda was then well on its way to becoming a transnational non-state armed group of a new calibre. As such, the organisation had become an entity that could attack within and across state boundaries, based on sophisticated networks of communication and information, and empowered by globalisation and information-age technologies. In effect, Al Qaeda was pushing war forward more innovatively than its opponents.[36] That should not come as a complete surprise, for, as Hew Strachan reminds us, 'War is not a one-sided activity, but assumes resistance'. Indeed, as he goes on citing Carl Von Clausewitz, 'martial agency', as we can term it here, is possibly a fundamentally reactive activity:

> Clausewitz is helpful on this point: war, he observed, begins with defence not attack. The invader might be only too pleased to gain his objectives without fighting; it is the defender who resorts to war to oppose the invader's intentions. Even when the invader uses force, if there is no response, the result will be not a war but a massacre. This element of reciprocity is critical to any definition of war and to all that follows.[37]

What followed on the part of Al Qaeda was a reinvention of terrorism as war (Table 1.1).

Al Qaeda started as an Arab-dominated group set up outside an Arab country in an Asian context, with a radical Islamist agenda designed principally to counter perceived Western, specifically American, hegemony in Muslim lands, and to respond to that dominion through the use of force targeted at the United States – at home and abroad – and its allies. With Bin Laden taking up residency in Afghanistan in May 1996, following his time in Sudan (1991–6), the operational implementation of Al Qaeda's battle plan was accelerated. In November 1995 and June 1996, two key centres of US military activity in Saudi Arabia were targeted, killing 26 soldiers and servicemen. These first two attacks were characterised by a familiar approach in which the group had clearly stepped up a gear, with their smuggled explosives and truck bomb *modus operandi* still in effect akin to earlier attacks against United States' interests in the Middle East, notably the October 1983 suicide attack in Beirut, Lebanon on US Marines and French paratroopers. The attacks were also indicative of

Table 1.1   Al Qaeda's major transnational operations, 1995–2005

Date	Target(s)	Location	Deaths
13 November 1995	US-operated Saudi National Guard Training Centre	Riyadh, Saudi Arabia	Seven, including five American servicemen
25 June 1996	Khobar Towers	Dhahran, Saudi Arabia	19 American soldiers
7 August 1998	US embassies	Nairobi, Kenya and Dar es Salaam, Tanzania	242
12 October 2000	USS *Cole*	Off the coast of Aden, Yemen	17 American sailors
11 September 2001	World Trade Centre in New York, the Pentagon and White House/Capitol (failed) in Washington, DC and Somerset County area over Pennsylvania	New York, Washington, DC and Pennsylvania, United States	2,977
12 October 2002	Night clubs (Paddy's Irish Pub and Sari Club)	Bali, Indonesia	202, mostly Australian, tourists
12 May 2003	Al Hamra residential complex, housing US and UK staff	Riyadh, Saudi Arabia	39, including twelve US citizens
11 March 2004	Atocha, El Pozo, Alcalá de Henares and Santa Eugenia train stations	Madrid, Spain	190
7 July 2005	Three subway stations and a double-decker bus	London, United Kingdom	56

the fact that Bin Laden had not yet refocused his attention fully on the 'far enemy', still indulging his desire to punish 'the near one'. Indeed, the November 1995 attack on the Saudi National Guard location followed the issuance, in August of that year, of an open letter addressed by Bin Laden to the King of Saudi Arabia, Fahd bin Abdulaziz Al Saud, in which Bin Laden criticised the nature of the kingdom's relationship with the United Stated, and stated:

Was it not the American President [Bill] Clinton on a visit to the country who refused to visit you in Riyadh? Did he not insist that you submissively and humiliatingly go to meet him in the American bases in Hafr-al-Batin? With that kind of behaviour, the American president wanted to prove two points: First, to emphasise that the nature of his visit was basically to inspect his forces stationed in those bases. Second: to teach you a lesson in abjectness and scorn so that you are aware that he is your true guardian even in your alleged kingdom which, in reality, is nothing else but an American protectorate governed by the American Constitution.[38]

An indication of the importance given by Bin Laden to military matters is provided in his comment in the same letter that:

There is no justification for leaving the nation's army to experience a state of incapacitation and negligence whereas it was supposed to safeguard the land of the Muslims and defend their causes in addition to protecting the holy lands. It is not reasonable to keep one's silence about transforming the nation to an American protectorate to be defiled by the soldiers of the Cross with their soiled feet in order to protect your crumbling throne and the preservation of the oilfields in the kingdom.

A year later, following the Khobar Towers attack in June that also struck at US interests in Saudi Arabia, on 23 August 1996 Bin Laden issued a first declaration of war on the United States. The very nature of that document – 'Declaration of War against the Americans Occupying the Holy Lands' (i.e. the cities of Mecca and Medina in Saudi Arabia) – encapsulated the shift-in-the-making, with Al Qaeda's rerouting of its violence and the reordering of its priorities. A second declaration of war would be issued on 23 February 1998 at the occasion of Bin Laden's meeting with three Islamist leaders – Abu Yasir al Rifai Ahmad Taha (Egypt), Sheikh Mir Hamza (Pakistan) and Fazlul Rahman (Bangladesh) – to set up a World Islamic Front for Jihad against the Jews and the Crusaders (Al Jabha al Islamiya al 'Alamiya li Qital al Yahud wal Salibiyin).

From that point forward, and although pressure would continue on the local Middle Eastern powers, and although Al Qaeda *qua* Al Qaeda was still being assembled, the group led by Bin Laden would turn its attention to what it considered the main event, namely engagement with the United States on a global scale. On 7 August 1998, the group conducted a simultaneous attack comprising two coordinated operations on the US embassies in Nairobi, Kenya and Dar es Salaam, Tanzania, killing a total of 242 people. The near-instantaneity, multiple-site lethality, lengthy preparation and military-style nature of the attacks confirmed the movement towards professional operations as well as Al Qaeda's growing stature as the main Islamist group worldwide – one able to 'take on' the world's superpower in contrast to other regional radical Islamist groups. That orientation and martial nature of the Al Qaeda plan was confirmed two and half years later when, in October 2000, the organisation led a speedboat suicide attack on a US destroyer, the USS *Cole*, killing 17 American sailors and injuring 39. The sequence would culminate in the 9/11 attacks, the ultimate transnational manifestation of a then-new type of violence produced and beamed by a non-state armed group on to a state power. The multiple temporalities of dissent – Bin Laden's recriminations to King Fahd and to the United States – encapsulated into that attack also spoke of an expanded spatiality of action, as the attacks had been designed in Kuala Lumpur, Malaysia; supervised from Khost, Afghanistan; planned in Hamburg, Germany; financed from Abu Dhabi, the United Arab Emirates; rehearsed in Tarragona, Spain; and launched on two cities in the United States from three airports, in under two hours, involving 19 individuals from four nationalities.

The McDonaldisation of Terrorism

The third and final way in which Al Qaeda heralded the emergence of IS was the manner in which, in the wake of the 9/11 attacks, it enabled the autonomisation of force in its own midst. Instead of indulging the time-tested tendency of terrorist leaders to centralise all decision-making around their person and demand loyalty and submissiveness, Bin Laden embraced independence of action on the part of his followers. In so doing, he set the stage for the emergence of a number of subgroups, offshoots and so-called franchises round the world, which in time grew into their own important entities. Eventually, IS would become the most important, transcending the legacy of Al Qaeda. This strategy of corporate dissemination on the part of Al Qaeda's leadership also owed a lot to the manner in which the group made innovative and creative use of the information technology revolution.

As 9/11 affected the US leadership (as late as 18 October 2001, six weeks after the attack, the US senior leadership was still edgy and prone to fear of further attacks),[39] the legend behind Al Qaeda developed rapidly among radical Islamists around the world. The nature of the blow dealt to the United States in the heart of its capital, and the extensive global media coverage of the event, combined to provide the group with unexpected international publicity. In time, when the George W. Bush administration decided to invade Iraq in March 2003, misleadingly linking that war with the attacks of 9/11, Al Qaeda would be provided with the next phase of its *modus operandi*, and would use that territory to plan new attacks – much as it had done in Afghanistan two decades earlier to rally troops in its *jihad* against the Soviet troops. However, the immediate aftermath of the 9/11 attacks was not so obvious for Al Qaeda, which in many ways became a victim of its own success. Its 9/11 operation was simply too big, triggering events too large and a sequence that played out too rapidly. The manner in which Al Qaeda managed the aftermath of what it referred to in its literature as the 'raid on Manhattan' (*ghazzou Manhattan*) gave it the keys to survival, opened the door to sustenance and prepared the way for its eventual replacement by IS.

For all its earlier consequential proactive planning, Al Qaeda found itself having to improvise after its attacks in the US. The group had sought to build a base from which to launch its war. Now it had, with one main operation, engineered a result it could not realistically top. With New York 'castrated' and Washington 'on its knees' – 'Here is America', uttered Bin Laden slowly and in guarded satisfaction, yet quite theatrically, in his first message five weeks after the attacks, as if to let his followers know that he had delivered on his promise – the group could plan a second wave of attacks, while attending to its survival in Afghanistan following the launch of the US invasion of that country on 7 October. Once it managed, with great difficulty, to survive the US assault, and though it had lost a few key operators – killed (notably military chief Mohammed Atef, known as Abu Hafs al Masri, hit during a US airstrike near Kabul on 16 November 2001) or arrested (in particular Ramzi Bin al Shaiba and Khaled Sheikh Mohammed, respectively coordinator and organiser of the 9/11 attacks on New York and Washington, detained on 11 September 2002 in Karachi and on 1 March 2003 in Rawalpindi, Pakistan; and Zein al Abidin Mohammad Hussein, known as Abu Zubayda, senior chief of operations, captured in Faisalabad, Pakistan on 28 March 2002) – the organisation pursued a new course of action that sought to spread its enemy under a logic of dispersion. Dissolving its physical, pinpointable presence, Al Qaeda rendered its centre of gravity fluid and itself evanescent. In so doing, it frustrated the advancing US special forces in Afghanistan from a fight which they had been bracing themselves for, luring them into a more difficult cat-and-mouse game. Bin Laden and al Dhawahiri then opted to forestall and relocate their attacks on US allies round the world. Accordingly, the group conducted six mid-scale operations in Karachi, Pakistan in May and June 2002; Sana'a, Yemen in October 2002; Riyadh, Saudi Arabia in May and November 2003; Casablanca, Morocco in May 2003; Istanbul, Turkey in November 2003; and Amman, Jordan in November 2005. These attacks were paralleled by two major operations in Madrid on 11 March 2004 and in London on 7 July 2005. The years between 2002 and 2006 thus constituted the final moment in which the group Bin Laden set up in 1988 was pushing its agenda. Terrorism in effect became the dominant issue of our times around this period, with the world engulfed in a violence that was playing out daily and descending to levels of mutual hostility unprecedented in the contemporary history of Western and Muslim relations; torture and humiliation begetting beheadings, in turn generating further killing – on both sides, a spiral of hatred and mayhem. The generation that would become IS grew up in these (de)formative years.

As Bin Laden began seeing the limits of what his 'base' could achieve operationally, and as he sought to morph himself into a statesman-like figure talking *de tú a tú* to Western leaders and addressing their societies in a series of messages meant to influence their domestic debates and electoral decisions, he introduced another important innovation that would characterise the history of his movement, namely the franchising system. While concentrating on the Iraq conflict, in effect treating it as a second Afghanistan (see Chapter 2), his organisation saw merit in formally embracing the decentralisation it was inevitably moving towards. To be certain, the assertiveness of the movement in that phase, which allowed it to take a back seat, sprang primarily from its battle-hardened status. Al Qaeda's leadership decision was not, however, wholly fatalistic, flippant or opportunistic. It was more adaptive, in the sense that, above and beyond its inability to oversee operations as it had done earlier, *upping the ante* by cloning the group and multiplying its centres of gravity could both confuse and put its enemies on the defensive in a larger number of spots around the world. Such orchestrating of different strata kept to the group's globalisation-influenced mindset. Al Qaeda is, in that respect, arguably more the child of globalisation than it is the product of the evolution of radical armed Islamism. In bottling his concept of transnationalised and militarised professional terrorism visited upon the states and citizens of the West in the heart of their metropolises, in retaliation for their governments' foreign policies, Bin Laden had achieved his goals. His ultimate disappearance (much later as it turned out, in May 2011) was in effect already a foregone conclusion of planned obsolescence. Such Che Guevarasation of Bin Laden was prefigured, however, by a final step, namely the transformation of Al Qaeda into a mass-market commodity.

Between 2004 and 2008, the central Al Qaeda organisation I have referred to as Al Qaeda al Oum, or the 'mother Al Qaeda', developed, inspired or welcomed into its fold several other organisations. One of those would go on to top it and become IS. Accordingly, in a span of four years (2003–7), Al Qaeda established the following six official branches: Al Qaeda in the Arabian Peninsula (AQAP, Tandhim al Qaeda fi Jazirat al 'Arab), the Secret Organisation of Al Qaeda in Europe (Jama'at al Tandhim al Sirri li Munadhamat Qaedat al Jihad fi Europa), AQI (Tandhim Qaedat al Jihad fi Bilad al Rafidayn), Al Qaeda in Egypt (Tandhim al Qaeda fi Misr), AQIM (Tandhim Al Qaeda fi Bilad al Maghrib Al Islami) and Al Qaeda in Afghanistan (Tandhim al Qaeda fi Khorasan). In November 2011 and in September 2014, in a different context and as a reaction to the growing emergence of IS, two more branches, Al Qaeda in the Sinai Peninsula (Tandhim al Qaeda fi al Sinai) and Al Qaeda in the Indian Subcontinent (Tandhim Qa'edat al Jihad fi Shibh al Qarra al Hindiya), were added (Table 1.2).

These different entities displayed the same *modus operandi* as Al Qaeda, with high-profile and coordinated attacks against symbolic targets, lengthy preparations and studied timing as well as an active use of the media. A key development in this phase was the use of technology and communication. Al Qaeda had long been preoccupied with communication matters, and as early as 1996 Bin Laden had convened a press conference at which he and their leaders announced the set-up of their organisation. Later, he welcomed a number of journalists for one-on-one interviews (John Miller, Scott MacLeod, Peter Bergen, Rahimullah Yusufzay, Robert Fisk, Ahmad Zaidan, Hamid Mir and Abdel Bari Atwan). After the 9/11 attacks, the organisation took that effort one step further, introducing a dimension that would be expanded fully by IS later on. In October 2001, as US and UK troops initiated their assault on Afghanistan, Bin Laden and al Dhawahiri appeared in a video aired on Al Jazeera. From that point on, regular pronouncements by the two men, and in time their lieutenants (such as Oregon-born Adam Gadahn), would be released, as would the videotaped 'wills' of the members of the 9/11 commandos (IS would top that technique with near-live videos of attack perpetrators minutes before initiating their suicide operations,

Table 1.2 Al Qaeda's franchises, 2004–14

Name	Location	Original leader(s)	Established	Relationship to Al Qaeda	Relationship to IS
Al Qaeda in the Arabian Peninsula	Saudi Arabia (2003–6), Yemen (2009–)	Yusuf al Ayeri, Abdelaziz al Moqrin, Nasser al Wuhaychi, Said Ali al Shihri	2003 (Saudi Arabia); 2009 (Yemen)	Official offshoot	No pledge of allegiance; competition
Al Qaeda in Iraq/Mesopotamia	Iraq	Abu Mus'ab al Zarqawi	27 December 2004	Official offshoot	Forerunner
Al Qaeda in Europe	London, Madrid and Rome	Unknown	7 July 2005	Claimed the 7 July 2005 attacks in London on behalf of Al Qaeda	Unknown
Al Qaeda in Egypt	Egypt	Mohammad Khalil al Hukayma	5 August 2006	Official offshoot; short-lived	None
Al Qaeda in the Islamic Maghreb	Algeria and the Sahel (northern Mali)	Abdelmalek Droukdel	11 January 2007	Official offshoot; restructuring of Salafist Group for Predication and Combat (Algerian group)	No pledge of allegiance; soft competition
Al Qaeda in Afghanistan	Afghanistan	Mustapha Abu al Yazid	23 May 2007	Official offshoot	No pledge of allegiance
Al Qaeda in the Sinai Peninsula	Egypt	Mohammed Eid Muslih Hamad; Ramzi Mowafi	November 2011	Offshoot, merger with Ansar al Jihad (Egyptian group)	No pledge of allegiance
Al Qaeda in the Indian Subcontinent	India and Pakistan	Asim Umar	3 September 2014	Official offshoot	No pledge of allegiance

uploaded online within hours). Al Qaeda was also the first terrorist organisation to create an official media branch, Moussassat al Sihab (the clouds' organisation). In the 1970s, a number of groups had published statements or manifestos, or produced regular magazines (such as the PFLP's *Bulletin*), but none set up a fully fledged parallel entity devoted solely to producing and disseminating 'news' about the group's activities. Indicative of both the mimetism that Al Qaeda inspired, and things to come later with IS, Moussassat al Sihab influenced AQIM, which set up its media branch, Al Andalus. In turn, AQIM's offshoot, Al Murabitun, created its own agency, Ribat. Al Qaeda also pioneered the use of regular video releases (from short videotaped messages in 2001 by its leaders, to hour-long online documentaries displaying graphs and computer simulations in 2005), peaking at 67 video messages released in 2007. The development of a dedicated Al Qaeda magazine was an important element in this phase. Upon its release, that magazine, entitled *Inspire* and developed by the American citizen Anwar al 'Awlaki, was indicative of a turn whereby the organisation was inviting individual operators to take matters of violence into their hands (see Chapter 4).[40]

By the time the aggrieved and ruminative Bin Laden (talking history and issuing truces) was replaced in 2014 in the public imagery of radical Islamist terrorism by the cocksure and menacing Jihadi John (beheading Western prisoners), the matrix Al Qaeda had introduced long ago had been cemented and transcended, occupying the period between 1988 and 2011. After the death of Bin Laden – whose persona and charisma had nonetheless been routinised[41] – the group that survived and continued to exist gradually became secondary to the actions of the several regional subgroups it has spawned; one of which, AQI, soon to be known as IS, superseded it. Twenty-two years after it was set up in Afghanistan, and ten years after it had conducted its most lethal operation in New York and Washington, Al Qaeda had mutated into a movement that no longer resembled its original form. From a hierarchical and centralised group led by the bicephalous leadership of Osama Bin Laden and Ayman al Dhawahiri, it had become a regionalised and decentralised organisation with several competing leaders following the death of Bin Laden in May 2011. By the end of its run, Al Qaeda had been successful in its offensive asymmetrical combat mode and was influencing its enemy's way of war. As the agility-focused strategic modes of the US and Al Qaeda began increasingly to mirror each other,[42] the net result was in favour of the armed group which, in effect, managed to proto-'statify' its military capacity. Such a dynamic was not wasted on the many armed groups observing this self-empowerment through a different type of mobilisation. Among the first to capitalise on such professionalisation was the Lebanese armed group Hezbollah, which had itself been growing in sophistication, as demonstrated by its military defeat of Israel in the July–August 2006 conflict. Al Qaeda's influence over Hezbollah was visible particularly in the course of that conflict, with 'Hezbollah react[ing] not as a culturally-captive, but as an evolving, adaptive force. The July [2006] war has been interpreted as a signpost conflict for the future, pointing towards a post-modern, hybrid and ever more complex environment.'[43]

Mainstream journalism, terrorism expertise and policy accounts often present the history of Al Qaeda as an organisation that had been decimated by US military efforts, when arguably the group objectively achieved its goals (to serve as a base for a radical Islamist war against its Western enemy states, principally the US) and went out through studied mutation. Contradicting themselves, these analyses speak of a process whereby the group had metastasised, although Al Qaeda has not technically ended even 30 years after its formal creation. The early successes of Al Qaeda masked, however, a self-inflicted structural defeat. If initially the rapid proliferation of the regional representations of Al Qaeda were arguably an added indication of the organisation's impressive global reach (in Europe, the Nile Valley, the Levant, the Maghreb and the Gulf) and its ability to operate transnationally years after the War on Terror had been launched against it, it gradually emerged that the regional entities differed significantly and their relationship to the mother Al Qaeda was now, at best, tenuous (with offshoots of offshoots multiplying, as in the notable case of AQIM).[44] Whereas in its first 15 years Al Qaeda had been able to advance globally, cumulatively and against important odds – for each tactical loss, Al Qaeda came to earn strategic gain: retreat in Afghanistan but advance in Iraq; confined leadership but proliferating cells; curtailed physical movement but global, transnational impact; additional enemies but expanding recruits – during 2006–11 its leadership had morphed into a meta-commandment ultimately offering only politico-religious and military-strategic commentary, not operational direction. All in all, what can be read as a regionalisation strategy of Al Qaeda ended up confusing the global picture of the organisation for its militants. The necessary elasticity the group adopted – partly voluntarily, partly as a way to adapt to the international counter-terrorism campaign – created an ever-growing distance with already independent units. The aesthetic authority of Al Qaeda was now merely anthemic for its anticipatory milieu. Woven in the fabric of its disruption of global affairs was, more importantly, a lasting *matrix* for radical political action that IS would, in time, come to inherit and build on.

As a terrorist military initiative, Al Qaeda peaked with the London July 2005 attack, itself a mini-replay of 9/11. Operationally, in leaving the protean sophistication of its violence there, it created a situation to be picked up by the franchises and the operatives in Western societies. An open-source Al Qaeda was born. Politically, the peak was reached a bit earlier, in November 2004, with Bin Laden's speech three days before the US presidential election of that year, which led to the second mandate of George W. Bush. Simultaneously resolved and resigned, Bin Laden expressed a muted turmoil in a way that sought to reverse the interrogation in his region and towards the West. His statement in that speech to Americans that their security was in their hands not their leaders', was an indication of a changed logic as to how the violence would play out in the next phase – while in effect closing his own chapter eight years before he was declared dead by the US.[45] Bin Laden's disappearance from Al Qaeda and the War on Terror scene marked the end of an era for the original group set up in Afghanistan. It opened a new phase in which the regional franchises would further enact their existing independence, and in so doing endow the larger conflict with a novel configuration by stretching the centre of gravity of transnational terrorism. Though the franchising exercise was complex and not fully mapped out by Al Qaeda, everything in that story had stayed in lockstep, as IS could next logically reinvent Al Qaeda, proving its mettle without necessarily differentiating itself from it. So much so indeed, that IS could claim Al Qaeda's legacy without being explicitly tacked on to it. This is the subject of Chapters 2–4.

2

Apocalypse Iraq

We'll have to work sort of the dark side, if you will.

Dick Cheney (2001)

To not understand the mythic underpinnings of our response to 9/11 is, in a fundamental way, to not understand ourselves, to be so unknowing about the way we inhabit our cultural roles that we are stunned, insensible, when confronted by a moment that requires our full awareness.

Susan Faludi, *The Terror Dream* (2007)

If the first layer of understanding IS is to be located in its Al Qaeda lineage, and how IS came to be profoundly impacted by that indelible experience, the second level rests in the legacy of what the United States acted out in Iraq after 2003. There is no overstating the harm done by the American invasion to that country, to the region's geostrategic balance and, more generally, to international affairs. The actions performed by the George W. Bush administration and the new Iraqi authorities they installed in Baghdad bear a direct correlation with the birth of IS, and the brutality the new group came to display in Iraq and other places. Beyond the grammatical legacy of what Al Qaeda introduced as a *modus operandi*, the type of terrorism, force patterns and transnational dissemination, there is, similarly, an important parallel to be established between the earlier 'AfPak' (Afghanistan-Pakistan) and the subsequent 'Syraq' (Syria-Iraq) theatres of conflict, and the connection with the rise of Al Qaeda and that of IS. Both Al Qaeda and IS partake in key ways in geopolitical dynamics that have, at different periods, moulded them into the entities they are. Specifically, war, occupation, destruction and violations by external actors and corrupt local regimes have contributed to both the rise of the groups and the fuelling of their radical agendas. In deciphering the nature of such continuities, we are able to see the deeper logics of recurring violence at the hands of such extreme groups, and in this case the further radicalisation of a new generation within an existing radical organisation.

Al Qaeda's September 2001 terrorist attacks on the United States unleashed, two years later, an imperial reaction in Iraq on the part of America, which in turn gave birth, ten years later, to IS. The challenge to the United States by Al Qaeda had led to the reassertion of American imperial might, in turn leading to a second armed group rising in the form of IS. Specifically, the degenerated sequence at the end of which an entity like IS could emerge with the violence that would come to characterise it, played out in relation to three key dimensions, namely: the dispossession and alienation consequences of *the reinvention of colonialism* under the guise of an international trusteeship to rebuild and democratise Iraq; *the brutalisation of Iraqi* society in the context of that episode in ways that left deep psychological and physical scars constitutive of societal trauma; which birthed a new generation of radicals fuelling their explicit *desire of revenge* through the use of upgraded terrorism.

Colonialism Redesigned

Reflecting on the reasons for which many US policymakers often choose to ignore the links between US foreign policy and violent reactions to it, Jon Schwarz reminds us[1] that the very official 9/11 Commission admitted in its report about the 2001 terrorist attacks on US soil that: 'America's policy choices have consequences. Right or wrong, it is simply a fact that American policy regarding the Israeli-Palestinian conflict and American actions in Iraq are dominant staples of popular commentary across the Arab and Muslim world.'[2] That remark was made in reference to the long-standing American support of the Israeli occupation of Palestinian lands, and the US prosecution of the 1991 war in Iraq to dislodge Saddam Hussein's army from its occupation of Kuwait and subsequent international embargo imposed on Iraq (which lasted from 6 August 1990 to 22 May 2003, and until 15 December 2010 as concerned US and UK control of Iraq's oil revenue). In the middle of that sequence, in May 1996, the United States ambassador to the UN, Madeleine Albright, was asked by the CBS television programme *60 Minutes* whether containment of Hussein's Iraq was worth the lives of half a million children. She replied: 'I think this is a very hard choice, but the price, we think, the price is worth it'. Those policy choices and those specific initial US actions in Iraq were referred to by Bin Laden as reasons for his attacks on the United

States. Extensively documented, the economic privations during these years impacted a full generation of Iraqis, who were born in conditions of malnutrition and grew up amid a war-torn country.³ The control of Iraq by an international community led by the United States during this period was extensive and unprecedented. Between May 1991 and December 1998, 3,845 disarmament inspectors were deployed in Iraq in the context of 276 UN inspection missions, during which 392,000 visits took place using 2,957 helicopters flights and 140 surveillance cameras placed in 29 sites (in addition to 434 U2 spy plane overflights). During these years, 1,378 Iraqi officials and technicians were interrogated for 2,359 hours, on nine kilometres of microfilm. These, however, were acts of instrumentalisation of international law and abuse of norms – as they went beyond the letter of the resolutions – to force the government of Saddam Hussein, which had not been defeated militarily in 1991 but merely compelled to withdraw from Kuwait, to bend to the will of the United States and its allies, be humiliated and ultimately collapse. The strategy pursued by the United States was explicitly about regime change, and all three US administrations (those of George H. Bush, Bill Clinton and George W. Bush) throughout those years provided support to the Iraqi opposition and sponsored coup attempts against Hussein's regime (notably in 1994 and 1996, with action taken by US special forces in 2002 to target the Iraqi president).

What took place when the United States established direct control of Iraq in April 2003, after it had launched a military invasion on 20 March, with the support of the United Kingdom and without the authorisation of the United Nations Security Council (UNSC), was of a different order and magnitude and constituted in effect an update of earlier colonial practices. The United States' invasion of Iraq in 2003 rebooted colonialism and, in addition to the independent legacy of Al Qaeda, set the stage (due to its brutality) for the birth of IS. The US invasion was illegal and the actions performed there criminal. The invasion was motivated by national and personal emotions, led by political calculations and constituted a strategic blunder. It followed explicit calls for colonising Muslim lands that had come less than a month after the 9/11 attacks, voiced in the columns of one of the most influential newspapers in the United States: 'America may have to accept long-term political obligations ... America and her allies may find themselves, temporarily at least, not just occupying with troops but administering obdurate terrorist states ... These may eventually include not only Afghanistan but Iraq, Sudan, Libya, Iran and Syria. Democratic regimes willing to abide by international law will be implanted where possible, but a Western political presence seems unavoidable in some cases.'[4] Importantly, the invasion is directly related to the birth of IS. A video released by IS on 18 April 2017, entitled *The War Recorded*, presented a history of the group that starts with the US invasion in 2003, kicking off the narrated story with images of US tanks rolling victoriously into Baghdad.

The Iraq War, as it has come to be known, is generally regarded as a failure. The conflict is depicted in terms of 'incompetence', a 'defeat' and a 'fiasco', 'unraveling' with 'no end in sight', a 'hell' that has left the country in 'fragments'.[5] The war is denounced as not having worked, but the discussion remains for the most part at a level where what is essentially being criticised is the prosecution of the war, and what is being regretted is that it failed to accomplish its goals.[6] In other words, from that perspective, had a better job been done at seeing it through, the war would have been acceptable. Discussion of the US invasion of Iraq is, in that sense, further marked by two traits, namely a tendency to focus on the tactical and military aspects and a desire to 'move on'. The analysis proceeds from criticism of the management rather than the nature of the actions. 'Missed opportunities', 'adventure', 'why we lost', 'why we couldn't win', all of it *lamento* for a scene where the travails of the US platoons are presented as 'epic' and 'tragic',[7] just as those of the Centurions in French Algeria were, with such celebration of SEALs in Iraq continuing the tradition and imagery of *The Green Berets* (1968) in Vietnam and *Black Hawk Down* (2001) in Somalia.

As attested to by the Pentagon's showing of *The Battle of Algiers* – the 1966 Gillo Pontecorvo film depicting French paratroopers battling Algerian independence fighters in French Algeria in 1957 – to its officers in 2003,[8] the GWOT's counter-insurgency matrix was eminently imperial in design and explicitly colonial in reference.[9] In spite of the illegality of the Iraq War that came to be linked to the GWOT, the nature of that enterprise as a *de facto* modern-day, proto-colonial exercise is not registered as such. Yet it is precisely this aspect which holds the second key to the birth of the IS phenomenon. Specifically, the Iraq question was unrelated to the 9/11 attacks, Iraq was not a terrorism menace to the United States (as the CIA noted before the invasion),[10] the Saddam Hussein regime did not hold nuclear weapons and the UNSC did not authorise the use of force by any member state in relation to that issue. Regardless, the United States, with the support of the United Kingdom:

invaded the country; arrested its president; took over its political, military and civilian administration; installed a government it had hand-picked; altered the laws of the nation; secured control over its resources; positioned thousands of troops throughout the land from March 2003 to December 2011 (with 73 per cent of all active US soldiers having been deployed there or Afghanistan)[11] and dispatched them anew since 2014; and built the largest embassy in the world in the heart of the country's capital. According to the organisation Iraq Body Count, 268,000 violent deaths occurred as a result of these actions since 2003, out of which 190,000 were civilian deaths. With sound reason, Ralph Wilde concludes:

> To be sure, colonialism had never gone away in some places, ... but Iraq perhaps marked the first time in the unipolar era that something *new* was criticised in mainstream commentary via direct colonial comparisons; the imperial hyper-power had shifted into an activity with echoes of post-Renaissance European colonialism, not only toppling a local government, but also administering the territory and attempting to profoundly reorient its economic, political and cultural system.[12]

The rapid fall of the Ba'ath regime – with its leadership reduced trivially to a set of playing cards (known as Personality Identification Player Cards) circulated by the US military to help its soldiers recognise and detain the most-wanted members – gave way to a lawlessness that has not disappeared since, 15 years later. Nir Rosen describes the mood as it materialised in the chaos-founding mid-2000s:

> The atmosphere of lawlessness that pervaded the country in those first few days and weeks never went away. Eventually, it allowed for criminals, gangs and mafias to take over; it replaced the totalitarian state and the fear it had imposed with complete indifference to the idea of a state. It was a shock from which Iraqis did not recover. In Baghdad, the dominant man in any area was called a *shaqi*. He was normally a thug who would sometimes engage in extortion and other small crimes; after the war these *shaqis* were recruited into armed groups and even religious militias.[13]

Such societal drift was institutionalised per an instrumentalisation of international law that was neither surprising nor anomalous. Rather, what took place was part of 'a long history of the uneven application of international law in situations of colonial and imperial conquest and the routine disregard and subordination of non-European peoples to the interests of European powers'.[14] Indeed, to a large extent the US administration replayed, after 2003, the sequence which had been pursued by the British in the 1920s. The so-called de-Ba'athification – whereby in May 2003 the US-led Coalition Provisional Authority ordered the removal of all Ba'ath party officials from the Iraqi political system – was not so different from the disbanding of the Ottoman structures that had ruled the provinces of Mosul, Baghdad and Basra in the late 1910s and early 1920s. Following the fall of Baghdad in March 1917, the British had initially opted for a sharp increase in direct rule. Considering the Iraqis incapable of managing their own country, they had abolished Ottoman governing institutions (such as the elected municipal councils) and installed British political officers in their stead.[15] Similarly, the British put together an Iraqi army in the 1920s that was essentially an amalgamation of conscripts, who were initially needed as support troops to quell the 1920 revolt against their rule. The problematic nature of that hodgepodge military force nonetheless gave it too strong a role in the early formation of the political structures of the country, leading in time to a series of coups as early as 1936. Sixty-seven years later, the rebuilding of the Iraqi army envisioned by Donald Rumsfeld, Paul Wolfowitz and Doug Feith at the Pentagon was similarly done in a way that inevitably invited further trouble. The remilitarisation of Iraqi society since 2003 was, for instance, reflected in the total number of people employed by the security forces, who, by 2012, came to equal 8 per cent of the country's entire workforce and 12 per cent of the total population of adult males.[16] Finally, just as would happen later, the first resistance movements to the British takeover were of the Islamist kind – the Society of Islamic Revival had been formed in Najaf and Karbala in late 1918 – and the tribal one.

If the US occupation of Iraq holds some of the crucial keys to the rise of IS, it is because it created a new type of colonialism anchored in the past, but also embedded in a contemporary and persistent dispossession, which maintains the appearance of legality and the pretence of sovereignty. 'Liberated', 'democratised' and 'self-ruling' Iraq was a message beamed (to Iraq, to the US and to the world) to conceal the backstage control of the actors and the dispossessing nature of the process. As in the old colonial days and under British influence, Iraqi culture now became Americanised. The country was ethnicised – the Iraqi Governing Council, which the US set up in July 2003, was the *first* entity in Iraq's contemporary history in which people were selected on the basis of their sectarian identity – and remade from afar, and a new flag designed for it (which was subsequently dropped).[17] Yet precisely in the same manner as it did under classical colonialism, the might of the new colonial power and its control of the lands and processes yielded a type of violent resistance – what the United States called 'the insurgency' – which was nothing but the mirror image of the imperial power's actions. Noting 'the similarities between US direct imperialism in the late nineteenth century with the late twentieth century', Julian Go highlights this replayed to and fro between centre and periphery: 'For both the declining hegemon and the rising contenders, direct imperial aggression becomes the tactic of choice; a means of warding off rivals, tempering the challenge from competitors if not undercutting them and securing position in the field. In this way, global competitive field breeds imperial aggression.'[18] This was a back and forth between foes that was not lost on some of the actors themselves. In a November 2004 interview with Walter Russell Mead for *Esquire* magazine, profiling US Vice President Dick Cheney, a senior US administration official established the link between the original 1991 US intervention in Iraq, the reaction by Bin Laden, the 9/11 attacks and the price of empire:

But what were the real reasons for going into Iraq? I'd asked a senior administration official ... And the connection between containment and Al Qaeda? I asked. Between our Iraq policy and 11 September? The official pointed out *fatwas* from Osama that cited the effects of sanctions on Iraqi children and the presence of US troops as a sacrilege that justified his *jihad*. In a real sense, 11 September was part of the cost of containing Saddam. No containment, no US troops in Saudi Arabia. No US troops there, then Bin Laden might still be redecorating mosques and boring friends with stories of his *mujahedeen* days in the Khyber Pass.[19]

At the heart of all colonialism, we find a *push to reaction* which is triggered once the occupied reaches the dead end of powerlessness. As Claudine Haroche explains: 'All colonisations are more or less violent, more or less brutal, open or insidious, extended or restrained, but all go back to absence, privation, denial of autonomy and of self-worth of the colonised, and as such are about humiliation; all generate the feeling, the sentiment, and consequently the conscience of oppression, alienation, enslavement, dependency and ultimately powerlessness.'[20]

There is also a striking similarity between the violence that took place in the context of the Vietnam War and that of the Iraq War. The state violence perpetrated in Iraq was a direct continuation of the tradition pioneered in Vietnam, with a similar systemic logic at play. What Nick Turse identified in relation to Vietnam applies to American Iraq:

[T]he stunning scale of civilian suffering in Vietnam is far beyond anything that can be explained as merely the work of some 'bad apples', however numerous. Murder, torture, rape, abuse, forced displacement, home burnings, specious arrests, imprisonment without due process – such occurrences were virtually a daily fact of life throughout the years of the American presence in Vietnam ... [T]hey were no aberration. Rather, they were the inevitable outcome of deliberate policies, dictated at the highest levels of the military.[21]

The role of the CIA is a case in point. After it was launched in 1965, its Phoenix Programme became part of the Civil Operations and Revolutionary Development Support programme in 1967, headed by William Colby (who served as CIA director from 1973 to 1976). The extrajudicial assassination nature of the programme, as well as its reliance on modern-day 'mercenaries', became characteristic of a pattern that would be updated anew in the 2000s. As Harlan Ullman, who in 1996 developed the rapid dominance military doctrine known as 'Shock and Awe' that was adopted in 2003 during the invasion of Iraq, writes:

Phoenix operatives were a mix of CIA, US and Australian Special Forces and South Vietnamese personnel and mercenaries. Until it ended in 1972, Phoenix 'neutralised' some 80,000 NLF [National Liberation Front] and Viet Cong of which about 30,000 were killed. In many cases, assassination was too kind a term and torture and barbaric interrogation practices were part of the standard operating procedure. Compared with Phoenix, enemy combatants killed so far by drone strikes have been a miniscule percentage as technology bypassed the need for 'terminating with prejudice' at close range.[22]

The pattern in Iraq also provided an eerie parallel to the well-documented human rights abuses committed by US-advised and -funded paramilitary squads in Central America in the 1980s.[23] Iraq bridged these different types of extrajudicial killing, collapsing the physical and virtual.

The process initiated by the US in 2003 has been playing out since with a grammar of degenerated conflicts that echoed from one country to another on a mimetic mode; the so-called 'Lebanonisation of Iraq' leading to the 'Iraqification of the Middle East'.[24] This took place in the context of a history of the Iraqi state which has fundamentally been one of resistance adopted by various groups of Iraqis trying to come to terms with the force, whatever force, the state represented.[25] That Iraqi state has been captured frequently by distinct, usually unrepresentative groups, and it has generally been incapable of socialising the population into accepting the ruler's vision of society and history other than by resorting to naked forms of coercion.[26] There has also been a defining historical measure of transnationalism at the heart of Iraq, which informed the nature of the subsequent radical Islamist groups (see Chapter 3), notably with actors coming from the Arabian Peninsula. What, however, gave further impetus to the violence unleashed in 2003 is that the previous Iraqi generation had itself been born in the midst of unceasing violence since 1980. As Faleh Abdel Jabar notes on the *differentia specifica* of that group:

> The generation who fought the eight-year Iran-Iraq War had to fight two more devastating wars in 1991 and 2003 ... During the war years, several age groups were drawn into the war zone. Those who were at the age of four in 1977 were fit for recruitment in 1991 [...] Hence, we [can] use the term 'generation of war' in two temporal senses: as young age groups across the national space, which developed under the impact of the Iran-Iraq War and those who were recruited before they could enjoy the fruits of civilian life in adulthood. ... While some other age groups shared this experience, the war generation had the misfortune of confronting it while on the verge of beginning what other age groups had already achieved: self-realisation, education, career-building, family-building and so on ... [W]ar became an obstacle to the normal development of careers at the very beginning of active life.[27]

To this history were added the more immediate brashness of the US control effort, the tensions between the new Iraqi ministries (notably defence and interior), the ferocity of the Shi'a victors' justice, the bypassing of parliamentary oversight by Prime Minister Nuri al Maliki, bureaucratic inefficiency, poor strategic planning, extensive and widespread corruption at all levels, and more importantly the *nature* of the violence introduced by the American occupier, which, within a year, had produced a genuine 'barbarisation' of the country.[28]

The United States went into Iraq in 1991 to wash away the 'Vietnam syndrome', and in 2003 ended up creating an 'Iraq syndrome' of a different nature. By 2016, one analyst could note that:

> The United States had a great window into its past with the Vietnam War, and although there were a number of differences between intervention in a Southeast Asian civil war and the occupation of an Arab country, anyone who bothered to look through that window could have forecasted much of the folly and fatality of Iraq. Instead, Americans boarded the window, tied yellow ribbons around their eyes and proved the accuracy of Gore Vidal's assessment of the country as the 'United States of Amnesia'.[29]

In such an important context for the creation of IS, the early twenty-first century then marked a reimagining of colonialism and a renewed form of imperialism ushered in by the US decision to invade and take control of Iraq. Violence by US stormtroopers against civilians in Iraq (and in Afghanistan) took place repeatedly and with impunity. Colonial-type violence (e.g. trophies taken by bone- and finger-collecting US kill teams, desecrations of bodies, flushing and burning of Qur'ans) was manifested regularly – 'such news reports, though a recurring feature of contemporary life, trace a predictable arc in and out of public consciousness ... Even a cursory reflection on the available facts, however, shows that these atrocities were not aberrations committed in a political vacuum'[30] – and was therefore revealing in terms of its inevitable time-delayed consequence on the colonised. The brutality of domination was also unpacked by the Iraqi Shi'a on their fellow Sunni citizens. Signs of the arrogant Americanised Arab military and police were already familiar in Jordan and Egypt, but in Iraq a new man was created; walking, talking and behaving like the colonial actor that violently moulded him in his image. Crucially for the IS story, many an Iraqi came to internalise their observations of torture performed by American soldiers, and replay them later on.[31]

Monstering in American Iraq

The control which the United States had secured over Iraq allowed it initially to achieve two unspoken goals that nonetheless stood at the heart of the motivations for the American war effort, namely closure of the 1991 Gulf War and revenge for 9/11. On the one hand, George W. Bush sought to achieve that which his father could not and had been criticised for, namely bringing down Saddam Hussein and delivering a clear victory to the US in the face of a 'defiant' Third World leader in the Middle East. (Shortly before the 20 March 2003 US invasion, the situation had acquired almost Shakespearean or Greek tragedy accents, with the son of a president, now president himself, issuing a 48-hour ultimatum to another president – who had fought the former's father – to step down along with his two sons.) On the other hand, the United States, which had been at war in Afghanistan since October 2001 in pursuit of Bin Laden and the rest of Al Qaeda's leadership, sought to demonstrate that they had punished Islamists and Arabs and taken control of their lands (regardless of the fact that Iraq had nothing to do with 9/11). A third, more insidious, less visible objective, but arguably even more relevant to the origin of IS, would be introduced subsequently, namely the torture and humiliation of Iraqis suspected of being part of the insurgency. In the immediate aftermath of the 9/11 attacks, the United States had embarked on a course in which human rights violations rapidly took place in the name of fighting terrorism. Within a year after 9/11 (September 2001–September 2002), the US-based Lawyers Committee for Human Rights was in a position to document that first batch of violations in the United States.[32] Among many in the United States, a dramatically expanded resentment towards Arabs and Muslims combined with limited knowledge of foreign affairs to allow for perceptions of 'the Iraq matter' as being related to the 9/11 attacks. Tellingly, an American citizen whose son had died in the 9/11 attacks contacted the Pentagon to ask that the name of his son be inscribed on one of the bombs to be dropped on Iraqis in 2003. The Department of Defense later informed him that this had been done and had been a 'one-hundred per cent success'.[33] Whereas the Afghanistan conflict – which had started on 7 October, less than a month after the New York and Washington events – could be linked to the terrorist attacks, since Al Qaeda was enjoying sanctuary in that country, the issue of Iraq that had lingered since 1991 and throughout the embargo years was instrumentalised to assert the United States' new global stance once it had been attacked on its own soil. The George W. Bush administration therefore consciously – with the support of the governments of Tony Blair (UK), José Maria Aznar (Spain), Silvio Berlusconi (Italy), Nicolas Sarkozy (France) and Hosni Mubarak (Egypt) – pursued a plan to take control of

Iraq both to give an appearance of dealing with the Muslim perpetrators of 9/11 to the none-too-regarding US population, and to send a global message about its willingness to be extreme in retaliating against those that dared conspire against it. In so doing, however, the US gave birth to a generation more brutal than the previous one, which is itself willing to pursue extreme violence to exact revenge on the United States.

This consequential US policy path was illustrated specifically and most problematically by the illegal, illegitimate and counterproductive usage of torture, notably between 2002 and 2005. As time and public inattention have gone by, responsibility for what took place has become murky and the issue of torture in Iraq is referred to metaphorically, generically casting the discussion in vague geostrategic, security or legal terms. The extent of the torture has, however, been well researched, documented[34] and reported by several insiders,[35] although not all the information has been released yet. A reconstruction of the events reveals that a political decision was taken at the highest levels of the US government to subject Arab and Muslim suspects in Iraq to methods unacceptable in a democracy. To the extent that, as it is argued here, such treatment sowed the seeds for the IS generation's brutality, it is important to review the facts in detail. Three days after the 9/11 attacks, President George W. Bush signed a military order, the 'Declaration of National Emergency by Reason of Certain Terrorist Attacks', by which he declared a national emergency in the United States. Shortly thereafter, that same month, he asked the CIA to 'capture or kill' all the leaders of Al Qaeda around the world. On 19 January 2002, US Secretary of Defense Donald Rumsfeld wrote a memorandum to the joint chiefs of staff, entitled 'Status of Taliban and Al Qaeda', in which he 'determine[d] that Al Qaeda and Taliban individuals under the control of the Department of Defense were not entitled to prisoner of war status for purposes of the Geneva Conventions of 1949'. The next month, on 7 February, President Bush wrote a memorandum to Vice President Dick Cheney, Secretary of Defense Rumsfeld and the heads of the intelligence agencies, in which he declared that the United States would not be bound by the Geneva Conventions' protections for prisoners of war when it came to Al Qaeda. Four months later, the head of the Office of the Legal Counsel of the Department of Justice, Jay Bybee, wrote a memorandum to Alberto Gonzales, counsel to President Bush, in which he noted that, specifically 'in the context of interrogations outside of the United States', torture can be considered in a restrictive manner; '[W]hile many of these techniques [defined as torture in the Convention] may amount to cruel, inhuman or degrading treatment, they do not produce pain or suffering of the necessary intensity to meet the definition of torture. From these decisions, we conclude that there is a wide range of such techniques that will not rise to the level of torture.'[36] The same day, in a heavily redacted memorandum to the CIA (ten of the 18 pages released are blacked out fully), Jay Bybee noted that 'to violate the statute, an individual must have the specific intent to inflict severe pain or suffering. ... [W]e believe those carrying out these procedures would not have the specific intent to inflict severe pain or suffering.'

Following a series of related memoranda detailing that 'harsh' measures could be used,[37] the US Department of Defense asked – as a May 2007 Pentagon report would later admit – the Survival, Evasion, Resistance, Escape programme of the US Army to look into 'aggressive interrogation techniques' (sleep deprivation, stress positions, sensory overload, mock executions) which could be used to interrogate the apprehended suspected Al Qaeda members and 'break' them. On 2 December 2002, Donald Rumsfeld approved a memorandum authorising the use of these aggressive measures (including nudity and use of dogs), annotating it personally and sending copies to the heads of the prisoners' camps in Guantánamo Bay and Afghanistan. Rumsfeld then dispatched Deputy-Under Secretary of Defense for Intelligence, Lieutenant-General William Boykin, to Guantánamo Bay, where he met the head of Camp X-Ray, Geoffrey Miller, who was instructed to travel to Iraq and implement there the interrogation techniques developed in Guantánamo Bay. Accordingly, in early 2003, a special missions unit in Iraq wrote up a protocol for prisoner interrogation based on the techniques used by US forces in Afghanistan; a document which the commander of the coalition forces in Iraq, Lieutenant-General Ricardo Sanchez, adopted on 14 September. A few months later, on 13 January 2004, a young military police officer, Joseph Darby, assigned to the Abu Ghraib prison on the outskirts of Baghdad, reported to the Criminal Investigations Division of the US Army that abuse of prisoners was ongoing at that facility. Darby sent a computer disc with pictures and videos of sexual abuse, including the humiliation of an Iraqi man and his son. On 16 January, a report was sent to Secretary of Defense Rumsfeld who informed President Bush of the situation.[38] The same month, Major-General Antonio Taguba launched an internal investigation which assigned responsibility to elements within the US Army, as well as the CIA, as regards the actions committed in Abu Ghraib. Taguba noted that, before the initiative taken independently by MP Darby, Lieutenant-General Sanchez was already aware of what had been taking place in Abu Ghraib since 2003, and that Geoffrey Miller had been sent to set up a torture model similar to the one used in Guantánamo Bay.

On 28 April 2004, the CBS News programme *60 Minutes II* aired some of the pictures of the acts committed in Abu Ghraib, which were also published online, two days later, by the *New Yorker*. On 6 May, Taguba was called in by Rumsfeld who, in the presence of Paul Wolfowitz, complained of not having been informed of the situation in Abu Ghraib. The next day, under oath, Rumsfeld denied any knowledge of what was happening in Abu Ghraib before the US Senate, and the nature of the actions that had been reported to him on 16 January. In December, in the wake of the leaking of a confidential report by the International Committee of the Red Cross (ICRC) that mentioned 'practices equivalent to torture' by the United States in Iraq,[39] the Department of Justice termed torture 'abhorrent' and appeared to bring an end to the practices adopted since 2002. However, in February 2005, under Alberto Gonzales, a new secret memorandum was drafted explicitly authorising a series of psychological and physical measures, including waterboarding. Eventually, in June 2006, the US Supreme Court decided that Common Article 3 of the four Geneva Conventions of 1949 applied to all US detainees. However, on 17 October of that year, the US Congress adopted a Military Commissions Act, which authorised the US president to determine the specific interrogation techniques to be used, and nine months later President Bush authorised the CIA, by presidential order, to use interrogation methods prohibited to the military. According to US soldier Michael Keller, who was posted in Abu Ghraib, resort to torture was persisting in the facility one year after the revelations had been made.[40] As late as 2009, the US administration was using secret prisons in so-called 'black sites'.[41]

The Guantánamoisation of Abu Ghraib clearly took place. Explicitly and bureaucratically. Though this was later officially denied by US authorities, methods of torture used initially on prisoners at Guantánamo Bay[42] (most of whom had been captured in Afghanistan from the autumn of 2001 onwards, or 'rendered' by countries cooperating secretly with the United States) were exported ('migrated' to use Pentagon phraseology) to the Abu Ghraib prison in Iraq. As the Taguba report also revealed, several agents of private military contractors (CACI and TITAN) were 'directly or indirectly' involved in the violations. In a 14 February 2007 confidential report, the ICRC noted that the United States also used torture on suspects in other sites kept secret and operated by the CIA. In spite of these violations, and the eventual release by the US Senate Select Committee on Intelligence, on 9 December 2014, of a 514-page report on torture (*The Senate Intelligence Committee Report on Torture: Committee Study of the Central Intelligence Agency's Detention and Interrogation Program*), Abu Ghraib has in effect been whitewashed and 'swept under the carpet',[43] erased from the American collective memory, and beyond. As was the case with Vietnam, the crimes that were committed there went largely unpunished and the visceral horrors that took place have not all been revealed. More than 60 children may have been interned at Abu Ghraib. Some of them may have been tortured and at least one child may have been abused while a woman took pictures.[44] Abuse of women, related to prisoners or prisoners themselves, contained cases of bestiality.[45] Indeed, according to those present, like US Army Military Intelligence Sergeant Sam Provance, who was involved in the acts committed, 'Abu Ghraib was *Apocalypse Now* meets *The Shining*'.[46]

Lied about, reported euphemistically ('in 2004, in the aftermath of revelations that the Bush administration was waterboarding terrorist suspects, ... *The New York Times*, *The Los Angeles Times*, *USA Today* and *The Wall Street Journal* almost never referred to waterboarding as torture'),[47] portrayed as the action of bad apples, whitewashed within the US Army (years after the crimes, stories kept surfacing, often with irresolution and impunity)[48] and forgotten quickly only to be reintroduced later ('it's quite an astonishing thing: torture, which used to be illegal, which used to be anathema, has now become a policy choice' remarked Mark Danner in 2014),[49] the partially disclosed crimes of human experimentation[50] at Abu Ghraib left an indelible imprint on the Iraqis who experienced them directly – those who were lucky to escape them – or indirectly, and those others observing with shock and revulsion. Accusations of similar actions were levelled at the United Kingdom. Though on a smaller scale, British authorities were accused of engaging in a systemic practice of torture in Iraq throughout the years 2003–8.[51] Abu Ghraib was a formal staging post for a level of atrocity, authorised at the highest levels of US defence officialdom,[52] which purposefully meant to impart to those insurgents fighting the United States that the gloves were off and that extreme prejudice would be pursued to bring them down by way of an ubiquitous system of suffering and humiliation. Healthcare professionals, physicians and psychologists assisted in the development of so-called 'enhanced interrogation techniques',[53] which were explicitly 'culturalised' to humiliate Arabs and Muslims in ways perceived by these professionals as most effective in a Middle Eastern environment. Inspired by Raphael Patai's Lombrosian phrenology-flavoured 1973 book *The Arab Mind*, a secret Pentagon programme known as 'Copper Green', designed to physically coerce and sexually humiliate prisoners, was developed by the US authorities in the aftermath of 9/11. Culturally informed interrogation techniques were introduced among some 24 methods used by the Department of Defense – these included two known as 'Fear Up Harsh' and 'Pride and Ego Down'. Upping the ante, with a view to both exorcise the 9/11 syndrome and punish those it chose to associate culturally with the attacks of 2001, the United States' leadership unleashed a fury which did not immediately step out to exact revenge in turn, but rather, and more problematically for the United States, grew slowly into a 'monstered' form of extreme radicalism. 'The relentlessness, day in day out, of these techniques – walling, close-confinement, water-dousing, water-boarding ... rectal re-hydration and various other disgusting and depraved things – and the totality of their effect when taken together is ... revolting.'[54] Abu Ghraib – which formed a pattern with Camp X in Guantánamo Bay, Bagram in Afghanistan and the black sites operated secretly around the world (considered as an option to be continued in 2017)[55] – was hardly an isolated scene of violence in Iraq, since at least two massacres of civilians imputable to US forces took place in March 2005 in Haditha and in March 2006 in Mahmoudia, with respectively 15 and 24 civilians killed.

As the United States processed 9/11, it experienced a combination of fear and desire for revenge, which fed the very cruelty that was displayed in this systemic fashion in Iraq. Whereas the crimes in Vietnam had been born in the context of a conflict evolving gradually over three administrations, in which US soldiers would operate with increased impunity as their government raised the political and military stakes, Iraq was an invented conflict to allow for immediate societal venting. It lent itself both to policy planning specifically designed to target the Islamist enemy that had conducted a terror attack in the metropolis, and, in terms of communication, to that segment of the US citizenry that only half-candidly went along with the misleading Iraq-as-an-international-nuclear-threat hoax, seduced by the unspeakable punishing mission. Unsurprisingly, and simultaneously with these torture practices, the 2000s witnessed a popular cultural revival of the horror films in the US that had first arisen during the 1970s Vietnam era (*The Texas Chainsaw*

Massacre, The Exorcist, Halloween). In a reflection of the Iraq War context, these new productions combined primal fear of the unknown with more straightforwardly sadistic illustrations such as *Saw* (the fastest franchise in film history, with seven releases in six years between 2004 and 2010), *Hostel* (2005) and *Torturer* (2008), the tag line of which was 'In a post-September 11 world, no one can hear you cry'. At times, it was almost hard to distinguish the trailer for the new *Saw* film and news footage of the latest leaked pictures from Abu Ghraib; real-life cases of *Apocalypse Now* meeting *The Shining* indeed.[56] Fear also manifested itself through the return of paranoid conspiracy political thrillers, just as they had featured prominently in the 1970s (*The Conversation, The Parallax View, Three Days of the Condor, All the President's Men*), as post-9/11 malaise replaced post-Watergate confusion, with productions such as *Bug* (2006), *Body of Lies* (2008), *State of Play* (2009) and *Duplicity* (2009). In *Munich* (2005), Steven Spielberg established a direct analogy between 1972 Black September terrorists and 2001 Al Qaeda operatives, and between the Israeli hunt of Palestinian operators across Europe throughout the 1970s and the United States' international pursuit of Bin Laden and his men. The manner in which these extra-legal issues were affecting the public debate, arts and life generally in the United States – with apathy nonetheless dominant[57] – was suffusing Americana in a striking way. Not even the popular, modern-day fairy tale *Star Wars* escaped those gloomy days where authoritarianism took the guise of righteousness, with Episodes II (2002) and III (2005) of that saga not-so-subtly echoing the ambient ethical dissonance in the face of terrorism, and the fall of a republic succumbing to the corruption of its ideals by the rise of obscure and unseen manipulative forces fighting rebels in the name of democracy. 'So this is how liberty dies, with thunderous applause', registers a distraught Queen Padmé Amidala (Natalie Portman). 'If you are not with me, you are my enemy', declares Anakin Skywalker (Hayden Christensen), already falling to the dark side, with director George Lucas near-explicitly denouncing George W. Bush's State of the Union phrase uttered in January 2002: 'Either you are with us or you are with the terrorists.' The full-circle sequence from Vietnam to Iraq by way of Hollywood would, however, be closed by the filmmaker Brian de Palma, who in 2006 shot *Redacted*, a modern *vérité*-style remake of his own 1989 *Casualties of War*, in which a young Iraqi girl, now replacing a young Vietnamese girl, is raped and killed by US soldiers (denounced by a whistle-blower but covered by their superiors) – both cases inspired by true events.

In the aftermath of 9/11, the United States engaged in the practice of torture. With overwhelming evidence of cases in Iraq, Guantánamo Bay, Afghanistan and elsewhere,[58] that practice was ordered at the highest levels of the state and was designed to function in a systemic way. In spite of its celebration, with scenes of waterboarding in television series such as 24, *Homeland*, *Sleeper Cell*, and *The Grid*, or films like *Zero Dark Thirty* (2012), torture did not work. Many detainees had nothing to do with terrorism, and indeed many of them *went into terrorism* after their torture experience at the hands of the US forces. Torture continued after the matter was allegedly closed in 2006. The Army Field Manual on Inter-rogation, amended that year, still allowed for sleep deprivation, separation and stress positions to be used in interrogation:

> Detainees were shackled in painful positions, locked in boxes the size of coffins, kept awake for over one hundred hours at a time and forced to inhale water in a process known as water-boarding. Interrogators sometimes went far beyond what Washington had authorised, sodomising detainees with blunt objects, threatening to sexually abuse their family members and, on at least one occasion, freezing a suspect to death by chaining him to an ice-cold floor overnight.[59]

In truth, the extent of the horrors in which US soldiers and private contractors casually engaged in Iraq, Afghanistan, Guantánamo Bay and several secret sites around the world, may never be known (particularly as some embedded American journalists who witnessed extrajudicial killing by US troops, including women and children, did not report it).[60] The crimes are likely to be much worse than acknowledged. Crimes have been left unpunished and hidden, and of little concern to the authorities which half-authorised them in the first place. In effect, the abuse of Iraqis took place with impunity for several years – few trials were brought up and most cases have been dismissed.[61] Ultimately, then, the militarisation of American society – increasingly fearful, paranoid, violent and insensitive to the brutality that its actions abroad were triggering[62] – can be looked upon as the expression of the trauma of 9/11, and a desire for revenge which gave birth to a type of cruelty that manifested itself in the midst of the US military. Indeed, during the autumn 2001 campaign in Afghanistan, a US soldier had suggested 'monstering' an Afghan prisoner.[63] The physical and psychological punishment, the normalisation of torture and the adoption of such practices by the Iraqis themselves vis-à-vis each other[64] helped create Islamic State in Iraq (ISI).

'I will see you in New York'

IS is derivative terrorism. The violent simulacra and the weaponisation of images it famously staged in the videos featuring 'Jihadi John' and others, followed Al Qaeda's actions and was inspired by the torturers of Abu Ghraib in the context of the modern subjugation of Iraq. Al Qaeda's radicalism had not, however, stepped into the level of barbarity that IS would come to perform regularly. The invasion of Iraq and the dehumanising torture acts committed in that context opened the road to a hellish new type of extreme radicalisation, which was different from the group Bin Laden had set up to pursue what could be termed 'political warfare terrorism'. Still, as discussed, the martiality of Al Qaeda was the first step in a process of IS's inception. By ushering in a new age of more proactive, battle-tested, non-state armed groups, Al Qaeda made available a functional matrix of self-empowered rebellion, which the Iraqi insurgency was immediately able to seize upon when it materialised between the spring and early summer of 2003 to face the US invader. The transformation of Al Qaeda that began with the US invasion of Iraq, and therefore the arguably inevitable passing of the baton to IS, is in fact an accidental development that owes as much to the actions and choices of the US as it does to the ones taken by Al Qaeda itself. For it is not at all evident – and indeed questionable – that had the invasion of Iraq not taken place, a similarly ultra-violent Al Qaeda offshoot would have materialised in the Levant or somewhere else. Al Qaeda had packed and left the Middle Eastern environment, in which its (Palestinian, Egyptian and Saudi) founders had developed their political views and underground radical militancy, to join a resistance movement in Asia, in the name of religious solidarity. At the close of the first chapter – the Afghan-Soviet war – and on the strength of its 'victory' over one superpower, Al Qaeda used its theatre of operation and experience as a jumping-off point to create a 'base' from which to attack another superpower (the sole remaining one by then). In effect, therefore, 9/11 was the culmination of that effort. The logical next step could only be envisioned, from Al Qaeda's viewpoint, as a series of further attacks on the United States on its soil. Yet a so-called second wave of attacks in the US did not materialise in late 2001 and 2002. Was it planned and could not be launched? It is not at all clear (arrested before the 9/11 attacks for a visa overstay violation, Zacarias Moussaoui was in all likelihood the original twentieth hijacker and not a sleeper accomplice planning more operations). Two small-scale operations were the work of copycats – on 2 December 2001, a Sudanese national fired a Stinger missile on a US military plane at the Prince Sultan airbase in Saudi Arabia, and on 22 December 2001, on board a London–Miami American Airlines flight, a British citizen of Sri Lankan origin, Richard Reid, attempted to detonate C-4 explosives hidden in his shoes. The logic of Bin Laden's 'to the far enemy' type of war had, it seemed, reached an impasse with the unexpected magnitude of the fall of the Twin Towers, the collapse of one wing of the Pentagon and the killing of close to 3,000 Americans. The subsequent moves on the part of Al Qaeda's leadership indicated that its mindset was still wedded to the displacement strategy. As both a rejoinder to the US response to the 9/11 attacks first in Afghanistan and later in Iraq, Al Qaeda struck once more at the larger territory of the 'far enemy', this time in Spain and in the United Kingdom. Although linked explicitly by Bin Laden and al Dhawahiri (in their speeches of, respectively, 15 April 2004 and 1 September 2005) to the support of the Aznar and Blair governments for the US invasion of Iraq, the attacks were essentially a variation on the 9/11 from-here-to-there mode. They also represented the last large-scale 'war' acts the group would conduct, and in effect the year 2005 closed the chapter on the group – again several years before the death of Bin Laden – as the strategy designed in Khost in August 1988 had reached its conceptual and operational limits. In invading Afghanistan in October 2001 and Iraq in 2003, the United States wrestled the initiative from Bin Laden. Tactically, he could and did respond lethally in Madrid and in London, but strategically the arrival of the 'far enemy' on his 'near' territory altered the game.

This mid-2000s juncture marked precisely the point at which *the logic of an 'Islamic State'* could emerge. More so than the Afghanistan conflict, which featured a wider set of actors (the international coalition, the Taliban), the occupation of Iraq brought back the perfected Al Qaeda *modus operandi* to inform the birth of a local insurgency, which would both borrow that method and develop its own narrative. The military influence of Al Qaeda on the local Iraqi actors was perceptible even before the Iraq insurgency started to form in mid-2003, and before that influence reached state actors themselves. Thus, whereas in 1991 Saddam Hussein's regime had prepared for classical state-on-state third-generation warfare by fronting its Republican Guard divisions, in 2003, as the battle was looming with the US, it shifted to asymmetrical fourth-generation warfare.[65] A special group known as Saddam's Fedayeen was set up, which in effect sought to replicate the partisan type of war that Al Qaeda had made its distinguishing feature in Afghanistan (while echoing nationalist-secular Palestinian terminology of the 1970s). A group of suicide bombers even emerged, and at least one woman was arrested as she was about to carry out an operation. The days in late March and early April 2003 during which the Iraqi army in effect refused to fight – some of its leadership reportedly striking deals with the US forces, the lower ranks defecting – opened the door to the formal emergence of a rebellion across the country. By June, what came to pass was a second consequence of Al Qaeda's 2001 attacks on the United States that Bin Laden did not envision nor could control.

The social make-up of that first generation of Iraqi insurgents featured a number of strands, which continued to coexist in the following years as the rebellion evolved and took on different forms; soldiers, local Islamists, tribesmen, average citizens and regional operators (again, mostly Islamists from the Gulf). Internationally, Al Qaeda was witnessing the Iraq War alter the nature of its operation. Besides the two small-scale attempts in December 2001 and the conflict raging in Afghanistan, the following two years saw stepped-up regional and international attacks by Islamist groups that increasingly escaped Al Qaeda's control – Jerba, Tunisia on 11 April 2002; Karachi, Pakistan on 14 June 2002; Sana'a, Yemen on 6 October 2002; Bali, Indonesia on 12 October 2002; Moscow, Russia on 23 October 2002; Mombasa, Kenya on 23 November 2002; Riyadh, Saudi Arabia on 12 May 2003; Casablanca, Morocco on 16 May 2002; Jakarta, Indonesia on 5 August 2003; Riyadh, Saudi Arabia again on 8 November 2003; and Istanbul, Turkey on 15 and 20 November 2003. This international sequence ran parallel with the events in Iraq, where the first two major operations of the insurgency took place in 2003, on 7 and 15 August, with the respective bombings of the Jordanian embassy and the UN compound. The year closed with the arrest of Saddam Hussein on 14 December, and his execution three years later on 30 December 2006.

The hanging of Saddam Hussein on a day of Muslim religious celebration, Eid al Adha, was a key moment in the degeneration of politics in Iraq and an accelerator of the radicalisation of the soldiery-to-be of IS. The videoed execution – grainy, snuff movie-like footage leaked by a high-ranking Shi'a official present at the event – was internalised by many Sunni Iraqis as the ultimate expression of their brethren's humiliation, the colonisation of their consciousness and a confessional war now in full swing, pitting them against vengeful segments of the Shi'a community. Present in the room were many Shi'a taunting Hussein as he was about to be hanged with shouts of 'Long live Imam Mohammad Baqr al Sadr!' and 'Muqtada! Muqtada!', in reference to Shi'a political leader Muqtada al Sadr. Eight years later, in June 2014, IS would, among its first acts as IS, seek out the judge who sentenced Hussein, Raouf Abdul Rahman, and kill him. For many radicalised Sunnis, the choreographed violence functioned from thereon both as an explicit motivator and as a trauma-like repressed memory, whose responsibility they laid at the feet of the new Iraqi authorities and the United States. The former Iraqi national security advisor who oversaw the execution, Mowaffak al Rubaie, recalled how the decision to hang Hussein was taken: 'Saddam's execution was set in motion after a video conference between [then Iraqi Prime Minister Nuri al] Maliki and then-US President George Bush, who asked the Iraqi prime minister: "What are you going to do with this criminal?" Maliki replied: "We hang him." Bush gave him a thumbs up, signalling his approval.'[66] The years of war in the 1980s and the sanctions of the 1990s had gradually led to an Islamisation of the Ba'ath party. The process started as the rhetoric of religion was increasingly introduced into the political communication of the party, and this continued in 1991 as the words *Allahu Akbar* (God is Great) were added to the Iraqi flag a few days before the start of the US operation on 15 January 1991. What had started as a tactic, and became a strategy after the Kuwait matter and the Shi'a revolt in April 1991, turned into an element of the identity of latter-day Ba'athism. The death of Hussein sealed the sequence by sacralising that add-on religiosity. The future IS leadership took this predisposition with it.

One man who lived through this period of Iraq's degenerated descent into violence and hatred, absorbing it all, was Ibrahim Awad Ibrahim al Badri. Upon his release in September 2009 from Camp Bucca (an inmate site named after a New York Fire Department marshal, Ronald Bucca, killed in the 9/11 attacks), the prison in Iraq where he had been held for the previous three years since his capture in Fallujah on 9 December 2006, the man turned to his captors and reportedly uttered the following words: 'I will see you in New York, guys'. He allegedly went on to become the leader of IS, as Abu Bakr al Baghdadi. US Army Colonel Kenneth King later recalled the words[67] as coming from an inmate who was not even among the more radical in the prison (who were quarantined in a special section). There is a lingering lack of clarity on the matter, and al

Baghdadi is also reported to have been released from prison much earlier, in December 2004, having been held there since the previous February. In effect, the man released in 2009 may not have been al Baghdadi at all but another Al Qaeda militant. Regardless, the symbolic nature of such a statement metaphorically closed the circle on Bin Laden's promise to visit violence on the United States, 20 years later. That resolve, however, had now come from a different place and it would first play out locally, then regionally and ultimately internationally.

3

From Qaedat al Jihad
to Al Dawla al Islamiya

Beware of pursuing savage speech in your quest for eloquence.
Abdullah Ibn al Muqaffa, *Al Adab al Saghir* (750)

Spirits that I've called, my commands ignore.
Goethe, *The Sorcerer's Apprentice* (1797)

Al Qaeda was once the mightiest radical Islamist group, revolutionising terrorism in the 1990s and 2000s and introducing novel patterns of transnational force projection. In the aftermath of the American occupation of Iraq, led in response to the attacks Al Qaeda had conducted in the United States in 2001, one of the group's own offshoots, IS, dislodged it between 2011 and 2014 and went on to acquire greater capability and impact. The evolution, within the same movement, of an entity stressing its 'base' (*qaeda*) nature to one seeking to become a 'state' (*dawla*) was an important marker of the shape and direction things were taking – within months, in 2011, the Arab Spring broke out, Bin Laden died and the United States left Iraq. As we have seen, Al Qaeda's push-and-pull extremism had come to represent a strategic reorientation of contemporary political violence, which owed its fundamental nature to globalisation. Whereas earlier generations of terrorism had sought to destroy (Nihilists and Anarchists of the late nineteenth century), capture (nationalists of the 1950s and 1960s) or usurp (left-wing revolutionaries of the 1970s) statehood, Al Qaeda had moved to declaring the Arab and Muslim states' military function obsolete, stressing its own militarised might and reach. Such self-capacitation met with success for a while, but in spawning franchises it paradoxically held the keys to the end of its own meticulous planning. The more Al Qaeda invited its subgroups to act independently and assert themselves regionally, the more it was hollowing out its core and rendering itself irrelevant, and not merely operationally.

Evanescence and hybridity came logically to take over a sequence closed neatly by the death of Bin Laden in May 2011.

The United States' withdrawal from Iraq on 18 December 2011 (the process had started in December 2007) opened the way for the local Al Qaeda franchise, AQI – which had already renamed itself Islamic State in Iraq (ISI) five years earlier, in October 2006 – to occupy that space by stepping up its insurgency in Iraq, but also, in time, growing to harbour wider and more consequential ambitions. Those aspirations would match the global plans once envisioned by Bin Laden, turning them into the reality of a transnational army, but they would also remap the strategic landscape his group had dominated for two decades by merging the original Al Qaeda logic with a centralised statehood aim which Al Qaeda had explicitly avoided. The shift from Qaedat al Jihad (the Base of Jihad), as Al Qaeda officially referred to itself, to al Dawla al Islamiya (Islamic State), as the new group would, in time, formally label itself, was a shift of lasting consequence, as IS eventually broke ranks publicly with Al Qaeda and declared it finished. How and why did that shift occur? What were the implications of IS's replacement of Al Qaeda? Towards which horizons was IS moving and for what discernible purpose? As the sequence played out during the first half of the 2010s, three dimensions, indicative of the nature of the emerging group, manifested themselves. First, whereas Al Qaeda had privileged the export of rebellion, IS engineered a *refocusing on the local*, specifically in Iraq in the wake of the change of political guard from US occupation forces to the Shi'a government of Nuri al Maliki. Second, IS seized on an unexpected opportunity afforded by the Syrian civil war, which started in March 2011, to assert itself regionally and pursue a complex *Levantine expansion* meant to widen its scope, power and performativity. Finally, the displacement of Al Qaeda – which IS would partly achieve violently and unstintingly, but also by passively observing Al Qaeda's drift into extraneousness – spelled the introduction of *a state-building project*. As IS achieved these three aims, it shifted to capture and pursue Al Qaeda's transnational dynamic, but doing so in a manner replacing franchises with regions, as part of an organic rather than a decentralised entity, with a deft use of information technology. Understanding the complex tapestry of the genealogy of IS holds the key to its multifaceted nature, and points to the different influences in its midst. Ultimately, was IS primarily an Iraqi story? Or was it an Iraqi story evolved into a Syrian one and a regional one? Or, as the original Bin Laden association would indicate, was it a project that always harboured a global dimension? The group is more accurately understood as all of the above.

Mesopotamian Recentring

IS was born six times: in 1999 as Jama'at al Tawhid wal Jihad (the Group of Unity and Jihad); in 2004 as AQI; in 2006 as Majliss al Shura al Mujahideen (the Council of the Assembly of the Fighters); again in late 2006 as ISI; in 2013 as ISIS; and, finally, in 2014 as IS (see Table 3.1). When, on the afternoon of 4 July 2014, its eventual dominant leader Abu Bakr al Baghdadi (announced dead by Russian authorities on 16 June 2017, but unconfirmed at time of writing) climbed the stairs of the Imam's *minbar* (pulpit) – pacing himself one step at a time – to deliver the sermon of the Friday prayers at the Great Mosque in Mosul, Iraq, an important moment in the saga initiated by Al Qaeda in 1988 and transformed by IS played out. A few days earlier, on 29 June, the spokesman for ISIS, Abu Mohammad al 'Adnani, had announced (in a statement released in Arabic, English, French, German and Russian) the birth of an 'Islamic State', with al Baghdadi (identified per an extended lineage meant to establish religious credentials and nobility pedigree: Ibrahim ibn Awad ibn Ibrahim ibn Ali

Table 3.1   Evolution of IS

Configuration	Period	Leader
Jama'at al Tawhid wal Jihad	October 1999–17 October 2004	Abu Mus'ab al Zarqawi
Al Qaeda fi Bilad al Rafidayn	17 October 2004–15 January 2006	Abu Mus'ab al Zarqawi (killed on 7 June 2006)
Majliss al Shura al Mujahideen	15 January 2006–15 October 2006	Abu Ayyub al Masri (also known as Abu Hamza al Muhajir)
Islamic State in Iraq	15 October 2006–9 April 2013	Abu Ayyub al Masri (killed on 18 April 2010) Abu Omar al Baghdadi (killed on 18 April 2010) Abu Bakr al Baghdadi
Islamic State in Iraq and al Shaam	9 April 2013–29 June 2014	Abu Bakr al Baghdadi
Islamic State	29 June 2014–present	Abu Bakr al Baghdadi (reportedly killed on 28 May 2017)

ibn Mohammad al Badri al Hashimi al Husayni al Qoraishi) as 'leader Caliph Ibrahim'. On 1 July, al Baghdadi himself had issued a 'Message to the Islamic Umma' calling on Muslims from around the world to migrate to the new Caliphate. The coincidence of al Baghdadi's sermon in Mosul – a city his group had captured three weeks earlier – with the first Friday in Ramadan and with the United States' independence day, was hardly fortuitous, and such timing was indicative of the flaunt-it-if-you-have-it theatricality that the group would continue to use in pursuit of its own domestic, regional and international marketisation.

To understand the full significance of that mid-2014 episode, which reveals the accelerated rise of a bellicose group that would later boast thousands of fighters and control a vast territory over two countries, is, first and foremost, to register how the organisation that had been established in Iraq in 2004 as a franchise of Al Qaeda moved to recentre itself in Iraq, temporarily dropping the transnational aspects of Al Qaeda's fight in order to focus primarily on the post-US fast-changing situation in that country. Between 2004 and 2011, the AQI group had seesawed between the two dimensions of the local vs. transnational struggle, as the Iraqi group would experience a difficult relationship with Al Qaeda. To be certain, IS's exceptionalism within Al Qaeda's trajectory had a long history, and it was arguably just a matter of time before the derivative group sought its full emancipation from the mother organisation. In point of fact, the entity that would become ISIS, and later IS, predated Al Qaeda's mid-2000s franchising model, which it joined in 2004 while constantly chipping away at Al Qaeda's influence and retaining the very functional independence that was subsequently played out.

A few months after the creation of Al Qaeda, in winter 1989, a 24-year-old Jordanian known as Abu Mus'ab al Zarqawi (Ahmed Fadil Nazzal al Khalayla), from the Jordanian city of Zarqa, travelled to Afghanistan where he took part in the last phase of the insurgency against the Soviet Union and met with Bin Laden. A year later, Zarqawi returned to Jordan and set up a militant Islamist group named Junud al Shaam (the Soldiers of the Levant). Shortly thereafter he was arrested and jailed by the Jordanian authorities, and on his release in 1999 he returned to Afghanistan, where he met with Bin Laden again and secured the latter's support for a new radical Islamist group named Jama'at al Tawhid wal Jihad (the Group of Unity and Jihad). In May 2002, that organisation moved to northern Iraq, where it remained underground until the United States' invasion in March 2003, at which time Jama'at al Tawhid wal Jihad became the first organised group to lead insurgency operations against US and UK troops, as well as the UN mission. Al Zarqawi then gained an international profile – he was featured in a 5 February 2003 UNSC briefing, during which US Secretary of State Colin Powell presented him as a leading emergent threat – and became of operational interest to Bin Laden's Al Qaeda, after the attacks he conducted that year on the Jordanian embassy in Baghdad on 7 August and on the UN compound on 19 August. Of key importance was that al Zarqawi's Afghan experience was subsequent to and separate from that of Bin Laden. Coming out of prison in Jordan, Al Zarqawi had moved late to Afghanistan. Setting up his own small-scale group in the Western province of Herat where he led and trained around a hundred Jordanians and Palestinians, away from Bin Laden's camps in Kandahar, he was already making a power statement about independence, as he had done earlier with his religious mentor in Jordan, Mohammad al Maqdisi, from whom he had eventually become estranged. For all intents and purposes, al Zarqawi was in effect the first brand of 'street Al Qaeda'. Less disciplined, more violent and often terroristically more efficient, al Zarqawi opened space for new groups under Al Qaeda owing to his 'rep.' among militants. His high-profile operations (notably the attacks on the Jordanian embassy and on the UN office) enabled his rapid, spectacular and ultimately ill-fated rise.[1] This also signalled the onset of Al Qaeda's faltering control of key battlegrounds such as Iraq, Afghanistan and the Sahel.

Following contacts established with Al Qaeda's number two, Ayman al Dhawahiri, and in the context of the group's mid-2000s franchising strategy, Al Zarqawi announced on 17 October 2004 that his Jama'at al Tawhid wal Jihad was folding itself into Bin Laden's Al Qaeda and becoming Tandhim Al Qaeda fi Bilad al Rafidayn (the Organisation of Al Qaeda in the Land of the Two Rivers, known as AQI). This second incarnation of what would ultimately become IS was important but relatively short-lived when compared to other franchises such as AQIM or AQAP. AQI was associated essentially with al Zarqawi's high-profile staccato attacks in Iraq in 2004–5. Al Zarqawi also distinguished himself from Al Qaeda by introducing two key elements which remained important in this context in the following years, namely his intra-Islam factionalist attacks on the Shi'a and his brutality (encapsulated in the videotaped beheading of US citizen Nicholas Berg on 7 May 2004, whom he dressed in the orange prisoner suit worn in Abu Ghraib and Guantánamo Bay, starting a referential trend IS would replay ten years later). Al Zarqawi's story and his late association with Al Qaeda is important and complex. It highlights the perennial conundrum posed to a central organisation that constantly needs to project its force and implement a global vision while having to rely on local actors who bring in their specific concerns, and often their ambiguous relations with their immediate environment, including friend and foe.

Al Zarqawi was killed by a US air raid on 7 June 2006, north of Baqubah in Iraq. With his disappearance the local Iraqi link to the global project of Al Qaeda started declining. In an audiotaped message released on 1 July 2006, Bin Laden would pay posthumous homage to the 'fallen soldier'. Four months later, on 15 October, ISI was created, overtaking AQI. Importantly, the first mention of the project of setting up an 'Islamic State' had come from al Zarqawi himself in his last videotaped message, aired on 21 April 2006. Earlier, on 15 January, the first umbrella organisation to which AQI had adhered, Majliss al Shura al Mujahideen, had been set up briefly and its head, Abu Abdulla Rashid al Baghdadi, had been the first to release a formal statement on al Zarqawi's death, on 16 June. Led successively by Abu Hamza al Muhajir (also known as Abu Ayyub al Masri), Abu Omar al Baghdadi (Hamid Daoud Mohammed Khalil al Zawi) and Abu Bakr al Baghdadi (also known then as Abu Du'a), ISI remained the dominant radical Sunni extremist group in Iraq until that third and lengthy phase – it lasted six and a half years – was reworked, for a fourth time, on 9 April 2013 into an expansion of ISI under the name of Islamic State in Iraq and the Levant (ISIL, al Dawla al Islamiya fil Iraq wal Shaam, or ISIS for Islamic State in Iraq and Syria). Finally, on 29 June 2014, Abu Bakr al Baghdadi, who had remained at the helm of the different incarnations of the group since May 2010, announced the creation of IS as the re-establishment of the Islamic Caliphate with himself as new 'Caliph' under the name Ibrahim.

In the immediate aftermath of the American withdrawal from Iraq in 2011, the Nuri al Maliki regime led a widespread repression of Sunnis, with thousands arrested across the country and hundreds killed in near-daily extrajudicial executions committed by several Shi'a militias. The relationship between the Sunni and Shi'a communities had already degenerated dramatically after the fall of the Saddam Hussein regime in the spring of 2003, and, over the next few years, the communal violence had reached unprecedented levels in the country's modern history. However, the events in late 2011 and early 2012 brought another dimension, and a logic of accelerated purging of Sunnis was discernible as al Maliki drove this plan forward. In addition to the individual killings, which were particularly intense in and around the greater Baghdad area, the Sunni tribes were alienated politically and kept out of the power-sharing bargaining. Two elements then helped al Baghdadi's reinvention of the AQI project: first, al Maliki's increasingly brutal repression – notably in Ramadi in January–March 2013, in Hawija in April 2013 against approximately 300 Sunni protestors and in December against senior Sunni parliamentarians – leading to extended large-scale Sunni demonstrations (supported financially by Iraqi businessmen such as Khamis al Khanjar); and second, the fact that the troop increment (commonly known as the 'Surge', an increase of 20,000 men positioned around Baghdad to battle the insurgency) which the United States had overseen in 2007 had left only the most battle-hardened elements of the original AQI and of ISI standing. Al Baghdadi would in effect (re) build his group on a pre-filtered, solid base of vengeful and experienced insurgents, such as former al Zarqawi right-hand man, Abd al Rahman Mustafa al Qaduli. These assertive elements were joined by remnants of Hussein's Ba'ath party and special military forces, in particular from the once-feared Hammurabi Division of the Republican Guard, and former senior military advisors of Hussein, such as Ezzat Ibrahim al Duri and Fadel Abdulla al Hiyali (Abu Muslim al Turkmani) – men with 'superior counterintelligence and security skills'.[2] Many of these men had also been imprisoned and tortured by American forces at Abu Ghraib and elsewhere, and others had suffered at the hands of the Shi'a militias. The radicalising prison experience and repression was not limited to local Iraqi actors. Several of the early foreign fighters coming from Europe experienced the same torture at the hands of American and Iraqi troops and ended up joining IS. One such case is the Belgian-Moroccan national Oussama Atar, who was held first at Abu Ghraib and then at Camp Cropper (the same camp where Hussein had been held), and eventually at Camp Bucca from February 2005 to August 2012, where he met al Baghdadi. Upon release, Atar re-established contact with al Baghdadi, and allegedly went on to oversee the operations leading to the attacks in Paris in November 2015 and Brussels in March 2016. To further reinvigorate the backbone of this rising new insurgency, al Baghdadi initiated a series of prison breaks in 2012–13, from the Abu Ghraib prison itself, to release inmates who went on to join his emerging group.

In effect then, IS rose from the deliberate actions of the most fiercely independent and violent lieutenant of Bin Laden (al Zarqawi) only to be taken over by battle-hardened local Iraqis, such as al Baghdadi, who recalibrated the group's orientation towards a domestic path and upgraded violence. Such a to-the-far-enemy-and-back indigenisation of a transnational group produced the uncertain transformation of a hybrid organisation that was expanding outwardly while remaining wedded to local goals. Similarly, the specialisation in coercion witnessed a dedicated reconfiguration with, in time, that refocusing translating into military patterns. Whereas, for instance, suicide attacks were being carried out predominantly by foreigners against civilian targets, as was the case circa 2004, IS's suicide attacks from 2014 onwards were primarily perpetrated by local operatives against military targets (923 attacks were, for instance, conducted in one year alone during that period, between December 2015 and December 2016).[3] To be certain, the recentring on Iraq, which culminated in the capture of Ramadi and Fallujah in early 2014, did not alter the fundamentals of a movement that still remained in key aspects transnational and regional, and in which, for instance, the Arabian Gulf area had always played a key role in terms of soldiery. Saudi recruits had indeed remained steady (around 2,000 men) and were motivated by a sense of pan-Islamism,[4] and this took place in the wider context of a loss of Sunni leadership across the region, filled by insurgents and hardliners. Similarly, the international radical Islamist movement – still led officially by Al Qaeda and al Dhawahiri, who had replaced Bin Laden – had remained significant in the late 2000s. One of the most successful operations for Al Qaeda had, for instance, taken place during that period. On 30 December 2009, Khalil Humam al Balawi, a Jordanian-born Al Qaeda double agent working for the Jordanian intelligence services and the CIA, and pretending to have penetrated the upper ranks of Al Qaeda, conducted a suicide operation inside the CIA camp in Khost, Afghanistan, in which he killed the seven top CIA operatives in the region.[5] However, the shift in Iraq – what we can term an *umma* (community) to *qabila* (tribe) transfer – was important, as it effectively confirmed a path that had been adopted haphazardly as early as 2006 in the wake of al Zarqawi's disappearance. Al Zarqawi's pre-Al Qaeda materialisation in Iraq in 2003 was itself indicative of a rerouting of the journey of transnational Islamism. In offering to lead the fight against the Americans that had been brought to Iraq, the Jordanian's group was now performing under a theme of *min al adou al qarib ila al 'adou al ba'eed* (from the near to the far enemy), to a new one of *wusul al 'adou* (the arrival of the enemy). All in all, IS's multiple births betray this essential dialectic, namely the recurring question within its ranks of which battle to pursue, what level of engagement to prioritise and in which particular direction to move. The local vs. international options were not the only ones, and the key event that would accelerate the rise of ISIS and then IS would come from an unexpected regional situation.

Into Levantine Battle

By mid to late 2011, ISI was at a strategic dead end. In the interregnum between the disappearance of Bin Laden in May 2011 and ISIS's April 2013 arrival, there was a transitional period wherein the global soldiery of Al Qaeda was looking more for strategic direction than for a cause. What was to become of the organisation the Saudi millionaire had set up? Where was it heading after the fall of its iconic leader? What should the movement's priorities be, as uprisings and upheaval proliferated unceasingly around the Middle East and North Africa? While Arab Spring-driven analyses decreed the end of Al Qaeda,[6] and Bin Laden's deputy al Dhawahiri sprang forth as the new formal but impotent leader, a global power vacuum deepened in radical Islamism – and Iraq remained, as it had been since 2003, its centre of gravity. Three unexpected events allowed IS to occupy that fluid space successfully: the transitional chaos that followed the social rebellions of the Arab Spring, starting in Tunisia and Egypt in December 2010 and January 2011; the anticlimactic death of Bin Laden the following May; and, most importantly, the Syrian civil war from March 2011 onwards. Immediately seeing the rebirth opportunity offered by this coincidence of events, and particularly the Syrian conflict, in July al Baghdadi set in motion a plan aimed at positioning his group at the centre of these changes. The first component concerned the revamping of ISI's soldiery in Iraq itself, in the context of Sunni disenfranchisement. As noted, al Baghdadi oversaw his replenishing of manpower through a number of prison breaks to free the most ruthless operators, whom he then appointed – alongside hardcore, middle-aged veterans and former Iraqi army officers (in its heyday, up until the early 2000s, the Iraqi Republican Guard had been an efficient and well-organised corps) – as his lieutenants to increase the group's lethality. During this period (July 2012–July 2013), eight high-profile prison breaks were organised in a campaign dubbed 'Breaking the Walls', using an upgraded military capability featuring vehicle-borne improvised explosive devices – culminating in a night-time assault on the prison of

Abu Ghraib on 21 July 2013, from which some 500 inmates were freed.[7] In the middle of this sequence, first in August 2011 and then in January 2012, al Baghdadi dispatched representatives to Syria to meet with the newly formed Jabhat al Nusra (the Victory Front), a Syrian radical Islamist group opposed to Syrian President Bashar al Assad, which had coalesced in the wake of the uprising and was being set up officially (it would be announced on 23 January 2012), to discuss operational collaboration across the Iraqi-Syrian border. (On 28 July 2016, Jabhat Al Nusra would be renamed Jabhat Fath al Shaam, or the Front of Opening of the Levant.) Eventually, on 9 April 2013, recognising an opportunity dovetailing the crisis in Syria, al Baghdadi stepped out to announce the creation of IS in Iraq and al Shaam – in effect adding Syria to his existing Iraq dominion. In that statement, al Baghdadi declared that Jabhat al Nusra was joining his movement as the local Syrian branch of ISI. Yet the next day, al Nusra's leader, Abu Mohammad al Jolani, rejected the integration, stating that 'neither the al Nusra command nor its consultative council nor its general manager were aware of this announcement. It reached them via the media and if the speech is authentic, we were not consulted.' This then led to a split within Jabhat al Nusra, a wing of which opted for integration into the newly formed ISIS, which also secured the support of Harakat Ahrar al Shaam (the Movement of the Free Men of the Levant), another powerful rebel group set up in Syria in 2011. Stepping in to settle the dispute, on 23 May al Dhawahiri disavowed the announced ISI-Jabhat al Nusra merger ('Sheikh Abu Bakr al Baghdadi was wrong when he announced the Islamic State in Iraq and the Levant without asking permission or receiving advice from us and even without notifying us; the Islamic State in Iraq and the Levant is to be dissolved, while the Islamic State in Iraq is to continue its work'), and called again for ISIS's disbandment on 7 November.

Such an extraordinary sequence of statements and counter-statements was unprecedented in the annals of Al Qaeda, and was indicative of the rough-and-ready threat IS had come to represent to Al Qaeda. Never before had Al Qaeda aired its disagreements so explicitly, and never before had its leadership been questioned so openly and its lack of control over matters revealed so plainly. Above and beyond the divisive contestation, this was arguably a revealing moment in the end of the cycle. Simply put, al Dhawahiri had failed to inherit Bin Laden's leadership. In contradistinction, the then-ISIS group saw strategic value in the Syrian civil war and opportunistically moved to harness it, with a view to both engineering the group's design and remapping the very environment in which it existed. As one analyst noted, in such an intervention-filled context:

> catastrophes are large-scale or mega-disasters that affect multitudes or entire populations and leave their marks on many people's space and time. *Space is marked by the de-territorialisation of a whole region and then by a re-territorialisation of a special zone within it ...* This is the area where former order crumbles, normal expectations become meaningless, the self-evident dimension of everyday life is lost ... amidst ruins of all kinds.[8]

Al Dhawahiri's 2013 statements were indicative of Al Qaeda's weakness and ISIS's rising power. Upping the ante, al Baghdadi chose to ignore the injunctions he had received, and moved to accelerate his group's plan in a second phase he dubbed the 'Soldiers' Harvest' (July 2013–July 2014). In December 2013/January 2014, he entered in the most ambitious phase of the group's history. ISIS initiated a two-step plan to try and position itself as the leading insurgency force in both Iraq and Syria within six months (before Ramadan of 2014). During that phase, the group battled a coalition, known as Jaysh al Mujahidin (Army of the Fighters), of eight small- and mid-sized Gulf-sponsored Islamist groups in the area around Aleppo, which it managed to defeat, as well as the Supreme Military Command of the Free Syrian Army (Jaysh Souriya al Hor), and went on to establish control of key sectors in north-eastern Syria, in particular the city of Raqqa. Subsequently, most Syrian cities straddling the border with Iraq were captured by the group: Tal Hamis, Shaddadi, Markada, Suwar, Hraiji, Abu Hammam, Hajjin and Bukkamal. On the strength of this show of force, ISIS turned back to Iraq, where it then seized control of Iraq's second biggest city, Mosul, on 10 June 2014. The fall of Mosul was a turning point and arguably the single event that allowed the group to materialise as 'Islamic State' on the strength of its recent military victories, the territory it now held and the cadenced momentum it rode in both the Iraqi and Syrian insurgencies – all against the focused attention of the global Islamist movement observing its actions in awe. Over the next months, and while positioning a force of 3,000 or so men in Raqqa as the centrepiece of its presence in Syria, the group moved on from Mosul to seize the Iraqi cities of Qayyara, al Shirqat, Hawija, Tikrit, Siniya, Saadiya, Anah, Rawah, Habbaniya, Tal Afar, Fallujah, Mahmoudiya, Traybil, Sinjar, Yarmouq and Al Qadisiya.

The Iraqi group was also able to count on the presence of a similarly fertile Islamist and tribal terrain in Syria. In October 2013, as ISIS was gaining ground in north-east Syria, a ceremony was organised in Raqqa during which 14 Syrian tribal leaders publicly announced their support for the group. To be certain, extremist Islamists had long been present in Syria, coexisting with the tribal structure – al Tali'a al Muqatila (the Fighting Vanguard) was, for instance, among the early groups in the mid to late 1970s, long predating the 2010s whirlwind of new formations. In 1982, a large-scale rebellion of Islamists in the city of Hama had led to a massacre of thousands ordered by Bashar al Assad's father, President Hafez al Assad. As the radical Islamist militancy persisted in Syria in the 2000s, it gradually became influenced by Bin Laden's Al Qaeda, and, in time, merged with the post-2011 rebellion. Just as it had done in Iraq, ISIS now capitalised on the rising tensions between the Syrian state and the tribes, which had historically controlled eastern Syria. In losing their clientelism with the state and their ability to deliver security locally, the tribes found themselves in an uneasy position whereby they had to negotiate with the armed groups not merely politically but operationally. In that context, it is important to note that, for all its different social *'asabiya* anchoring the armed group's religious call, Arab tribal structure was never fundamentally problematic for IS. Rather, as a time-tested and organised source of power, the tribe offered a ready-made and legitimate local construct, which the group could engage with and enlist in its opposition to the Iraqi[9] or Syrian state, and indeed align itself with; *shuyoukh wa 'ashayr* (chiefs and tribes) fighting alongside *mujahideen* (religious warriors) was not an unfamiliar scene in the region, and specifically in the Levant, and such a relationship was often displayed as alliance imagery in the videos of IS. For instance, when it sought to establish its dominion over the Deir Ezzor area, IS had to navigate the local power configurations between various tribes such as the Bukeyr, the Buchamel and the Shuheil.

The history of IS that emerges from these first two configurations – of a post-Al Qaeda national focus on Iraq and the regional Syrian expansion – is a picture of a passive entity present in Iraq before the US invasion in 2003 which seizes that opportunity to unleash its operations, before folding itself temporarily into Al Qaeda and then joining in a nationwide Iraqi insurgency platform, before using a second opportunity afforded by the Syria conflict to reactivate its operations and move on to claim a regional and ultimately international leadership of radical Islamism. In the event, IS was therefore driven by its provincial ambition, the deterioration of the Iraqi situation under Prime Minister Nuri al Maliki's rule, post-Bin Laden indecisiveness on the part of Al Qaeda and the unexpected situation provided by the Syrian conflict.

State-Building from Franchise to Region

ISI's April 2013 decision to expand officially to Syria took Al Qaeda by surprise. Just as he was not able to take Al Qaeda's project forward after Bin Laden's death, al Dhawahiri failed to address the issues raised by the gradual independence and, in time, the full break of al Baghdadi's organisation. Indeed, al Dhawahiri weakened his position in August 2015 by pledging allegiance to a new Afghan leader, Mullah Akhtar Mansour, in effect relinquishing the sovereign leadership status Bin Laden's death had bequeathed on him. In reacting indecisively – as noted, he twice called unconvincingly for a cancellation of the ISIS project in May and November 2013, and also failed at an attempted mediation in January 2014 between ISIS and Jabhat al Nusra – al Dhawahiri opened the way for al Baghdadi to make a full run for the leadership of the global Islamist movement. This was forcefully embodied in IS's June 2014 dual statement about the birth of IS and the claim to the Caliphate. From that point onwards, Al Qaeda and IS were formally on different trajectories and tempos, with the original group playing catch-up. Al Qaeda was able to push back operationally through the association with Jabhat al Nusra, which became its local representative in Syria until July 2016 (when it became Jabhat Fath al Shaam and adopted an ambiguous stance towards Al Qaeda), but that owed much to the latter's own initiative in (temporarily) choosing to side with it. However, two caveats are in order as we observe this evolution. First, Al Qaeda and IS share a common history, with IS having been Al Qaeda's franchise in Iraq between October 2004 and January 2006. Second, limitations in their competing and oppositional stances after 2013 were, to a significant extent, inevitably self-imposed on both sides, as Bin Laden and al Zarqawi were key founding figures shared by both groups. Ultimately, however, Al Qaeda was falling slowly and IS rising fast. The rupture with Al Qaeda was then nevertheless the result not merely of classical group competition or turf wars, but of a deeper shift in strategy. Part of this was historical – the waxing and waning of irredentist armed militancy – and part of it behavioural. For all IS's actions, it must also be kept in mind that Al Qaeda's 20-year saga since 1989 was naturally beginning to slow down by the late 2000s. With Bin

Laden's death and al Dhawahiri's inability to take the project forward, Al Qaeda's story was slowly closing. This in effect opened a window for *any* group willing and able to fill that vacuum. It took an Al Qaeda franchise to do it, with al Baghdadi in Iraq forcefully, opportunistically and decisively positioning himself. The key decision on his part was to capitalise on the post-2011 strife in Syria to both expand his domain of operation – ISI was now folding the Levant in its envisioned wider jurisdiction – and to gain added military experience. The result, two years later, was a reborn entity that was eminently hybrid, with some seven layers in its midst (see Table 3.2): part Al Qaeda; part Iraqi Islamist insurgency; part Ba'ath renaissance movement; part Syrian armed rebellion; part regional post-Arab Spring political and security phenomenon; part global Islamist movement taking the place of Al Qaeda, from West Africa to the Indian subcontinent by way of the Sahel; and part Western metropolis-based rebel. IS was therefore able to pursue and deepen Al Qaeda's transnational mode of force projection while focusing on the territorial centre of gravity it controlled between Mosul and Raqqa.

Table 3.2   The seven layers of IS

Identity	Environment	Purpose
1. Heir of Al Qaeda	Global franchise system	Perpetuating Al Qaeda's war
2. Iraqi Islamist insurgency	US occupation of Iraq and Shi'a government	Leading armed national Sunni movement
3. Iraqi military insurgency	US occupation of Iraq and Shi'a government	Avenging Ba'ath regime defeat
4. Syrian insurgency	Syrian civil war	Unseating Syrian regime
5. Regional Islamist group	Post-Arab Spring, Middle East and North Africa	Seizing governance opportunity
6. International Islamist group	Muslim world	Replacing Al Qaeda
7. Transnational post-modern radical	United States and Europe	Rebelling against alienation

On the surface, the differences between Al Qaeda and IS grew ever more visible from 2013 onwards, both at the leadership level and among their respective followers. The relationship between al Dhawahiri and al Baghdadi was itself strained, competitive and irreconcilable. The men were of different generations, experienced different battlefields

(Afghanistan 1980s vs. Iraq 2000s) and harkened back to different social backgrounds; a bourgeois surgeon from Cairo thinking strategically, on the one hand, and a working-class student of religion from Samarra versed in tactical operations, on the other – everything conspired to keep them estranged from one another. In the aftermath of the Paris attacks in January 2015, there was conjecture about an alliance between Al Qaeda and IS, although no tangible evidence of such potential partnership materialised. Specifically, the issue arose because Chérif Kouachi, one of the two brothers who had led the attack in Paris on the offices of the *Charlie Hebdo* satirical magazine, declared to the French news channel BFM that he had been sent by AQAP and had been financed by its then-senior operator Anwar al 'Awlaqi; while his likely co-conspirator, Amedy Coulibaly, who led a follow-up attack two days later on a Jewish supermarket, stated in a video message that he was affiliated with IS. Yet Kouachi's alleged AQAP connections went back to an earlier, pre-IS phase, with al 'Awlaqi now dead (killed by a US drone attack in the Al Jawf region of Yemen on 30 September 2011), and Coulibaly's statement was more akin to a unilateral pledge of allegiance than a revelation of pre-set operational links. Beyond that undecided episode, the larger relationship was much more one of competition in the Levant, in the Gulf, in North Africa and in Afghanistan.

In the wake of its coup on Al Qaeda and expansion into Syria, paradoxically IS started going down a path towards the type of organisation that Bin Laden and his associates had set up in Afghanistan in 1988. As IS firmed up its power in Iraq and Syria, secured control of large swathes of territory and embarked on a wider regional strategy, the conditions that obtained were reminiscent of what took place a quarter of a century earlier in that arc bridging Afghanistan and Pakistan, when Osama Bin Laden, Ayman al Dhawahiri and Abdallah Yusuf al 'Azzam set up Al Qaeda in the summer of 1988 following the Soviet retreat. Witness the similarities: a context of lengthy armed conflict born out of occupation and domestic strife (Afghanistan from 1979 to 1989, Iraq since 2003 and Syria since 2011 – IS was *also* born in war); a globally expanding transnational militant front ('Arab Afghans' then, 'foreign fighters' now); the complex tapestry of guarded but real superpower involvement (Soviet Union and US then, US and Russia now); active and competing powerful regional actors with colliding agendas (Pakistan and Afghanistan; Iran, Saudi Arabia, Turkey and Qatar); shadowy proxy-war dynamics (the Pakistani ISI and the Mujahideen then, Lebanese Hezbollah, Iranian Al

Quds and others later); powerful local insurgencies (Northern Alliance and Taliban in Afghanistan, all manner of Sunni and Shi'a groups in Iraq and Syria); and in both cases sporadic tactical victories by a rising group, cumulatively generating further strategic momentum. The sum total of these parallels was consequential, as the new group continued to experience a complicated relationship with the mother organisation that spawned it, with IS seeking to replicate Al Qaeda's successful militarised matrix but with a view to introducing important innovations of its own.

There were, however, key differences in the related stories, and the parallel during that phase should ultimately be relativised because it moved towards a different horizon. First, IS was immersed in a territorially defined struggle (a romanticised Levant or Shaam, which is real to many militants but which never existed administratively in the past), whereas the original Al Qaeda had been eminently about transcending boundaries, with Afghanistan being the springboard on to the American 'far enemy' (*al 'adou al ba'eed*) in lieu of the Arab regimes 'near enemy' (*al 'adou al qareeb*). Second, the ideological component of IS remained thin[10] and ranked behind its identity (Levantine) and confessional (Sunni) dimensions when Bin Laden consistently stressed political goals and religious unity among Islamists of all hues, including non-Arabs and non-Sunnis. Finally, the increasing inroads of IS were mostly attracting a motley crew of fighters from around the world who had come, almost overnight, to regard Syria as the new *cause célèbre* of 'jihadism', whereas Al Qaeda had been painstakingly constructed in several stages in Asia – Al Qaeda was set up in Khost, Afghanistan and Bin Laden died in Abottabad, Pakistan – under a logic of *homogenising and exporting operators* and opening fronts in various other geographical centres (East Africa, Western Europe, North Africa, the Arabian Gulf). In other words, IS was concerned with securing an inwardly driven, regional centre of gravity (coalescing somewhere between Fallujah, Iraq and Raqqa, Syria) for primarily regional purposes, while Al Qaeda rewrote the transnational rulebook to beam out its politico-religious fight internationally. Notwithstanding the subsequent smartphone tweeting of its flag in front of the White House to reach and frighten the US,[11] for the new group, the prize was Baghdad and Damascus. For the older one, it had been New York and Washington.

The IS story thus indicated that, for all the decentralisation, there remained among international Islamist militants a yearning for a global leadership, as had once existed during the heyday of Bin Laden's Al Qaeda al Oum (1995–2005). IS certainly filled the vacuum, and regenerated a brand that was successful among those militants, but it did so without establishing unquestioned political legitimacy. In the mid-2000s, Al Qaeda's franchising had been accepted internally because it was decreed by Bin Laden's authoritative figure and because it made sense tactically to the group's militants, as Al Qaeda avoided structural collapse by proactively embracing generational shift. Al Qaeda, which again refers to itself officially as Qaedat al Jihad (the *Base* of the Jihad), saw itself as an enabler, whereas IS's centrifugal dynamics indicated otherwise, revealing the limits of the franchise model under such an evolved logic. Similarly, al Baghdadi's in-your-face ruthlessness was the consequence of the urgency of the battle scene he inhabited in ultra-violent 2000s Iraq, and the outcome of mixed results, demanding and battle-hardened management of ISI-to-ISIS-to-IS since 2006, rather than distant inspiration by Bin Laden. If most insurgent groups are born from pre-war politics,[12] both Al Qaeda and IS were forged in war. The martiality that presided over the birth of Al Qaeda was what allowed IS to take Bin Laden's real legacy, 'Al Qaedism' – a loose ideology, rather than Al Qaeda the physical group – to the next level.

The campaign al Baghdadi orchestrated was undeniably a qualitative milestone in the larger Al Qaeda story, which in effect closed the Bin Laden era and displaced al Dhawahiri, as the new strongman in Mosul proclaimed himself Caliph ('I have been plagued with this great matter, plagued with this responsibility and it is a heavy responsibility', he said in his 4 July 2014 address). Yet framing IS merely within the logic of Al Qaeda would be missing the novelty of the group, as it introduced a dimension previously neglected by Al Qaeda, namely state-building. Just as Al Qaeda was an emanation of both globalisation and transnationalism in the late 1980s and early 1990s, IS during the 2010s was a testimony to the mutating manifestation of international insecurity in the form of weakened states, increasingly 'militiaised' in the Levant but also of those so-called 'ungoverned spaces'[13] that had been materialising in the Middle East, in the Sahel and in sub-Saharan Africa, and which IS now sought to govern differently. And so, just as al Baghdadi expressed a desire to unite ('It is time for you to end this abhorrent partisanship, dispersion and division', he remarked in his Mosul lecture), the strategy of his group was to build up momentum towards physical expansion. In that respect, it was IS's very existence, not its tactics or cadence, that were offsetting its enemy, and so bombings such as those ordered by US President Barack

Obama in August 2014, and by France and Russia starting in September 2015, were likely to achieve little in terms of lasting resolution of the problem. Reflecting on the relevance of Von Clausewitz's ideas regarding the Great Arab Revolt, T.E. Lawrence captured a key marker of such an asymmetrical engagement: 'Clausewitz had said that rear-guards modulate the enemy's action like a pendulum, not by what they do, but by their mere existence.'[14]

The evolution of IS during this phase was therefore a combination of an independently moving battle plan – now focused on Iraq, now centred on Syria – and an adaptation to domestic and regional contingencies. Tellingly, the move on to Syria was not isolated, but from the beginning part of a regional logic – at the time al Baghdadi also reportedly met with Egyptian fighters from the Sinai,[15] which eventually would become Ansar Beit al Maqdis (as discussed below). In this inherent duality and flexibility resided the initial strength of IS, namely its forward-looking versatility. This is what allowed it continuously to present its struggle as driven by urgency: the immediate need to resist the US invasion in 2003–6; the necessity to oppose Iraqi Prime Minister Nuri al Maliki and his Shi'a militias in 2006–11; the imperative to go to battle against Syrian President Bashar al Assad and his Alawite troops in 2012, and their Russian ally in 2015; the obligation to resist the Iraqi and American troops advancing on Mosul and Raqqa in 2016–17; and so, on open-endedly. In other words, the ability to stay the course and reinvent itself continuously – a feature of modernity – is what made IS potent in that way. The brand that IS physically stamped on a conspicuously displayed flag in lieu of the distant and ethereal Al Qaeda name ensured a stronger impact on the new group's social and religious milieu. Most importantly, and in spite of the prevalence of that narrative, IS managed to avoid the perception among its soldiery that it could, at any given time, be finished, since each new episode appeared to lead logically to the next one. Seen as such, IS was the natural culmination of the United States' failed adventurism in Iraq, Maliki's authoritarianism, Assad's ruthlessness and post-Bin Laden Al Qaeda's discomposure. The central question was less the pull of IS in the eyes of its fighters, or its grandstanding towards the *umma*, than its real reach and impact on the ground. As al Baghdadi reintroduced the street style of al Zarqawi, and focused on prison breaks to staff his group with ruthless operators, he also pursued a centralised conquer-and-hold approach to seizing territory, instead of an open-ended, evanescent and sporadic insurgency. With the 'Islamic State' announcement in 2014, this became coupled with symbolic, overreaching state-building claims.[16]

Realistically, IS's state-building project started in earnest in mid-June 2014. The fall of Mosul – the second largest city in Iraq and an extended urban centre with a population of over two million people – was, for IS, a moment akin to what 9/11 represented for Al Qaeda; namely an unexpected success of enormous magnitude with unforeseen strategic implications to which they needed to adapt. Instead of bunkering down and using Mosul as a base merely to continue its insurgency and the attacks it had actively led that year (notably against Baghdad), the IS leadership produced a more ambitious plan which was revealed to the world at the end of that month. On 29 June, the group's spokesman, al 'Adnani (who would be killed by a Russian airstrike on 30 August 2016 in Aleppo) delivered a 34-minute audiotaped speech in which he announced the creation of an 'Islamic State':

The time has come for those generations that were drowning in oceans of disgrace ... The time has come for the *umma* ... to wake up from its sleep, remove the garments of dishonour and shake off the dust of humiliation and disgrace, for the era of lamenting and moaning has gone and the dawn of honour has emerged anew. The sun of *jihad* has risen ... The signs of victory have appeared ... Here the flag of the Islamic State, the flag of *tawhid* [religious unity] rises. Its shade covers land from Aleppo to Diyala. Beneath it, the walls of the *tawaghit* [religiously illegitimate rulers] have been demolished, their flags have fallen and their borders have been destroyed. Their soldiers are killed, imprisoned or defeated. The Muslims are honoured ... Prisoners are released by the edge of the sword. The people in the lands of the [Islamic] state move about for their livelihood and journeys, feeling safe regarding their lives and wealth ... *Jizya* [religious taxation] has been enforced ... *Zakat* [alms] have been collected. Courts have been established to resolve disputes and complaints. Evil has been removed. Lessons and classes have been held in the mosques ... The Islamic State ... resolved to announce the establishment of the Islamic Caliphate, the appointment of a Caliph for the Muslims ... descendent from the family of the Prophet, Ibrahim Ibn 'Awad Ibn Ibrahim Ibn 'Ali Ibn Muhammad al Badri al Hashimi al Husayni al Qurashi by lineage, al Samarrai by birth and upbringing, al Baghdadi by residence and scholarship ... Thus, he is the imam and the Caliph for the Muslims everywhere. Accordingly, the 'Iraq and Shaam' in the name of the Islamic State is henceforth removed from all official deliberations and communications, and the official name is the Islamic State from the date of this declaration.

On 16 June – two weeks earlier and five days after the fall of Mosul – al 'Adnani had released another overlooked but equally important message entitled 'Apologies, Emir of Al Qaeda', in which he referred explicitly to Bin Laden's earlier calls to the Iraqi people to rise up against the occupiers and praised fully *that* legacy (Ayman al Dhawahiri and Abu Yahya al Libi, another former senior leader of Al Qaeda, were also mentioned in that speech):

> This is the base of Al Qaeda [*qaedat al jihad*], this is Al Qaeda as we have come to know it, this is its path and whoever changes it we change him, this is Al Qaeda as we have loved it, as we have inherited it and as we have made it victorious, this is Al Qaeda, this is Al Qaeda that has terrorised the enemy, this is Al Qaeda that runs in our hearts ... this is our relationship to Al Qaeda ... but sorry, Emir Al Qaeda, the [Islamic] State is not a branch of Al Qaeda ... *a state cannot be part of a group.* (Emphasis added)

In so doing, IS was unambiguously connecting its project with that historical Al Qaeda lineage – in effect to show its colours to its constituency – but in addressing al Dhawahiri in such less-than-complimentary terms it was severing the relationship and already embarking on the writing of its own history. Lest it be misunderstood, the 16 June message was a polite divorce. The new armed group went on at once to flesh out its ambition to become an institution able to deliver services to a community and beam a message – however embryonic and however fledging – of statehood. To that end, religion was enlisted with a view to sacralising this project – something that was not too difficult to achieve given that Islamist armed groups benefit from the fact that the pursuit of state-building has been assumed in its militant cosmogony, with the notion of an 'Islamic state' regarded as the natural and self-evident demand of a religion such as Islam that is steeped in politics and state formation.[17] Conceived as the natural order of things, the group's envisioned role as a state-in-the-making was presented as merely that of an implementer. Therefore, declaring statehood is notionally relatively easy, and functions for any Islamist group as a circular logic. The question of statehood came equally logically into the IS saga, as it connected specifically with the unfinished debates of the Middle East a century ago, in the mid to late 1910s. At the time, '[T]he question of the Islamic state [had been] a major point of debate after the defeat and eventual dissolution of the Ottoman Empire after the First World War. A number of thinkers presented their ideas on the nature of the Islamic state when the new Turkish rulers decided to abolish the Caliphate and establish a republic.'[18] Bin Laden did not have to be too concerned with an actual discussion of that project as he was merely, by his own reckoning, setting the base for that effort. As his task was accomplished, territory gained and communities in need of services were in expectation, however, the IS leadership made the leap to a maximised vision of both religious legitimacy and historical statehood (combined in the Caliphate construct). In that regard, IS's state-building project could, arguably, be seen as classically linked to state-formation processes characterised by what Heather Rae terms a 'pathological homogenisation'[19] of peoples, namely a redefinition of a socio-political community as an exclusively moral one. Indeed, the homogenisation pursued by ISIS is here reconstitutive of a long-gone system and creative of a modern one, as well as destructive of the existing Iraqi and Syrian states. Moreover, the process pursued – as opposed to classical Tillyan state-building – was not led by an elite (it would have been if, say, Bin Laden had pursued it) but by lower elements in the group (regardless of al 'Adnani's cosmetic insistence on al Baghdadi's alleged Hashemite lineage). Nevertheless, whereas Al Qaeda's references to the Caliphate had been inconsistent and aspirational, IS positioned itself from the beginning of its history within a firm logic of statisation. Like most modern-day Islamists, IS ideologues therefore faced the challenge of reconciling modernity and tradition. As Nazih Ayubi explains:

[T]he neo-fundamentalists, or the proponents of political Islam, have actually introduced some novel, and radical, changes in the way the Islamic political tradition is understood. While they want to preserve the close link between religion and politics that the traditional jurisprudence had developed, they want to reverse the order within this link. The traditional jurists had forged a link between politics and religion by giving a religious legitimacy to political power. The political Islamists maintain that religion and politics cannot be separated, but because they are now in the position of resisting the existing state, not of legitimising it, they are seeking the politicisation of a particular vision of religion that they have in mind. To achieve this purpose, the contemporary Islamists are often inclined to be more innovative and less textual in their approach.[20]

This is precisely what IS did, as in the next phase it quickly moved on with its territorial administration project, alternating orthodox readings and modernising ones – all in explicit pursuit of statehood. Some of that had been done in Ramadi and Fallujah when the cities fell to the group six months earlier, but now the project was taken to a new level, with a view to institutionalising it on a lasting basis. Roads were refurbished in the Mosul and Raqqa areas in the summer of 2014, garbage was collected, telephone lines were fixed, 'police' were posted at traffic intersections, banking services were taken over and money distributed, salaries were established for foot soldiers (approximately USD400 monthly) and strict law and order was imposed terroristically (with public beheadings and individuals pushed from rooftops). In both cities, a proto-administration was set up with departments of water, electricity, communication and transport. Seizing the oil fields around Mosul, IS went on to establish control over their production sites, and set up black market routes to sell that oil (averaging 50,000 barrels a day in some sites during 2015). A chief financial officer was appointed to oversee an annual budget, and a team of 'consumer protection agents' were dispatched to conduct surprise visits in stores throughout the occupied cities to check on the prices set by store owners. Territory, finance, population and use of violence – the classical trademarks of statehood – but also armament as resilience came to the group, through an important volume of weapons seized. These were mostly those which the US Army had provided to the Iraqi military and counter-terrorist special forces it had set up and trained; small and heavy weaponry, M1A tanks, 155 mm artillery, truck-mounted machine guns, portable surface-to-air missiles, man-portable air-defence systems and bomb-proof Humvee vehicles.

The economic base of the group solidified during this phase, which witnessed a shift from small-scale financial support (wealthy Gulf benefactors, religious donations and Hawala system transfers) to an industrial-scale economic base with pirate oil sales and the sale of antiquities – historical cultural artefacts captured in both Iraq and Syria, most of which were put on the international market through private sellers. The group's coffers were also replenished by way of taxation established at checkpoints throughout the territory the group held in Iraq and Syria, including across the wheat fields in the region. In November 2014, the creation of a currency using the old Arabic Dinar was announced. Ten textbooks (on religion, geography, jurisprudence, grammar and history) and a school curriculum were issued in September 2015 (the corpus was a combination of Abu Mus'ab al Suri's globally oriented texts, the more regionally focused writings of Abu Mohammad al Maqdisi and the political and strategic messages of Ayman al Dhawahiri). A 6 July 2016 video entitled *Structure of the Khilafa* explained how the Caliphate worked. To be certain, IS's challenging of the Iraqi and Syrian states was facilitated by these states' incompleteness and nature as by-products of colonial continuity,[21] but the new group proceeded from a different place to delegitimise these state authorities, seeking to combine in turn a supra-authority with evidence of administrative efficiency in the face of its enemies' inaptness and ineptitude. The logic of state-building – vividly seen in the videos produced that summer with the chant *baqiya* (staying), as in 'the Islamic State is staying' (*al dawla al Islamiya baqiya*), becoming a leitmotiv of the group – was also based on a broadening of what that 'state' was seen as offering, namely institutional perennation and self-realisation. Whereas Al Qaeda was all about military output and warrior ethos, IS widened that by promoting a single target, aiming at statehood. In a June 2014 IS video entitled *There is no Life without Jihad*, inner peace and atonement with oneself (away from 'trouble in the West') is promised to the militant invited to join the group and find his or her place in the *dawla*. One fighter remarks in that video, in English, that 'the cure to depression is *jihad*'. As Christoph Günther and Tom Kaden note: 'IS can be regarded as both a socio-political movement and a quasi-state with different sources of authority and means of power pertaining to each of these two roles. Both of these dimensions of authority guarantee and reinforce each other, thus providing IS with a stability that is often overlooked in public debates about its aspirations and prospects.'[22] It is this pervasive, pragmatic, programmatic and regulatory authority that must be stressed in making conceptual sense of IS.

With shades of incomplete colonial episodes and a mix of political-military group logic and religious movement dynamics presiding over it, the IS state-building project, which carried with it obvious limitations, could not then be dismissed so easily as mere militant rhetoric. Its emergence was due primarily to the societally degenerated situation in both Iraq since 2003 and Syria since 2011. As, however, we find ourselves at a key moment in the evolution of the armed groups evolving in the larger Middle East and North African area, the IS trajectory must in turn be located in a wider history not fully of its making, and removed from its specific motivations and methods. The materialisation of IS also owes a lot to the changing contexts of politics in the region. This, in effect, was a third phase in an interlocked scene in which post-colonial battles had generated a first transnational moment in the 1970s. In that respect, Bin Laden was not the first to introduce a globally oriented struggle. The first to do so were the Palestinians, and a first transnational moment – albeit a secular one regarding a national struggle for liberation – had taken place in the early to mid-1970s.[23] The birth of Al Qaeda in the wake of the Afghan-Soviet war led to the rise of a second, more effectively transnational moment with completely different radical Islamist motivations. As Al Qaeda began receding in the late 2000s and early 2010s, and as the Syrian uprising mutated into an internationalised civil war, a third global moment was born, again for different reasons but building on the same state-weakening grammar as the previous wave. Whereas the Palestinian guerrillas had straightforward national liberation motivations and Bin Laden's agenda was politico-religious, IS's motivations – which, as noted, were partly derivative from Al Qaeda in that complex bilateral relationship – were expressed compellingly to their soldiery by way of a narrative about statehood ('a state cannot be part of an organisation', al 'Adnani had pointed out almost apologetically to al Dhawahiri, but also *de facto* defiantly). IS's motivations denoted agency but were unshakably circumstantial and derivative. Martial dynamics such as resistance (*muqawama*) and fight (*nidal*) in the 1970s and 1980s, and *jihad* (struggle) in the 1990s and 2000s, were replaced by the control and dominion logics of *dawla* (state) in the 2010s (Figure 3.1).

Although it was striking alliances in the revolts in Iraq and Syria and feeding off the neo-*fitna* (strife/dispute) between Sunni and Shi'a in the Muslim world, IS was not actually launching a global offensive on many fronts, as it was focusing on building a core. In so doing, IS had two previous examples of failed Islamist management to learn from: the Taliban in Afghanistan in the 1990s, and AQIM in the late 2000s and early 2010s. Both had chosen punitive approaches to their relations with the local population, which proved fatal to the groups. Missing an enabling environment and ready-made acceptance, both had artificially stretched their connections with the locals in Afghanistan and Mali, as these two groups relied primarily on ruthless and violent control. In

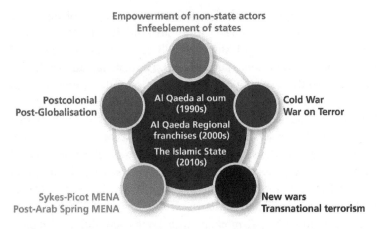

Figure 3.1 The changing contexts of transnational Islamism

contradistinction, Al Qaeda had been born out of a bureau of *assistance* in Afghanistan (Maktab al Khadamat lil Mujahideen). Therefore, IS adopted the posture of a firm, indeed extremely ruthless organisation (conducting routine public executions), but alternated that violence with an image of service delivery and administrative rule-enforcer. However, it must be noted that were it not for the tribal Sunni support in Iraq and the presence of other Sunni groups battling the regime in Syria for their own reasons, IS's strength might not have been sufficient on its own to change the dynamic in the region so radically. This then raises the important question of whether IS – which, as noted, can also be looked at as a neo-Ba'athi state resurrecting the military segments of that defunct political structure – was ultimately not merely a super-Sunni group. In 2007, the Sunni Sahwa (Awakening) tribal movement gained the upper hand on the then-ISI in high-profile engagements in the Diyala and Anbar provinces, and, seven years later, Sunni tribal revolt against al Maliki enabled IS's rise. Yet alliance with the Sunni tribes could not last, and talk of *khilafa* (Caliphate) was not reconcilable with Iraqi *wataniya* (patriotism), which in the past took secular forms and involved many different ethnic and confessional identities across Iraq. Tellingly, the Shi'a aspect per se was not problematic for Al Qaeda, and Bin Laden was always careful not to alienate the Shi'a, explicitly reprimanding al Zarqawi in 2005 for his attacks on them. That, however, was a different context before Saddam Hussein's December 2006 hanging amid Shi'a religious chants, which marked a turning point in the conflict between Sunnis and Shi'a.

It is no small paradox that, benefitting from the most globalised context ever, IS first behaved eminently locally. The reason for that lay in the initial refocus on Iraq, the desire to append neighbouring Syria to that project and the pursuit of contiguous, delineated, physical and territorial statehood. As, however, the group made forays in that regard in mid to late 2014, it saw merit in capitalising on an objective attraction phenomenon in Syria, whereby fighters were coming from other regional groups, from the diasporas in the West and from their ancestral homes. Amid these reinvented possibilities, each of these arrivals had several layers of motivations, and this served to open the purview of IS both in further territorialising it and in introducing a key spin on the Al Qaeda franchising system.

As IS led its coup on Al Qaeda in June 2014, closing the book on al Dhawahiri's indecisive leadership (which it regarded as weak and obsolete) more than on Bin Laden's original movement ('that is the Al Qaeda we love'), it had also shed its identity as a former franchise of that group. To that end, the announcement of the re-establishment of the Caliphate and the pursuit of statehood immediately served to project a new group identity, transcending the earlier one and eschewing factional bickering. Such a power move on the part of al Baghdadi was also meant visibly to discourage any attempt to question this new project. The concerns were not unfounded, as two other Al Qaeda franchises had, earlier, taken pole position in the global radical Islamist movement without taking off in that direction. In the late 2000s, as Al Qaeda al Oum began losing influence and started becoming evanescent, AQAP and AQIM gained visibility in, respectively, the Arabian Gulf and the Sahel, with the former riding high in security dangerousness rankings and considered the more lethal of the Al Qaeda franchises.[24] This meant then that a key element in the evolution of the Al Qaeda-IS rift could be the stance the other power houses in the Al Qaeda constellation would take vis-à-vis the matter, notably AQAP and AQIM. Initially, neither group adopted a clear-cut position regarding the IS power grab. Early, low-level reactions were guarded, with both resentment of IS and attraction towards it coexisting. Then, on 14 July 2014, AQIM leader Abdelmalek Droukdel rejected IS's call and reaffirmed his allegiance to al Dhawahiri and to Al Qaeda. This proved to be unsettling as, on 25 June, the head of AQIM's Central Zone had announced his support to IS. Similarly, the founder of AQIM offshoot Jama'at al Tawhid wal Jihad fi Gharb Ifriqiya (the Movement for Unification and Jihad in West Africa), Hamada Ould Mohamed Kheirou, had expressed, three days before Droukdel, his support of 'the Islamic Caliphate'. For its part, and while being enmeshed in the Yemeni post-Arab Spring political transition, AQAP remained silent officially, but on 3 July its leader, Nasser al Wuhayshi, issued a poem praising al Dhawahiri and implicitly criticising IS' pronouncements, although, as was the case with AQIM, AQAP commander Sheikh Makmun Hatim had previously indicated support to IS. Both AQIM and AQAP would officially remain unclear about their stance vis-à-vis IS: formally staying part of Al Qaeda, *de facto* fully independent and in effect espousing the same ideology as IS, which they also never criticised explicitly nor called on to cease what it was doing.

Over the next two years, IS would see its appeal grow internationally, and dozens of radical Islamist organisations round the world would pledge allegiance to or express formal support for it. As opposed to Bin Laden's project, there was, to be sure, more internal resistance to allegiance among the new groups towards IS (as evidenced by the different statements from operators within the same branch or region), but overall the movement was wider and faster. More importantly, it had acquired another nature: the groups were not so much inventing or reinventing themselves as franchises – that is, materialising as localised mini-versions replicating the nature of the mother entity (Al Qaeda al Oum) – as they were pledging allegiance to a 'state' and a leader they came organically to consider their own. Paradoxically, the elasticity of the Caliphate logic also worked to provide these groups with more independence – while they were pledging allegiance – than was the case with Al Qaeda, since as *wilayas* (regions) they could also claim sovereign control over regional matters, whereas Al Qaeda's original franchise system carried a measure of departmental discipline in relation to headquarter's directives (e.g. al Zarqawi circa 2005 being told by al Dhawahiri that Bin Laden did not approve of his targeting of Iraqi Shi'a). In quick succession, the pledges of allegiance and statements of support materialised after the June 2014 announcement of the Caliphate, providing a clear indication of the successful use of that narrative with the worldwide Islamist armed militancy. Within two years, the group had received the allegiance or formal support of 40 groups from 22 countries (see Table 3.3). On 13 July, Abubakar Shekau, the leader of the Nigerian group Boko Haram, expressed support, and his organisation followed that with a formal pledge of allegiance a few months later in

March 2015. In September 2014, an Algerian group, Junud al Khilafa (the Soldiers of the Caliphate), was created to support the establishment of IS, which in the context of the global Al Qaeda-into-IS story was particularly revealing, as an offshoot of Al Qaeda had effectively given birth to its own offshoot. In Libya and Tunisia, respective branches of Ansar al Sharia (Partisans of the Sharia) followed suit. In Libya, IS supporters faced fiercer competition among the dozens of organised militias, which had come to dominate the country's security landscape in the aftermath of the fall of Muammar Gaddafi's regime. Several engagements took place, notably with the Derna Mujahideen Council in Derna in July 2015, before IS was able to claim a *wilaya* on the Mediterranean coast that it controlled sporadically over the next two years.

Table 3.3   Pledges of allegiance and/or support to IS

Organisation	Date of pledge/support	Region/country
1. Mujahideen Shura Council	6 February 2014 (pledge to ISIS, before IS name change)	Palestine
2. Al Huda Battalion in the Islamic Maghreb	30 June 2014	Algeria
3. Liwa Ahrar al Sunna fi Baalbek (Brigades of the Free Men of the Sunna in Baalbek)	30 June 2014	Lebanon
4. Mujahideen Indonesia Timur	30 June 2014	Indonesia
5. Jaysh al Sahaba (Army of the Companions)	1 July 2014	Syria
6. Ansar al Sharia (Partisans of the Sharia)	4 July 2014	Tunisia
7. Tehrik-e-Khilafat (Caliphate Movement)	9 July 2014	Pakistan
8. Jama'at al Tawhid wal Jihad fi Gharb Ifriqiya (Movement for Unification and Jihad in West Africa)	11 July 2014	Sahel/Mali
9. Sons of the Call for Tawhid and Jihad	20 July 2014	Jordan
10. Itisaam al Qur'an wal Sunna (Spread of the Qur'an and Sunna)	1 August 2014	Sudan
11. Ansar al Khilafa (Partisans of the Caliphate)	13 August 2014	The Philippines

Organisation	Date of pledge/support	Region/country
12. Bangsamoro Islamic Freedom Fighters	14 August 2016	The Philippines
13. Ansar al Tawhid (Partisans of Unification)	4 October	India
14. Ansar al Sharia (Partisans of Sharia)	31 October 2014	Libya
15. Junud al Khilafa (Soldiers of the Caliphate)	14 September 2014	Algeria
16. 'Oqba Ibn Nafaa Battalion	20 September 2014	Tunisia
17. Al Tawhid Brigade in Afghanistan	23 September 2014	Afghanistan
18. Islamic Movement of Uzbekistan	25 September 2014	Uzbekistan
19. Junud al Khilafa fi Ard Kinana (Soldiers of the Caliphate in the Land of Egypt)	29 September 2014	Egypt
20. Heroes of Islam Brigade in the Khorasan	30 September 2014	Afghanistan
21. Tehrik-e-Taliban (Movement of the Taliban)	4 October 2014	Pakistan
22. Shabaab al Islam fil Darna (Youth of Islam in Darna)	6 October 2014	Libya
23. Ansar al Tawhid fi Ard al Hind (Partisans of Unification in the Land of India)	6 October 2014	India
24. Katibat al Imam al Bukhari (Brigade of the Imam al Bukhari)	29 October 2014	Syria
25. Ansar al Sharia	31 October 2014	Libya
26. Ansar Beit al Maqdis (Partisans of the Holy House)	10 November 2014	Egypt
27. Mujahideen al Yemen (Mujahideen of Yemen)	10 November 2014	Yemen
28. JundAllah (Soldiers of God)	17 November 2014	Pakistan
29. Ansar al Dawla al Islamiya fi Bilad al Haramayn (Supporters of the Islamic State in the Land of the Two Holy Sites)	2 December 2014	Saudi Arabia
30. Ansar al Islam (Partisans of Islam)	8 January 2015	Iraq
31. Leaders of the Mujahideen in Khorasan	10 January 2015	Pakistan

Organisation	Date of pledge/support	Region/country
32. Boko Haram	9 March 2015	Nigeria
33. Junud al Khilafa (Soldiers of the Caliphate)	31 March 2015	Tunisia
34. Jemaah Islamiyah (Islamic Group)	27 April 2015	The Philippines
35. Al Murabitun (The Almoravids)	14 May 2015	Sahel/Mali
36. Mujahideen Kairouan (Mujahideen of Kairouan)	18 May 2015	Tunisia
37. Caucacus Emirate	23 June 2015	Russia
38. Hezb-e-Islami (Islamic Party)	6 July 2015	Afghanistan
39. Jabhat East Africa (East African Front)	8 April 2016	Somalia
40. Ansar al Khilafa (Partisans of the Caliphate)	19 July 2016	Brazil

Shamasr, or the geographical combination in Arabic of *Shaam* (Levant) and *Masr* (Egypt), an area historically linked politically and militarily, came next. In Egypt, on 24 October, the speaker of a new group known as Ansar Beit al Maqdis (the Partisans of the Holy House), Kamal Allam, announced that his group was joining IS: 'Give the good news to al Baghdadi … Give the good news to the Caliph of the believers. Victory is coming and we are your soldiers.' A month later, on 10 November, the group's commander, Abu Osama al Masri, confirmed that statement, declaring: 'The Caliphate has been declared in Iraq and al Shaam … We have no choice but to welcome the invitation of God's caller. We therefore pledge religious and political loyalty to Caliph Ibrahim.' As was the case with AQIM and AQAP, there were internal disagreements, and an earlier pledge issued on 3 November had been denied the next day, again indicative of lingering uncertainty. This was also illustrative of the complexity of that particular scene, as the insurgency in the Sinai had been born initially in the aftermath of the 1978 Camp David Accords between Egypt and Israel and the subsequent Israeli withdrawal in 1982, but this particular incarnation of the movement was much more recent and closer to IS's perspective. Ansar Beit al Maqdis were in effect heirs to Al Tawhid wal Jihad fi Sayna (Unity and Jihad in the Sinai), which had emerged in July 2005; and that first generation, founded by Khaled Musa'id, had been visibly influenced by al Zarqawi. (In September 2015, a video by IS's Sinai *wilaya* paid homage to the Jordanian first leader of AQI.) A second group, Al Tawhid wal Jihad-Beit al Maqdis, was formed in 2009. The same themes about Jerusalem (the holy city formally known in Arabic as Al Quds is also referred as *beit al maqdis*) were appearing among Iraqi groups such as Ansar al Sunna, and early connections with them were visible. As was the case with ISI, that group's violence increased symmetrically with ruthless counter-insurgency and counter-terrorism operations led successively by the Hosni Mubarak, Mohamed Morsi and Abdelfattah al Sisi regimes, and the repression turned that violence inward. However, the 2014 allegiance to IS was an unprecedented event, particularly as the earlier Al Qaeda in Egypt franchise failed to take off in 2006. As Omar Ashour notes: 'The November [2014] pledge of allegiance ... to ISIS was perhaps the most critical and unprecedented development in the history of Egyptian jihadism. It was the first time that a local armed jihadist organisation of Ansar Beit al Maqdis' size declared transnational loyalty to a foreign organisation.'[25] Ansar Beit al Maqdis's choice of IS over Al Qaeda was indeed revealing – particularly in light of al Dhawahiri's Egyptian lineage – but it was essentially a choice dictated by the overwhelming power of IS and the appeal of its dangerousness. In effect, Ansar Beit al Maqdis's militarisation in the following months during 2015 spoke of its increasing emulation of IS's tactics, notably the use of improvised explosive devices. The group's military prowess and capture of Egyptian military material, including at least one tank, were also shown in a video entitled *Desert Flames* posted online by the group in August 2016, again using the same communication strategy that had by then been fully implemented by IS (see Chapter 4). This went along with investment in an effort to maintain the religious leadership claims of the group, which also impacted the international radical Islamists' scene – as, for instance, on 22 October 2015, the chief ideologue of Somalia's main radical Islamist group, Al Shabaab, Abdelqader al Mumin, shifted from his Somali group to IS.

The global appeal of the group continued to expand into places previously unreached by Al Qaeda, and by 2017 IS influence had reached Trinidad and Tobago, Indonesia and the Philippines.[26] As such dissemination played out, two dynamics were emerging. On the one hand, the groups appeared primarily to value the military might and power of the brand 'Islamic State', and supported its 'religiously sacred' fight. They therefore privileged presentations of themselves as *junud* (soldiers) and *ansar* (partisans/companions). IS, for its part, regarded these different entities as essentially formal regions of its dominion (as explicitly communicated in the 6 July 2016 video message), and sought to introduce the normative use of a term that had not been previously used by Al Qaeda, namely *wilaya* (region or province, but with an administrative and departmental connotation). Accordingly, in the different video messages that were produced and released officially by the group in the next phase, that terminology was used systematically for individual militants' operations or group insurgencies, notably in Libya, Egypt, Yemen, Afghanistan, Nigeria and Pakistan. In most cases, IS was essentially renaming the existing regional internal divisions of these countries (e.g. the three regions of Libya: Cyrenaica, Fezzan and Tripolitania), but in some cases it was purposely blending countries, with Bahrain for instance integrated into what were mostly Saudi provinces, or Nigeria standing in for all of West Africa (*gharb ifriqiya*). The core IS system was, however, focused on those Iraqi and Syrian *wilayat* (19 out of 35) that were most often referred to or featured in messages (Table 3.4).

Table 3.4   Wilayas (regions) of IS

Country	Wilayas (regions)
Afghanistan	Wilayat Khorasan
Algeria	Wilayat al Jazayr
Egypt	Wilayat Sinai
Iraq	Wilayat Ninawa, Wilayat al Jazira, Wilayat al Furat, Wilayat Jila, Wilayat Kirkuk, Wilayat Salah al Din, Wilayat al Anbar, Wilayat al Faluja, Wilayat Diyala, Wilayat al Shamaal,
Libya	Wilayat Barqa, Wilayat Fezzan, Wilayat Tarablus
Nigeria	Wilayat Gharb Ifriqiya
Russia	Wilayat Qawqaz
Saudi Arabia	Wilayat al Hijaz, Wilayat al Najd
Syria	Wilayat al Raqqa, Wilayat al Barqa, Wilayat al Khayr, Wilayat Homs, Wilayat Halab, Wilayat Hama, Wilayat Dimashq
Yemen	Wilayat Aden-Abyan, Wilayat Ataq, Wilayat Bayda, Wilayat Hadramawt, Wilayat Luaa al Akhdar, Wilayat Sana'a, Wilayat Shabwa

The elasticity of IS's positioning across the region also meant it could always find new territory to claim. Its territorial structure featured four different sectors: centres of immediate importance (Iraq and Syria), areas of control and action (Libya, Egypt and Yemen), places of active influence

(Somalia, Nigeria, Mali, Niger, Afghanistan, the Philippines) and locations with active operators (Turkey, Saudi Arabia, Lebanon, Algeria, Tunisia and Europe, notably France, Belgium and Germany). The group, however, headquartered itself in a 'capital' of twin cities in Iraq and Syria, namely Mosul and Raqqa, from where, until 2017, it directed its project under the leadership of al Baghdadi and his associates. In August 2014, as the Iraqi army was still reeling from its shock eviction from Mosul by IS (32,000 soldiers had fled the area in early June in the face of 1,500 militants), Iraq's military (with US aerial support) initiated engagements with the group around the city. The Battle for Mosul began in earnest, and for the next three years was presented by the Iraqi authorities and their Western counterparts as a key event in the envisioned defeat of IS. In October 2014, it was announced anew that plans to retake the city were under consideration. Later, Iraqi officials declared that the offensive was still under preparation. A year later, in December 2015, following the liberation of Ramadi, it was announced again that Mosul would be next. Eventually, the coalition assault on the city began the following year, on 20 October 2016, and lasted a year. Battling the United States (the first ground clashes between the group and US forces took place in December 2014 in Ein al Asad near Ramadi), Russia, the United Kingdom, France, the US-trained Iraqi military, the Iraqi official militia known as the Popular Mobilisation Forces (set up in mid-June 2014 specifically to battle IS after Mosul's fall), Turkey, experienced Iranian military advisers, battle-hardened Kurdish Peshmerga (in May 2016, following the advance of Iraqi troops, IS led several large-scale operations against the PKK/ YPG (Kurdistan Workers' Party/ People's Protection Units) groups in Manbij), Sunni tribes and the Shi'a Lebanese Hezbollah group, IS held on to the two cities for more than three years. Arguably, however, and as regarded their eventual retaking by the Iraqi and Syrian regimes, for all their tactical importance to the group the two cities were not crucial to IS's strategy. The capture of those regional urban centres by IS was, in the first place, the consequence of historical contingencies and the storm of deteriorating conflicts. In Iraq, as noted, the group's success owed much to Sunni resentment and Ba'athi vengeance, with tribesmen providing the soldiery and former senior officers becoming the cadre of the group. In Syria, Bashar al Assad's cautious focus on the 'useful' territory he had wanted to protect since the start of the Syrian civil war led to his shying away from adventurism further north in rebel-held lands such as Raqqa. With territory coming and going in fragmenting Levantine lands, for the armed group that IS was before it captured Mosul, territory itself was a malleable commodity. If the territorial approach failed and if the leaders were killed, transnationality and online space, which the group capitalised on, as well as the post-modern incarnations of its brand of terrorism, would provide equal opportunities for IS to evolve and to keep attacking. Fully aware of what it was doing, IS publicly recounted the logic of its emergence, writing in issue twelve of its magazine *Dabiq* (see Chapter 4), released in November 2015:

> It was not but a few years [ago] that the Islamic State made a great comeback on the scene of Iraq. At the same time, it had entered into Shaam [Levant] and prepared the foundation of *wilayat* there. The words 'the Islamic State is *baqiya* [remaining]' filled the air and echoed before this and also thereafter in various addresses of the Islamic State leadership. The Islamic State not only remained in Iraq, it had spread to the Arabian Peninsula, Shaam, North and West Africa, Khurasan (Afghanistan), al Qawqaz (Caucasus) and elsewhere.

Regeneration naturally came to the IS repertoire – from Caliphate legacy, from Al Qaeda reboot, from the continuing history of Iraq and from the uprising in Syria seeking a new order. What al Baghdadi simply had to do was to stage the re-incarnation of those interrupted narratives. At the same time, emphasis was placed on maximising the role played by operators located in the West.[27] As IS saw it, the project of a religious state garnered more impetus since opposition to it was simply ideological; on the one hand, the neo-authoritarian Arab state and, on the other, the European neo-colonial and US imperial states, as it regarded them. Problematically for them, all carried contradictions in their fight against IS. The Arab states often produced terrorism in the name of fighting it, and the Western countries often closed democratic space in the name of opposing the threat represented by the group. Was it ever clear to al Baghdadi – who was always less strategic and visionary than Bin Laden, and closer to the ruthless ways of al Zarqawi – how his organisation could simultaneously pursue its domestic plan of conquering, controlling and administrating large swathes of territory over Iraq and Syria, expanding regionally per its Caliphate logic and folding new provinces from the groups pledging allegiance to it, all while acting globally in attacking the West with its large contingent of foreign fighters? Ultimately, weren't the different identities and multiple layers of IS contradictory, in particular its combination of the local and the distant (whereas Bin Laden had simply privileged the latter)? It is in this sense that the eventual disappearance of IS as a group and its leaders will not necessarily be consequential. The logical next step for such a movement could, for instance, be relocation or rebirth in the name of a sacralised Mosul/Raqqa golden age. Alternatively, the lost Eden might be reconceptualised virtually or displaced transnationally (see the Conclusion).

The campaign launched by IS in 2014 generated deep fear among Western citizenry. Between June 2014 and June 2016, the group had conducted or inspired 75 attacks in 20 countries besides Iraq and Syria, killing a total of 1,280 people, with attacks continuing steadily throughout 2017. This staccato violence reached its apex in the summer of 2016 (see Chapter 4). Besides the different Western governments battling the group, sub-state entities in Europe and in the United States also reacted by threatening IS. The group Anonymous 'declared war' on IS on 16 November 2015 shortly after the attacks in Paris, and claimed subsequently to have closed 5,000 Twitter accounts. On 28 July 2016, a faction (known as '22 October') within the Corsican nationalist group, the Corsican National Liberation Front, said it would retaliate against any ISIS attack on the French island. In effect, Western state and non-state entities came to regard the group as an existential opponent – actions and reactions which closed the circle on what Bin Laden had wanted to do, namely wrestle the martial function from the regional Arab and Muslim state and locate it in the actions of non-state actors putting pressure on the West. IS appeared thus to follow an accelerated version of Al Qaeda. Too black, too strong, it experienced the same sequence as its begetter, with spectacular victories followed by a large-scale allocation of resources by its state opponents to target and kill its leaders. The new group invested in reorganising its 'army', with regional commanders reporting to a key senior structure and a military-style organisation comprising different types of uniformed special units with black fatigues and balaclava hoods. Holding ground meant proactively planning new operations, and this IS did by launching simultaneous campaigns on two fronts against the Yazidi areas of Sinjar in Iraq and the Kurdish-dominated city Kobani (Ayn al Arab) in Syria. Again, the two sectors were not of strategic importance to IS, and were recaptured in 2015 by the respective Kurdish and Turkish forces, but at that key moment they served an important tactical purpose in 'spreading the enemy' and buying time for the group as it settled in Mosul and Raqqa. Similarly, the group captured, in May 2015, the cities of Ramadi (Iraq) and Palmyra (Syria), which it lost the following year. On 26 and 29 September 2015, Russia and France respectively stepped up their involvement in the fight against IS, launching a series of aerial bombings on the areas held by the group, which responded by downing a Russian plane on 4 October, and conducted attacks in Paris on 13 November killing a total of 354 Russian and French citizens. With the other regional and international powers remaining active as well, the group would experience first a slowdown and then a gradual loss of the areas it controlled at the height of its advance in mid to late 2014. At that time, it had controlled over 60,000 km^2. By the summer of 2017, it had lost 23,000 km^2 but continued to hold most of Mosul and Raqqa, as well as the Euphrates River sector between the two countries and other pockets, carrying out regular local attacks.

Ultimately, as regards their common religious identity, Al Qaeda and IS were close enough as Sunni neo-Salafist radical Islamist groups. Ideologically, Al Qaeda was a transnational entity focused on displacement of its war on to 'the far enemy' (the US principally) and dealing secondarily with the 'near enemy' (local Arab authoritarian regimes). IS, for its part, worked in the opposite direction. It started off as a local Iraqi story, built up momentum with the Syrian issue and then moved to the global chessboard, inviting not so much franchises as Al Qaeda did but rather provinces. Politically, Al Qaeda was a post-Cold War and post-globalisation development representing the entry of radical political Islam on to the global scene. IS was a post-modern story, only partly related to radical Islamism and indeed to the Middle East and North Africa. There was always a larger dimension at play in the case of IS, which connected with the violence projected from the Western metropolis and with a series of military interventions. An understanding of the state-building project of IS goes a long way to explaining the emphasis on administration, taxation, legitimation and the conduct of 'foreign affairs', but it must be complemented by an examination of an additional, equally innovative element of communication. Following on from Bin Laden, IS had understood the importance of spectacle. Immediately after its takeover of Mosul – and therefore coincidentally with the announcement of its Caliphate-building project – in the summer of 2014 it unleashed a media *blitzkrieg* which would take the world by storm, raising Al Qaeda's professionalised communication to another level and, in so doing, introducing the third layer of IS's identity, one located in modernity and in the West.

4

Modernity and the Globalised Insurgent

The price of freedom is death.
Malcolm X (1964)

On the strength, the situation's unreal.
I got a raw deal, so I'm going for the steel …
As for the rest of the world, they can't realise.
A cell is hell. I'm a rebel, so I rebel.
Public Enemy, 'Black Steel in the Hour of Chaos' (1988)

In a 29-minute video entitled *A Year upon the Conquest*, posted online on 12 June 2015, IS celebrated the one-year anniversary of its takeover of the Iraqi city of Mosul. Starting with footage of SUV columns lining up at dawn on 4 June 2014 to launch the attack, and depicting the different phases over the next seven days – during which a group of approximately 1,500 irregulars overran the 32,000-strong Iraqi army force stationed in and around Mosul, forcing its disorderly retreat – the step-by-step video was the culmination of the second phase of IS's history, namely as a modern phenomenon with global communication playing a central role in that effort. Recognising the impact of this unique campaign, the international public relations firm Global Leadership later noted in its ranking for 2015 that the international brand recognition of IS or ISIS had come to surpass that of the Vatican.

The proverbial 'day after Mosul' for IS came under the theme of state-building and management of victory, but also under the theme of dissemination of an increasingly globalised narrative. In line with their three-tiered local, regional and international strategy of holding ground, developing resilience and expanding front, the group, now boasting 50,000 men (according to Al Jazeera on 19 August 2014), invested massively in a large-scale multimedia advertisement campaign. The organisation had already been deft at using social media, but in the summer of

2014 it launched a conspicuously more ambitious plan to let the world know about its presence and agenda. This was in effect the moment at which 'ISIS', as a news phenomenon, fully came to the attention of the mainstream public in the West and, indeed, when policymakers started paying attention to the group with more urgency.

IS's storming of the world stage in this fashion, and specifically the expert use of communication technology tools, enabled it to add a new layer to its identity above and beyond its Al Qaeda core: the Iraqi and Syrian insurgencies it rode and the regional groups it had begun influencing in North and West Africa and in the Gulf. The group would now come to tap into the very heart of European and North American cities and a tempest of political, cultural and socio-economic discontent and malaise in the West. As the tech-minded, self-empowered message beamed by the group from the territory it held in Iraq and Syria gained momentum in this way, putting pressure on policymaking at the highest international level to stop such a disrupting campaign (indeed an embarrassing one, years after the 'liberation' of Iraq boasted by President Bush in May 2004), IS unexpectedly started appealing to many a radical rebel-in-the-making across Europe and the United States – extremists of all hues, young and old, second- or third-generation Muslim immigrants and local religious or ideological converts. The extreme violence used by the group did not deter these individuals. To the contrary, many of them saw in it – as they made explicit in their recorded messages – a way to visit violence on their own societies. In so doing, these actors prioritised that specific adrenaline-heightened, violent release dimension over the state-building project of IS and the socio-political conflicts the group was immersed in in the Levant. As it entered this phase of its history, IS therefore continued to function as a political entity bent on power acquisition and informed by the different aspects of the ongoing Iraqi and Syrian conflicts, but also as one displaying an added dimension of privatised and individualised martiality driven from the West itself.

IS's rapid redirection towards a previously untapped dimension of its initial project was enabled primarily through *a Hollywoodised staging of violence* that was designed to appeal to a different militancy than merely its local and regional one. The impact of this effort was global, quickly leading to a so-called phenomenon of foreign fighters, which was large in scale but manifested particularly in Europe and best encapsulated in the *alienated youth networks in post-colonial Europe*. Those actors were driven primarily by a domestic experience of loss and disenchantment, which they connected with the Western military interventionism that had been playing out in a number of Muslim countries, in the Middle East, North Africa and the Sahel. In the event, this sequence of forward-looking dynamics furthering IS's game plan during the mid to late 2010s ended up unexpectedly but revealingly echoing *the 1970s societal malaise* that had dominated the social and political scene across the United States and Europe 40 years ago, indirectly reactivating many rebellions that were not related to radical Islamism per se, but which fed off this atmosphere of violence. In a further historical twist, this evolution and the reaction to it also laid the ground for the rise of a type of authoritarianism in these societies reminiscent of the 1930s climate.

Remixing Violence

In the years after the events of 9/11, Al Qaeda had overseen the asymptotic decentralisation of its operations and the capacitation of a number of new franchises around the world. From roughly 2007 onwards, the combined effect of these strategies started birthing a post-modern type of terrorism – in effect one that was already post-Al Qaeda. This new mode featured a number of traits, chief among which was a widened and facilitated private resort to terrorism, self-radicalisation on a heroic-punitive mode, a symbiosis of physical and symbolic violence moving from the battlefield to the virtual battlespace and organisational professionalisation anchored in an active and innovative use of information technology. The successfully Uberised bottling of the new terrorism by Al Qaeda was, however, only the start of its story in the late 2000s and early 2010s. The rapid succession of individual high-profile and mediatised attacks inspired by Al Qaeda – as illustrated by cases involving David Coleman Headley in Chicago in 2008, Nidal Malik Hassan in Fort Hood in November 2009, Omar Faruk Abdulmuttalab in Amsterdam in December 2009, Colleen LaRose in Pennsylvania in March 2010, Anders Breivik in Oslo in July 2011, Mohamed Merah in France in March 2012 and Dzhokhar and Tamerlan Tsarnaev in Boston in April 2013 – paved the way for a second generation exemplified by Chérif and Said Kouachi in Paris in January 2014, and many more that followed in subsequent years. The rise of those latter-day, variously-Al Qaeda-influenced terrorists was now accompanied, indeed facilitated, by a spider-net communication campaign designed by IS that would impact directly upon and mould a new brand of globalised insurgents.

In the summer of 2014, IS embarked on a media *blitzkrieg*. The project constituted a fully fledged component of its battle plan and functioned in a way that revolutionised communication by violent, armed non-state actors. Earlier generations of terrorist groups addressed communication matters after their operations. A message would be sent or a telephone call placed *ex post facto* to a news agency to claim an operation or formulate demands. Al Qaeda changed this approach by working upstream and pre-recording video 'wills' of its operators conducting the suicide attacks, which it then released to media outlets (Al Jazeera mainly) or uploaded online. IS took that logic to the next level by conceiving of communication as an integral, *in situ* component of its war, not merely to make demands or to inform but to strike the minds and expand.[1] The architecture put in place to that effect was large, complex and multifaceted. The group combined official releases with messages put out independently by its operators. This allowed it to ensure wall-to-wall, expanded coverage of its actions and, in so doing, generate an impression of omnipresence. Operations by the group were systematically recorded on video and published online, either near-simultaneously with their performance (in one instance – the killing of a married couple of police officers in their home by an IS sympathiser in France in June 2016 – the video was posted on Facebook by the killer while he was still on the premises) or shortly thereafter. Replacing an earlier media branch set up by ISI in November 2006, Al Furqan Foundation for Media Production (which continued to release IS messages), a new official media branch named Al Hayat Media Centre was launched in August 2014. Videos were released in Arabic, English, Spanish, French, Turkish, German, Italian, Dutch, Bahasa, Swedish, Polish, Chinese, Japanese, Farsi, Russian, Portuguese, Azeri, Somali and Hebrew.[2] With multiple media platforms used extensively, releases were of high quality and produced to professional standards. Closing the book on the early shaky cell phone footage uploaded hastily on rogue temporary YouTube accounts (predominantly from its Syrian operators during the first year of the civil war), these were now regular, high-definition videos shot professionally and staged with specific themes and narrative arcs: previews followed by main stories with cliff-hanger endings. The videos ranged from lengthy serialised features such as *Clanking of the Swords IV* (*Salil al Sawarim IV*, using Roman numerals)[3] – which opened with an aerial shot of Mosul – to 50-second 'coming soon' trailers such as *The Flames of War*, posted in September 2014, the day after a speech by US President Obama threatening the group with reprisals; with the subtitle *Fighting Has Just Begun* accompanied by imagery of the White House in flames. The powerful and colourful visuals (exaggerated hues of vivid red for gory blood and cut angles with shadows of fighters riding against orange sunsets) of the videos were directly, and at times explicitly, inspired by Hollywood productions; in particular Oliver Stone's frenetic editing style as seen in *JFK* (1991) and *Natural Born Killers* (1994), David Fincher's execution scenes in *Se7en* (1995) and Kathryn Bigelow's Copper Green military overtones in *The Hurt Locker* (2009). With super-slow motion, reverse motion, Go-Pro fight scenes, drone IMAX-like wide shots and mid-speech angle cuts (indicative of several cameras used during the filming and subsequent editing), these state-of-the-art videos, often emulating real-life special forces operations and depicting them with *Mission Impossible*-inspired visuals, represented the first time in history that a terrorist group was communicating in such a technically polished fashion, articulating its ornate propaganda (with 'top ten videos' listings) beyond that of states. During World War II, *Triumph of the Will* and *Why We Fight* had been state-sponsored films, *Clanking of the Swords IV* was the work of a non-state actor. Filmed with drones, suicide attacks were integrated into these videos and were often preceded by interview with the attackers, minutes before their assault generating a you-are-there, or rather you-should-be-there, feel for their mesmerised audience of radical extremist militants. A video released in February 2015 (*A Message Signed with Blood to the Nation of the Cross*) featured CGI special effects and apparent use of green screen to make IS executioners on a beach off the shores of Libya appear taller than their victims being marched dramatically in a single line to their death. The serialised logic was also featured in a number of verisimilitude health services videos (NHS-style, one featuring Australian doctor Abu Yusuf at the Raqqa General Hospital), history lessons (*Breaking of the Borders, The End of Sykes–Picot* presented by a Chilean national introduced as Abu Safiya), statistics on military operations and news reports (*From Inside Mosul, Lend Me Your Ears*) hosted by hostage John Cantlie in Kobani on 26 October 2014 and in Mosul on 3 January 2015. The group reached out to the American cable television programme HBO Vice News and, in July 2014, took them on a tour of positions held in Syria. A number of themes were repeated in these videos: punishment of the Safavids (the term used by the group to refer to Iraqi and Iranian Shi'a, associating them with the Safavid dynasty which ruled Persia from 1501 to 1736), resistance to the Crusaders (the term used for Western countries) and punishment of the apostate or *murtad* (the term used for the Arab and Muslim authoritarian regimes), as well as rejection of the modern boundaries of the region.

In print, the group introduced a series of glossy publications with an equally professional use of software (InDesign, Adobe and Photoshop) at times indicative of the likely involvement of trained graphic designers. An official magazine entitled *Dabiq* (the name of a city in northern Syria where in IS eschatology an end-of-days battle is expected to pit Muslims against Christians) was launched in July 2014 (with 15 issues as of July 2017). The same slick film imagery used in the videos was reproduced in the magazine (an advertisement for IS's upcoming currency in issue twelve used a visual from the 2001 film *The Lord of the Rings*), as were the recurrent gory details of beheadings. The magazine led every issue with a main theme, combining current questions and historical commentary: 'The return of the khilafa', 'The flood' (the cover of that issue was inspired by the 2014 Hollywood film *Noah*), 'A call to Hijra', 'The failed crusade', 'Remaining and expanding', 'Al Qaeda of Waziristan', 'From hypocrisy to apostasy', 'Sharia alone will rule Africa', 'They plot', 'The law of Allah', 'From the battle of al Ahzab [between the Meccans and the early Muslims] to the war of coalitions', 'Just terror', 'The *rafida*' [Shi'a], 'The *murtad* brotherhood' and 'Breaking the cross'. Other magazines followed in December 2014 with a French-language release, *Dar al Islam* (*House of Islam*), and, in June 2015, others in Turkish, *Konstantiniyye* (*Constantinople*), and Russian, *Istok* (*The Source*). In September 2016, a fifth magazine entitled *Rumiyyah* (*Rome*) was released in six languages; English, French, German, Russian, Indonesian and Uyghur, appearing to replace *Dabiq*, and, in March 2017, yet another one entitled *Al Haqiqa* (*The Truth*) was launched. Radio news bulletins were started in April 2015 in Arabic and Russian by an IS online radio channel entitled Al Bayan (the announcement) but subsequently discontinued. The group also released a mobile telephone app entitled The Dawn and produced a manual for evading geolocation.

With a strong impact on the seen-it-all globalised youth, such intricate, gear-shifting modern propaganda was allowing multiple narratives, and was depicting action, combat and killing rather than speeches – an important qualitative departure from Bin Laden's lengthy videotaped messages aired semestrially on news channels or summarised in newspapers. Indeed, al Zarqawi's bravado, rather than Bin Laden's gravitas, was more often featured in these IS videos, with footage of al Zarqawi in April 2006 showing him firing AK-47 rounds in the Anbar desert of Iraq as a recurring image. These innovations also superseded the first generation of hour-long documentary videos that had been released by Al Qaeda in the second half of the 2000s. As noted, the use of communication was also conspicuously proactive, and not an *ex post facto* afterthought, and in that sense communication was inherently part of the IS battle plan. Over time a pattern emerged involving what we can distinguish as three different types of videos released by the group. A first batch was concerned with religious commentary (e.g. *To Establish the Religion, Racing to the Villages to Spread Guidance, And You Will Remember What I Now Say to You, Of Their Goods Take Alms, Into Light, The Fortress of Perseverance, The Rejecters of Injustice, Answer the Call*), a second set depicted attacks and military-style operations (e.g. *The Generation of Epic Battles, Clanking of the Swords IV, Crushing the Enemy, Bangers of the Swords, Reaping Heads, The Warriors, The Harvest of the Soldiers, The Assault of the Righteous II, Raid of the Predators II, Kill Them Wherever You Find Them, No Escape, Strategy of War*) and a third cluster provided political messages and analysis (e.g. *From Humiliation to Dignity, They Are the Enemy, An Eye for an Eye, No Respite, Their Alliance and Our Terrorism, That They Might Stop, The Reality of the American Raid, The Battle to Achieve Good, A Birthed Nation*). To this could be added a dedicated line focused on education and social services (e.g. *The Path of the Righteous Fathers, Those Who Believed and Migrated, He Will Surely Establish their Religion for Them, Safety and Security in the Islamic State, The Office of Protection and Safety, Food Security*). Longer, documentary-style videos (such as *Hunters of the Shields*, released in December 2016) blended these different approaches. As regards communication from the leadership, it was handled primarily by al 'Adnani until his death in August 2016 (he was replaced formally by al Muhajir as spokesman in December 2016, but with much less visibility the following year). Learning the lessons from the fate of Bin Laden, who had been located by the US in 2011 through couriers tracing his communication, but also modulating the group leader's presence, only one video message was issued by al Baghdadi, on 4 July 2014, followed by three audio messages in August 2014 and March and December 2015, until the Russian announcement of his reported death (unconfirmed at the time of writing) on 28 May 2017.

As Twitter and Facebook accounts held by IS militants and sympathisers (45,000 accounts by mid-November 2014, generating an estimated 200,000 daily tweets during that period) were being shut down in 2015–16 (the first filtering measures were taken officially by Twitter in September

2014), the group launched a news agency known as Al 'Amaq al Ikhbariya. The agency was initially set up in October 2014, independently from IS, by a Syrian journalist named Re'yan Mash'aal who had previously managed an online news website in the city of Aleppo. As that site grew in technological sophistication (launching an Android application and delivering its bulletin in a dozen languages) and in ideological sympathy to IS, the outlet triggered the interest of the group's communication team, which in effect sought to integrate it eventually into its business plan. Dispatches by Al Amaq 'objectively' announcing operations and attacks started delivering the news on an encrypted mobile application, and in so doing widened the impact of what the organisation was trying to do beyond boastful messages. Though IS had lost the ability to have several simultaneous sources beam information, notably the Arabic-language use of the Twitter service by militants on the frontlines, the idea was that a centralised and more detached source would enable it to elevate its authority and only communicate consequential developments. Often, operations were also announced by official news agencies or news channels (notably the Arabic-language news channels Al Jazeera and Al Mayadeen) before IS itself would inform of such developments; Agence France-Presse, for instance, first reported the retaking of Palmyra by IS on 11 December 2016. For IS, Al 'Amaq's use of 'neutral' terminology was meant to provide credibility to the information relayed.

IS's mode of war was the centrepiece of the news relayed and of the videos posted; a combination of urban terrorism, guerrilla warfare, special forces commando-like strikes, exploding drones, war of attrition, siege of cities, informant-hunting, door-to-door combat and vehicle-borne improvised explosive device operations, performed by a soldiery made up of a mixture of battle-hardened Syrian and Iraqi defectors, local insurgents, inexperienced youth and sympathisers coming from around the world. (In October 2014, an IS video showed fighters training to fly warplanes seized from the Jarah military airport in Syria.) The commando-style approach to battle, which Al Qaeda had adopted with AQI, was rebooted by IS, and this was facilitated by the involvement of Saddam Hussein's former officers. In so doing, IS merged those innovations with earlier tactics of revolutionary warfare as developed historically by Mao Zedong. Specifically, a review of the evolution of IS makes it clear that its leaders had honed those techniques and the synchronisation of Mao's well-known critical elements of revolutionary warfare.[4] Such unrestricted asymmetrical combat also combined with references to classical Arabo-

Islamic tribal warrior warfare (images of Saladin's troops advancing towards Jerusalem in 1187 from the 2005 Ridley Scott film *Kingdom of Heaven* on the Crusades were used in several IS videos and in its French-language magazine *Dar al Islam*, as was footage from Mel Gibson's 2004 film *The Passion*). Digital networks and high-tech graphs staging that asymmetrical martial mode were on full display in these videos which, consequently, acquired a videogame feel (influenced specifically by the games *Counter Strike, Call of Duty, Splinter Cell* and *Metal Gear Solid*), and in turn these repatterns inspired the real-life militarisation of attacks, as witnessed in Paris and Brussels in 2015–16. In September 2014, the group released a trailer for its own video game based on the game *Grand Theft Auto*, with customised IS computer graphics and redesigned IS fighter profiles, and did the same the following December with the game *Hearts of Iron IV*.

The hobgoblinisation of this violence registered with a segment of the disenfranchised Western youth, as it illuminated their readings of political and historical conflicts in the Levant they knew little about and a world religion they were largely ignorant of, even when nominally of the Muslim faith, with a contemporary sociological lens that was determined primarily by the format of the message and the brutal manner in which such communication connected with their daily, Western, suburban lives. Whereas the tone of Bin Laden's and al Dhawahiri's messages in the 2000s had been slow, sombre and solemn, the fast-paced IS messages were now accompanied by a distinctive audio track that featured crisp sound effects of loud machine-gunning and blade-sharpening, but also *nasheeds* or anthems sung by a male chorus. Recorded and released in various languages, these original hymns were idiosyncratic a cappella war chants that merged religious litany with warrior cheer. The hybrid mélange of the martial rhetoric (e.g. 'clashing of the swords: a *nasheed* for the defiant, the path of fighting is the path of life, so amidst an assault tyranny is destroyed') with religious aesthetics and a totalising style of history framed as meta-narrative (images cutting back and forth from ancient history to current affairs) was subsequently reappropriated by IS's international followers. Strikingly, a new type of soundtrack developed in a second wave of IS videos: part religious, part tribal and part rap. These anthems became a dedicated line of release by IS. Language-specific versions started appearing in 2015 and traded online on *nasheed*-specialised sites (such as DankestNasheeds.com). On 5 July 2016, in the aftermath of the Brussels March 2016 and Paris November 2015 attacks,

a chant entitled 'Ma Vengeance' ('My Revenge') was released in French
by IS's Hayat Media Centre. The video for the chant, which played like a
rap music video, starts with an excerpt of French Prime Minister Manuel
Valls stating that France was at war with IS, followed by a chant in French
verse: 'Valls wants to threaten us and see our corps amassed, remember
the past O my brother, for they transgress against us, when their planes
take off and bomb our schools and when they take control of our lands
and plunder our oil, after all these years of fierce battles, the *khilafa* thrives
once again and the time has come for revenge.' The scene goes on: 'This
is for François Hollande. My Kalash [Kalashnikov firearm] is loaded, the
civilians isolated, I eliminate the French, so thank Valls, an explosive belt
is ready, I detonate it in the middle of a crowd, I blow up French people.'
And ends thus: 'You can all do it. My brother [Amedy] Coulibaly has
made them pay a heavy price. Carnage hypercasher.' (A similar chant
'Avance, Avance' – 'Advance, Advance' – had been released on 31 October
2015 two weeks before the attacks in Paris; and on the eve of those attacks
a chant in Russian entitled 'Soon, Very Soon' had been put out.) But for
the sex, the contemporary urban world of gangster rap and its modern
industrial cityscape was being visibly imported and exported in a form
and tonality which sought to reconfigure its aesthetics as militarised
political violence. Reworking a socio-economic delivery historically
pioneered long ago in American urban settings (from the Last Poets in the
1970s to Public Enemy in the 1980s), the violence-advocating soundscape
of these messages was now borrowing from a different imaginary than its
initial Middle Eastern one, redesigning the original religious and political
landscape of IS, martialising it and formatting it to the experience of
the young Western rebel-in-waiting familiar with the by-now globalised
musical form of rap. In sonically redefining the parameters of what was
once a local and regional message about political, social and economic
grievances, IS had in effect become an entity whose logic had arrived
in an altogether different cultural territory; one in which al Baghdadi
or the former Ba'athi officers fighting the Shi'a militias alongside him
had less control than the radicalised youth of French, British, German
or American suburbs and inner cities. The rat-a-tat-tat of the delivery
and the rigmarole of you-are-there accounts were now a distinct and
powerful trademark that made IS appeal to a new circle of militants who,
first and foremost, sought the turn-on and exhilaration of that particular
experience. The impact was rapid, global and enormous. For instance,
83 per cent of the individuals indicted by the United States Department

of Justice for IS-related offences between 2014 and 2016 had watched IS videos.[5] Indeed, as regards the attacks that took place in Europe and the United States, IS had explicitly called for operations of this kind. In a September 2014 message, al Muhajir, who would become the group's official spokesman in December 2016, had addressed sympathisers in the West thus: '[R]edouble your efforts and step up your operations ... Smash [the *kaffir*'s] head with a rock, or slaughter him with a knife or run him over with your car ... Attack them inside their houses, markets, roads and clubs and burn the land under their feet ... Destroy their vehicles, raid them ... in their shelters so they can taste some of your misery and do not talk yourselves into fleeing.' In the months following his call to terrorism, attacks perpetrated by individual operators, all claiming one way or the other a link to IS, had taken place in precisely these types of places in Europe and in the United States (see Table 4.1, later in this chapter).

One of the techniques that IS used to cement this approach further was to individualise the narratives. Whereas Al Qaeda's productions featured testimonials and 'wills' videos, IS's new films presented more personalised 'life stories'. These were shared either directly by the individuals in extended narrations or in homages paid to 'fallen soldiers'. In either mode, the attention paid to the lives and stories of their foot soldiers were indicative of a strategic investment at the level of the fighters, not merely the leadership. For instance, in the March 2017 issue of the IS magazine *Al Haqiqa*, an article opened thus: 'Abu Jandal was a *muhajir* [migrant fighter], who made *hijra* [journey] from The Netherlands. This is the remarkable story of his Life, his *da'wa* [proselytising], his *jihad* and his martyrdom in Shaam. It is told by his younger brother Abu Aicha.' The same approach was featured in several videos of French fighters recounting their life stories; Nicolas Bons, Jean Daniel and Kevin Chassin, for instance. The theatrics of the elevation of these individuals to glory status and the visuals used in video and in print endowed them, in the eyes of IS's audience, with a Marvel Comics-like narrative of the 'average kid' character turned superhero or supervillain overnight.

Half a decade after 9/11, a new generation in the West had become influenced by the fire Bin Laden had started in New York and had become radicalised within the West. Among the early figures giving shape to that first pattern was Samir Khan, a young Pakistani born in Saudi Arabia and living in the United States. By the time Khan left North Carolina, in October 2009, travelling to Sana'a, Yemen to join AQAP, he had travelled the road that many foreign fighters would tread five years later. As an

18-year-old, in 2003 he had set up a blog entitled *InshaAllahshaheed* (martyr, if God wills), which by 2007 had developed a large following. Khan represented the face of an emergent and diversifying radical Islamist digital media activism, which had started with grainy video uploads of al Zarqawi severing heads in Iraq.[6] Khan put out the first magazine that influenced Al Qaeda's own magazine, *Inspire*, which started in June 2010 (and released 15 editions until September 2015). *Jihad Recollections*, which was put out by Khan in a series of online PDFs in 2009 (the last issue came out in September that year), was the precursor to both Al Qaeda's *Inspire* and IS's *Dabiq*. Khan was in effect the link between cyber and field, as he himself noted, writing in an article entitled 'I am Proud of being a Traitor to America' – penned for the first edition of *Inspire* a year before he was killed in Yemen by a US drone attack on 30 September 2011 – that: 'I knew I could no longer remain in the United States as a compliant citizen. My beliefs had turned me into *a rebel of Washington's imperialism*' (emphasis added). Khan's odyssey – and Anwar al Awlaki's for that matter – came, however, more as a bookend to Al Qaeda's from-the-East-to-the-West-and-back trajectory than as a full building block of IS beaming its message to the West and tapping into a ready-made nest of alienated radical youth. As illustrated by hip hop bands such as Los Angeles-based Soldiers of Allah, which were expressing in music their political discontent and nostalgia for Islam's golden age well before 9/11 ('Salah al Din [Saladin] we are here ... How did they do this to you and me? We turn on the TV and all we see is a world full of casualties, a generation in agony, our *umma* is in misery, let us go back to beginning of the century and review our history', the group raps in a song entitled '1924' in reference to the date of the end of the Caliphate after the collapse of the Ottoman Empire), the issues which IS would awake violently had been buried in the post-colonial years and rediscovered gradually by a new generation, not of artists but extremists, many of them in the West. As the 2000s moulded that experience further with this youth living through the Al Qaeda and Iraq years, the experience became much more violent and the rupture with society more visible. By 2016, in Germany, the Kabul-born rapper SadiQ (who had posted pictures of dead children in Syria on his Facebook page) was releasing a video entitled 'Charlie Hebdo' in which he rapped: 'I shoot with the Arabs, the Parisians flee ... I burn the pages of Charlie Hebdo.' Denis Cusper, another German rapper known as Deso Dogg, had earlier joined IS and helped shape the content of its media releases (Cusper was reportedly killed in October

2015, with a first announcement of his death made by US authorities in April 2014),[7] as had Ahmed Abousamra (a Syrian born in France and raised in the US) and one 'Chechclearr' from The Netherlands.[8] Another example is that of a young Italian rapper, Anas el-Abboubi, who organised a demonstration against the anti-Muslim film *The Innocence of Muslims* (2013), set up a blog to express his radical political views and ultimately travelled to Syria to join IS – from where he posted a video about 'killing the Infidels' in October 2013.

The impact of IS's mid-2014 media offensive – to which the US State Department tried unsuccessfully to respond using Hollywood screenwriters[9] – was enormous and swift. Within months, approximately 30,000 foreign fighters had travelled to Mosul and Raqqa from some 80 countries. In the face of the phenomenon's unprecedented security implications, the UNSC adopted a resolution in September 2014 (2178) – the first text of its kind to register the transnational effect of these operators at the UN level ('foreign terrorist fighters increase the intensity, duration and intractability of conflicts, and also may pose a serious threat to their states of origin, the states they transit and the states to which they travel', the resolution noted). Although most of these foreign fighters were from the Middle East, North Africa or Central Asia (between 2012 and 2015, 4,000 individuals came to Iraq and Syria from Kazakhstan, Uzbekistan, Kyrgyzstan, Tajikistan and Turkmenistan), many were from Western countries. Within a year of the fall of Mosul to IS, by 30 June 2015, 677 Germans had departed Germany for Syria or Iraq, with an increasing number of women involved.

At the tail end of the 2010s, Somalis in Minneapolis, Moroccans in Brussels, Algerians in Paris, Pakistanis in London or Turks in Berlin, and many more, almost all citizens of the Western countries they lived in, had been involved in radical Islamist circles. Young British and French dyed-in-the-wool men and women – earning culturally hybrid media monikers such as 'Jihadi John' (whose real name was Mohammed Emwazi, a Briton of Kuwaiti origin who executed several hostages – seven Westerners and Asians and 21 Syrian soldiers – on video before being killed on 12 November 2015 in Raqqa by a US drone strike)[10] or 'the Beatles' (three British Islamists in addition to Emwazi, who tortured hostages in Raqqa) – were now drawn to IS, its state-building project and its mode of extreme violence. The profile of these individuals varied, with university graduates – Emwazi attended Westminster University where he earned a degree in computer science; Najim Laachraoui, one of the suicide bombers of the Brussels March 2016 attack, went to Catholic school and studied electrical engineering – and working-class profiles mixed. A June 2016 report by the World Bank reported that 69 per cent of IS foreign recruits in Syria had at least a secondary level education. Prior signs of the specific IS-inspired wave of terrorism in the West were noticeable when on 22 May 2013, as the latest strife in Iraq and Syria was picking up momentum in the media, Michael Adebolajo and Michael Adebowale (two British citizens of Nigerian descent) attacked and killed a British army officer in a London street, running him down with a car and hacking him to death in an attempt to decapitate him. In a video filmed by a bystander, to whom the perpetrators also handed a handwritten note explaining their act, Adebolajo declared:

> The only reason we have killed this man today is because Muslims are dying daily by British soldiers. And this British soldier is one ... [W]e swear by the almighty Allah we will never stop fighting you until you leave us alone ... [W]hen you drop a bomb do you think it hits one person? Or rather your bomb wipes out a whole family? ... An eye for an eye, a tooth for a tooth ... Do you think politicians are going to die? No, it's going to be the average guy, like you and your children. So get rid of them. Tell them to bring our troops back ... leave our lands and you will live in peace.[11]

This was the opening salvo of a wave of 60 attacks inspired or led by IS throughout the West over the next three years (see Table 4.1).

Two years into the IS Western offensive, the violence had spiralled and a significant mimetic effect had taken hold like a forest fire, producing a helter-skelter summer of terror in 2016 with a spike of attacks. On 12 June, a security guard killed 49 people at the Pulse gay nightclub in Orlando, Florida before calling the police emergency line 911 and declaring himself 'a soldier of ISIS'. The next day, in France, a snack-food entrepreneur killed a policeman and a policewoman in their home and pledged allegiance to IS on a video posted on Facebook. On 14 July, in Nice, France, a truck driver drove a truck into a crowd killing 86 people. Five days later, a young Afghan refugee armed with an axe injured four people in a train in Würzburg, Germany. On 22 July, an 18-year-old German shot and killed nine people in a shopping mall in Munich (five years to the day after the Anders Breivik attack in Norway). On 6 August, in Brussels, a 33-year-old Algerian man attacked a guard post outside a police station

Table 4.1 Attacks led or inspired by IS, 2014–17

Perpetrator(s)	Location	Modus operandi	Victim(s)	IS link	Date
1. Michael Adebolajo, Michael Adebowale	London, England	Axe attack and decapitation attempt	One British army officer killed	Predating IS (ISIS period); situation in 'Muslim lands' referenced by attackers	22 May 2013
2. Mehdi Nemmouche	Brussels, Belgium	Shooting at a Jewish Museum	Three people killed	Pledge of allegiance to ISIS	24 May 2014
3. Abdul Numan Haider	Melbourne, Australia	Knife attack on policemen	Two individuals wounded	Perpetrator profiled in IS magazine *Dabiq*	18 September 2014
4. Junud al Khilafa group	Tizi Ouzou, Algeria	French citizen kidnapped and beheaded	One person killed	Perpetrators pledge allegiance to IS	20 September 2014
5. Martin Rouleau-Couture	Saint-Jean-sur-Richelieu, Quebec, Canada	Soldiers hit with a car	One soldier killed and another injured	Expressed support online to IS	20 October 2014
6. Michael Bibeau	Ottawa, Canada	Shooting inside the Canadian Parliament	One soldier killed	Express support to group in video	22 October 2014
7. Zale Thompson	New York, United States	Hatchet attack on policemen	None	Expressed support online to IS	23 October 2014
8. Man Haron Monis	Sydney, Australia	Hostage-taking	Two hostages killed	IS flag displayed	15 December 2014
9. Bertrand Nzohabonayo	Joué-les-Tours, France	Stabbings	Three police officers wounded	Posted IS flag on his Facebook page	20 December 2014
10. Name undisclosed by French authorities	Dijon, France	Car driven into pedestrians	Thirteen people wounded	No known direct relationship	21 December 2014

Perpetrator(s)	Location	Modus operandi	Victim(s)	IS link	Date
11. Sébastien Sarron	Nantes, France	Van driven into pedestrians at street market	One dead, 13 wounded	No known direct relationship	22 December 2014
12. Saïd Kouachi and Chérif Kouachi	Paris, France	Shootings at offices of *Charlie Hebdo* satirical magazine	Twelve people killed and eleven injured	Perpetrators claimed affiliation with AQAP but alleged accomplice Amedy Coulibaly pledged allegiance to IS	7 January 2015
13. Amedy Coulibaly	Paris, France	Shooting of policewoman and, later, at a Kosher grocery store	Five people killed	Pledged allegiance to IS in a video	8–9 January 2015
14. Omar Abdel Hamid El-Hussein	Copenhagen, Denmark	Shots fired at forum featuring controversial cartoonist and at a synagogue	Two people dead	Swore fidelity to IS leader in video	14–15 February 2015
15. Yassine Labidi and Saber Khachnaoui	Tunis, Tunisia	Shootings at museum	Twenty-three dead and 36 wounded	IS claim of attack	18 March 2015
16. Elton Simpson and Nadir Soofi	Dallas, Texas, United States	Shooting outside cartoon contest	One person wounded	Online support to IS	3 May 2015
17. Seifeddine Rezgui	Port El Kantaoui, near Sousse, Tunisia	Shooting on tourist beach at hotel resort	Thirty-nine people killed, including 30 UK nationals	IS claim of attack	26 June 2015
18. Yassine Salhi	Lyon, France	Perpetrator's office manager decapitated	One person killed	IS flag attached to fence near victim	26 June 2015

Perpetrator(s)	Location	Modus operandi	Victim(s)	IS link	Date
19. Rafik Yousef	Berlin, Germany	Knife attack on policewoman	One person wounded	Linked to Ansar al Islam, an Al Qaeda-affiliated Iraqi group	17 September 2015
20. IS affiliate in Sinai	Airspace over the Sinai Desert, Egypt	Explosive in Russian passenger plane	224 people killed	IS claim of attack	31 October 2015
21. Faisal Mohammad	Merced, California	Knife stabbings	Four people injured	IS videos on perpetrator's computer	4 November 2015
22. IS operators in Lebanon	Beirut, Lebanon	Bombing in a Shi'a neighbourhood of the city	Forty-three dead and 200 wounded	IS claim of attack	12 November 2015
23. Bilal Hadfi, Brahim Abdeslam, Chakib Akrouh, Abdelhamid Abaaoud, Ismael Omar Mostefai, Samy Amimour, Foued Mohamed-Aggad, Ali al Iraqi and Ukasha al Iraqi	Paris, France	Six attacks with rifles and explosives on a stadium, a concert hall and cafés	130 people killed and 350 wounded	IS claim of attacks	13 November 2015
24. Syed Rizwan Farook and Tashfeen Malik	San Bernardino, California	Shooting at Inland Regional Centre	Fourteen killed and 22 injured	IS congratulates the attackers	2 December 2015
25. Muhaydin Mire	London, England	Knife attack	One man killed	Picture of IS flag in perpetrator cell phone	5 December 2015
26. Ali Salah	Paris, France	Axe attack against police stations	None	Drawing of IS flag displayed	7 January 2016
27. Edward Archer	Philadelphia, United States	Police officer shot	One person wounded	Pledged allegiances to IS	8 January 2016

Perpetrator(s)	Location	Modus operandi	Victim(s)	IS link	Date
28. Nabil Fadli	Istanbul, Turkey	Suicide bombing targeting foreign tourists	Thirteen dead	An IS fighter from Manbij, Syria	12 January 2016
29. Safia S. (last name withheld by German authorities)	Hanover, Germany	Knife attack on policeman	One person wounded	IS contact online	26 February 2016
30. Ibrahim El Bakraoui, Khalid El Bakraoui, Najim Laachraoui, Mohamed Abrini and Osama Krayem	Brussels, Belgium	Three coordinated suicide bombings at Brussels airport	Thirty-two individuals killed and 300 injured	IS claim of attacks	22 March 2016
31. Omar Matteen	Orlando, Florida	Shooting in nightclub	Forty-nine killed and 53 injured	Swore allegiance to IS in telephone call to 911 operator from attack spot	12 June 2016
32. Larossi Abballa	Magnanville, France	Police officers couple killed in their home	Two people killed	Pledges alliance to IS in video live on Facebook	13 June 2016
33. Rakim Bulgarov and Vadim Osmanov	Istanbul, Turkey	Suicide bombing and mass shooting at Atatürk Airport	Forty-five people killed	Turkey claims perpetrators were ISIS fighters in Raqqa, Syria	28 June 2016
34. Mohamed Lahouaij Bouhlel	Nice, France	Drove bus through crowds on Promenade des Anglais avenue on Bastille Day	Eighty-six dead, 434 injured	IS claim of attack	14 July 2016
35. Muhammad Riyad	Würzburg, Germany	Axe attack in a train	Five people injured	Video featuring the perpetrator posted by ISIS	19 July 2016

Perpetrator(s)	Location	Modus operandi	Victim(s)	IS link	Date
36. David Sonboly	Munich, Germany	Shooting in a shopping mall	Nine dead and 16 injured	No known direct relationship	22 July 2016
37. Mohammed Daleel	Ansbach, Germany	Suicide bombing at a bar	Fifteen injured	Perpetrator filmed himself pledging allegiance to IS	24 July 2016
38. Abdel Malik Petitjean and Adel Kermiche	Saint-Étienne-du-Rouvray, Normandy, France	Assassination of a French priest in a church and hostage-taking	One dead	Attackers posted a message online swearing allegiance to ISIS	26 July 2016
39. Aaron Driver	Strathroy, Canada	Shot by police before he could set off a bomb	None	Perpetrator filmed himself pledging allegiance to IS	11 August 2016
40. Name undisclosed by Swiss authorities	Salez, Switzerland	Stabbing of travellers and wagon in a train set on fire	One dead, seven injured	No known relationship	13 August 2016
41. Meza Hodzic	Copenhagen, Denmark	Shooting	Two police officers injured	IS claim of attack	1 September 2016
42. Dahir Adan	St. Cloud, Minnesota, United States	Stabbings in a shopping mall	Ten people injured	IS released claim of attack on Amaq news agency	17 September 2016
43. Ahmad Khan Rahami	New York, United States	Bombing in the Chelsea neighbourhood; two other devices found unexploded	Twenty-nine people injured	Cited IS in personal journal	17 September 2016
44. Hicham Diop	Brussels, Belgium	Machete attack on policemen	Two wounded	Established contact with Syrian IS operators	5 October 2016
45. Amina al Almaniyya	Mulheim, Germany	Knife attack on policemen	Two wounded	IS flag among perpetrator's belongings	31 October 2016

Perpetrator(s)	Location	Modus operandi	Victim(s)	IS link	Date
46. Abdul Razak Ali Artan	Columbus, Ohio, United States	Vehicle ramming and stabbing attack at Ohio State University	Thirteen wounded	IS claim of attack	28 November 2016
47. Anis Amri	Berlin, Germany	Truck ploughed into street market	Twelve killed, 49 wounded	IS claim of attack	19 December 2016
48. Abdulkadir Masharipov	Istanbul, Turkey	Shooting in nightclub	Thirteen dead	IS claim of responsibility	1 January 2017
49. Abdallah El-Hamahmy	Paris, France	Machete attack on policeman at Louvre Museum	None	Online support to IS	3 February 2017
50. Khalid Masood (Adrian Russell Ajao)	London, England	Car driven into people on pavement in front of Westminster Palace, police officer stabbed	Five dead and 40 wounded	IS claim of attack	22 March 2017
51. Akbarzhon Jalilov	St Petersburg, Russia	Bombing in metro station	Fifteen killed	Perpetrator trained with insurgents in Syria in 2014	3 April 2017
52. Rakhmat Alikov	Stockholm, Sweden	Truck driven into department store	Four people killed	Perpetrator pledge support to IS	7 April 2017
53. Kori Ali Muhammad	Fresno, California	Shootings in four different locations	Three people killed	No known relationship; killer shouts 'Allahu Akbar' (God is great) and claimed hatred of white people	18 April 2017

Perpetrator(s)	Location	Modus operandi	Victim(s)	IS link	Date
54. Karim Cheurfi	Paris, France	Shooting of policemen in their car	One policeman killed	IS claim of attack	20 April 2017
55. Salman Abedi	Manchester, England	Suicide bombing at music concert by singer Ariana Grande	Twenty-two dead and 59 injured	IS claim of attack	24 May 2017
56. Khuram Shazad, Rachid Redouane and Youssef Zaghba	London, England	Van driven into pedestrians on London Bridge, stabbings at restaurants in Borough Market	Seven killed and 48 injured	IS claim of attack	3 June 2017
57. Jessie Javier Carlos	Manila, the Philippines	Machine-gunning into the Resorts World Manila casino and tables set on fire	Thirty-seven dead and 70 wounded	IS claim of attack (rejected by Filipino police)	2 June 2017
58. Yacub Khayre	Melbourne, Australia	Hostage-taking in apartment building	One man killed and three police officers wounded	IS claim of attack	5 June 2017
59. Farid Ikken	Paris, France	Attack with hammer and kitchen knives	One policeman wounded		6 June 2017
60. Seriyas, Fereydoun, Qayyoum, Abu Jahad and Ramin (last names undisclosed by Iranian police)	Tehran, Iran	Simultaneous assaults with guns and explosives on the parliament and the Ayatollah Khomeini mausoleum	Seventeen dead and 43 wounded	Attackers had fought for IS in Syria; IS claim of attack	7 June 2017

with a machete. On 11 August, a 24-year-old Canadian, who previously filmed himself pledging allegiance to IS, was shot by the Canadian police in Ontario as he was about to set off a bomb in Strathroy, south of Toronto. Two days later, a 27-year-old Swiss man set a train wagon on fire in north-east Switzerland and stabbed six people. An 18-year-old French girl was arrested, the next day, in Clermont-Ferrand, France, on charges of supporting IS's messages and echoing them on the online application Telegram (an app that had also been used by Abdelmalik Nabil Petitjean and Adel Kermiche, two teenagers who had killed a French priest in France on 26 July). On 1 September a 25-year-old Dane of Bosnian origin shot two policemen in Copenhagen, an attack claimed two days later by IS. On 7 September, French police arrested three young French women accused of planning an attack on the Notre-Dame Cathedral in Paris. On 14 September, French police arrested a 15-year-old boy suspected of plotting to carry out terror attacks in the country and accused of links with IS, with which he had established contact via social media. On 17 September, a man stabbed ten people in a mall in Minnesota and was depicted three days later by IS as one of its 'soldiers'. The same day, a 28-year-old Afghan American was arrested on suspicion of detonating a bomb in the Chelsea neighbourhood in New York, which injured 29 people. On 16 December a German Iraqi boy tried to blow up a Christmas market in the town of Ludwigshafen, Germany.

As this international sequence of individual extreme violence played out from summer to winter, it became clear that these attacks had recommissioned and repurposed the substance of what IS had initiated, and were being used to vent all manner of violent local discontent and radicalisation. An entanglement of configurations developed whereby the perpetrators sought to anchor their violence in IS mythology, however superficially, IS itself claimed these attacks or congratulated the attackers opportunistically and belatedly, and the public perception increasingly linked the attacks to Islam and Muslims. By 2016, the conflict had morphed in such a way that Europe was literally bracing for hundreds of IS fighters to attack the continent in a 'wave of bloodshed'.[12] What was significant, however, was the fact that, just as the motivations were variegated, identity lines had become increasingly blurred, with Asians, Africans, Europeans and North Americans involved, as well as converts to Islam (e.g. Aaron Driver) and children of mixed marriages (e.g. Savoy-born Abdelmalik Petitjean). These new actors straddled a logic of notional historical revenge, immediate dispossession and imagined future. Theirs – 'jihad in the hood'[13] – was violence in search of local impact and recognition, and one which was equally performative.[14] Nowhere was that better seen than in the violently radicalised, post-colonial and post-modern youth of 2010s France.

Imperial Reconnections

Associations between IS's ambition to link itself with different communities beyond Iraq and Syria – following al 'Adnani's explicit September 2014 call – and Western actors located in the metropolis, were possible because the nature of these 'imagined communities' (linked traditionally to statehood and the nation, as Benedict Anderson had discussed the notion) were now also lending themselves towards a multiplicity of societal reinterpretations. As Diane Davis remarks, the territorialities of today suggest that political communities of reciprocity are no longer limited in the same way as before, owing to globalisation and the transnational flows of peoples and ideas, and to the fact that states are neither uniformly legitimate nor the only authority in an increasingly interconnected and globalised world. This does not mean that political communities of reciprocity (or imagined communities) have disappeared, only that they are transforming in scale and scope.[15] In that sense, the modernity of the movement triggered by IS rests in its *novelty*, which in turn is a combination of *displacement* into a different setting and the initial ability to escape recognition. As Michael North remarks, 'an innovation is by definition *something that has become new by being moved to a place unfamiliar with it*. Diffusion, that is to say, is itself tantamount to innovation. ... Even in its reduced form as innovation, then, actual innovation only exists at the very crest of the wave ... dependent on its relative unfamiliarity to a new audience.'[16] Therefore, what IS did in 2014 was to provide a different population than the Mesopotamian and Levantine one it was immersed in originally with a threefold narrative of nation (Caliphate) and community (*umma*), but also (and more importantly) actionable transformation (agency through rupture and the diffusion of violence), allowing it to express a pre-existing dormant radicalisation that was merely in search of a conduit. Explicitly aimed at Muslims – while inviting others to convert to Islam – and calibrated to influence those populations in the West, more so than, say, Africans, Asians or Latin Americans (although IS was present in these regions too), the calls acquired particular acuity in the context of post-colonial societies.

France, which had one of the largest colonial empires – colonising Algeria for 132 years – and which was now home to the largest Muslim population in Europe (as well as the largest Jewish population in Europe), was a theatre where these issues would predictably play out. Though the administrative heritage of colonial history is rarely recognised in relation to the manifestation of contemporary political violence and terrorism, understanding the conflicts over immigration and citizenship in France today necessitates a journey into this often overlooked aspect of the genealogy of France's political culture.[17] Just as it had trouble coming to terms with its years of collaboration with the Nazi regime during the German occupation and the deportation of Jews between 1940 and 1944, France has not yet been able to address its colonial past. Specifically, the national (non-)discussion of the issue has seesawed between amnesia and romanticisation, caged in by a dominant theme that this was a long-gone era whose relevance to contemporary developments is negligible. As Muslim migrants from the former North African and West African countries it had colonised started arriving in France from the 1960s onwards, a societal process of transformation of the country was inevitably set in motion. By the early 1980s, as the first generation of children of these migrants were coming of age, signs of cultural tension with the rest of society appeared, heightened by the fact that the vast majority of the population which moved in during the 1960s had been housed in large-scale, low-income housing projects. Known as *banlieues*, these densely populated areas (e.g. Les Minguettes, Vaulx-en-Velin, Clichy-sous-bois, La Courneuve, Sarcelles, Les Mureaux, Trappes) inhabited by working-class families were located on the outskirts of the major urban centres such as Paris, Lyon and Marseilles. Petty criminality, juvenile delinquency and insecurity became the staple of these places, and was compounded by poverty. This led to regular riots, starting in 1981 and running until the 2010s (with a major uprising in October–November 2005 that triggered a national state of emergency declared by President Jacques Chirac). In the face of police brutality, killing of suspects and socio-economic exclusion, the second generation of these populations – whose parents had mostly come from Algeria, Morocco, Tunisia, Senegal and Mali – became increasingly alienated from the rest of French society. Initially, the non-political resentment of some started acquiring undertones of a politics of identity and, soon enough, of culture and religion. Although, the majority of these youth had not been particularly religious, religion started gaining ground within the *banlieues*, pushed in further as a reaction to a number of stigmatisation measures adopted by the successive right-wing and left-wing French governments – notably opposition to the Islamic scarf (*hijab*) in September 1989, leading to a law prohibiting it in public schools in 2003 and a ban of the full body veil (*burqa*) in September 2010.

As a segment of France increasingly regarded these populations in its midst as alien, looked upon their religion as a threat and revisited the country's colonial history (in 2005, the French National Assembly adopted a law requiring high schools to teach the 'positive' values of colonialism, a bill that was later repealed), and as its highest officials called these youth 'scum' and 'riff-raff' (as did Prime Minister Nicolas Sarkozy in 2005), the societal rupture deepened and connections with far-away conflicts in the Middle East and North Africa increased, as did violence. By 2015, the country was experiencing a 'social, territorial and ethnic apartheid', according to French Prime Minister Valls. As one analyst summed it up:

> When it comes to *jihad* ... there is a French exception ... France's dis-tinctiveness arises in part from ... decades of economic hardship, the growing stigmatisation of cultural differences [and] the fervent indi-vidualism of new generations ... Above all, France has not been able to solve the problem of economic and social exclusion. Its system ... breeds angst all around. Young people in the *banlieues*, marginalised and with few prospects, feel like victims. They become prime targets for jihadist propaganda, often after a stint in prison for petty crimes. Neither Germany nor Britain faces the *banlieues* phenomenon, at least not on such a scale ... this growing gap is a source of pervasive distress. And so ... the weight of France's national identity has become a problem. It only heightens the discontent of young people with foreign origins.[18]

This situation had not escaped the attention of Al Qaeda, whose leaders issued calls in 2005 to the Muslim youth of France to rise up against their society. Ten years later, it was those young French men and women who were recording the videos and calling for violent action on their fellow citizens. The political sympathy or cultural affinities, which radicalised segments of the French Arab and Muslim population initially shared with the suffering populations in Palestine, Iraq or Syria, gradually turned into an existential and intimate issue, driven not-so-subterraneously by more local socio-economic issues of rejection and alienation. As some of these actors became more violent, French society became more intolerant and vice versa. The logic of forcefully suppressing social opposition was often associated with the need to rid society of a specific segment. Awash in a media landscape where ethnic minorities were also represented by what Cornel West termed non-oppositional instances of commodification,[19] the radicalised French Muslims became looked upon not merely as a discrete security threat (i.e. *specific* individuals related to *given* events), but more so as a loose ideological if not ontological *masse*, carrying a 'disease' that could affect the 'French French', through those converted to Islam and represented by the mainstream media as internal enemies.[20] Lurking behind every male Muslim in the city was the widespread unspoken suspicion of a born terrorist, and attacks on the Western metropolis never failed to trigger debates on the nature of Islam and of needed cultural responses. However, such societal drift created an unexpected danger for French society, as the unanticipated appeal of IS to young Western men and women became visible when the global foreign fighters phenomenon emerged so massively. In increasing the dangerousness of the young Muslim figure and featuring it non-stop in the media, it would seem the French and other Western authorities paradoxically and self-fulfillingly raised its symmetrical appeal for those willing to act as radical outlaws in their own societies and culture – and those were legion. At a time when transgression is commoditised and staged in every day ('thug') life, the extreme stance of IS and its followers became a lure for those individuals on their way to radicalisation. (Even the obvious sexism of IS was no deterrent, as the groups it spawned in the metropolis often featured women; in the 2016 French film *Le Ciel Attendra* (*Heaven Will Wait*), for instance, the experience of these young French girls, both of immigrant and local extraction, working and middle class, is depicted in all its contradictions.)[21]

Initially, however, the rebellion of these disenfranchised actors was about defence of social space and identity – constructs that were eminently local and Western.[22] In racialising its reading of the global order and linking that construct to a population in its midst, a segment of French society opened itself to being *racialised back* by these actors – and by those groups such as Al Qaeda and IS pushing from outside to facilitate that. French youth of recent immigrant origin thus coined a derogatory term, *souchiens*, to refer to the French of local, older origin (i.e. *de souche*), which conveyed a double entendre insult as the term also sounded liked *sous-chiens* (underdogs). Societal tensions of this nature in play well before IS (and even Al Qaeda) now became related to the way in which France came to interact with itself, and how foreign conflicts had evolved and violently inserted themselves into such a context. At the centre of this shift stand the motivations of the IS perpetrator of the Western type. 'Who fights, for whom and why'?[23] is a question that acquires new resonance in this context. As Tarak Barkawi remarks:

> In order to understand the nature of security relations in a post-9/11 world, we must revisit the most basic issues concerning war and armed conflict. Two factors dominate contemporary security relations. The first is the ways in which the new threats have arisen from, and develop in and through, long histories of interaction between the West and other parts of the world. The second is how these threats interact with the societies and politics of the West, not least by fostering *a self-perception that prevents full understanding of the situation.*[24]

A post-modern cultural landscape characterised by narcissism, self-absorption, constant distraction, incessant consumption and status obsession provided a facile platform for the fundamentalist expression of back-to-your-roots cleansing championed by IS's Western sympathisers, and the linking of that with terroristic violence. Yet paradoxically the new IS insurgent is also a consumer of celebrity culture – the Thanatos-like celebrity of his or her breaking news in the wake of a terrorist attack. That culture 'has taught us to generate, almost unconsciously, interior personal screenplays in the mould of Hollywood, television and even commercials. We have learned ways of speaking and thinking that disfigure the way we relate to the world'[25] – and this has been adopted by the new global terrorising insurgent. As events and fake news can now be manufactured more than ever, *nouveau* terrorism – wherein illusion dominates, staged under pornographic violence exposure and constant category-shifting – has emerged lethally in our midst.

This new domestic revolution, observed in accelerated fashion in 2010s France, appeared to seek to displace and transcend the territoriality in which it was boxed. Such spatial transformation was carried in earlier moments of radicalised violent revolt, but with IS's self-capacitation logic, and following Al Qaeda's transnationality, it becomes more qualitatively defining of the latter-day terrorist. The Kouachi brothers 'travel' to the heart of Paris to 'avenge the Prophet'. Yet, once their deed committed, for the next hours they are stuck in the Parisian 'space', precisely because their space is one of the no-man's land of transgression and contestation. The reification of IS as Southern violence playing out away from the North and only interacting with it when it travels to attack it (breaking news, terrorist attack) or when it calls Western youth to join it (foreign fighters) misses on this newly problematic hybrid dimension of the group. Indeed, the cold-bloodedness displayed by the perpetrators of the attacks in Paris and Brussels often played out in relation to a deeper, buried and unresolved set of multiple histories, which they carried intimately and which were largely unspoken – the key to which could not be found in their pseudo-religious statements. In the formation of identities, memory is not only invented, conjured up or reawakened, it is also purposely suppressed, erased and deleted.[26] Both the core of IS and its copycat followers function according to a logic of romanticisation of the past, with their respective creations of fanciful realms into which their different swashbuckling projections of global expansion are performed. The gory projected violence is indicative of a distant memory of the colonial period, but one that has not been experienced by these eminently Western youth. The original rebellion brewing in the French suburbs was getting more violent as the youth became increasingly alienated from the rest of French society. Depicted in the 1995 film *La Haine* (*The Hate*) directed by Mathieu Kassovitz, these life patterns were indicative of a profound split within French society which Al Qaeda tried to manipulate early on and IS would in time build on. For all its tragic poignancy, *La Haine* featured lost youth that had not yet been ideologised. The economic dispossession and social anger felt existentially by the three main protagonists – the Arab, Said (Said Taghmaoui); the Jew, Vinz (Vincent Cassel); and the African, Hubert (Hubert Koundé) – was arguably more related to familiar class disparities, and as such more reminiscent of the tragic fate of, say, *The Outsiders'* small-town working-class Greasers fictionalised in Francis Ford Coppola's 1982 film, or the more violent inner-city isolation of suburban African American, Latino and 'White Trash' gangs in Walter Hill's 1979 film *The Warriors*.

The new post-colonial and post-modern radical insurgent arises instead from *within* Western societies, because these societies have also developed an updated form of Orientalism beamed at (and representing) the 'Oriental' in their very midst, and that projection allows the violence to come out in the mode of connection-disconnection with the distant wars of the Middle East. In other words, the rebellion is essentially an open-ended release wherein the *choice* of violence and the *moment* of rebellion is the acme of local built-in frustrations connected to an external realm. Agency and desire to control one's own trajectory are prime movers of the rebellion at the core of this violence. Whether during suicide operations, attacks against targets in the metropolis or travel to Raqqa or Mosul, there is little calculation beyond the final, no-turning-back terroristic rupture. As Chris Hedges notes more generally on the nature of rebellion, 'There is nothing rational about rebellion. To rebel against insurmountable odds is an act of faith, without which the rebel is doomed. This faith is intrinsic to the rebel the way caution and prudence are intrinsic to those who seek to fit into existing power structures. The rebel, possessed by inner demons and angels, is driven by a vision.'[27] In a context where '[c]itizenship has been redefined in terms of consumer choice ... [and where] many citizens increasingly think of security in terms of individualised safety, and seek to secure themselves against anything that is deemed to put them at risk',[28] that very idea of a violent vision is adopted by the globalised insurgent who in effect makes a statement akin to 'my security is a product of the insecurity I can visit upon you'. At the heart of the new rebel's disposition often stands an urban context and a consumer lifestyle. However, inspired by distant conflicts and couched in religious terms, like all politics, such violence is inescapably local. It springs from and speaks to the frustration arising from the terrorist's vicinity – one from which he or she cannot escape (the Tsarnaev brothers circling Boston and the Kouachi brothers driving around Paris, for three days in both cases), or to which they are lured back in Dostoevskian fashion (Abdelhamid Abaaoud returning to his crime scene an hour after the explosions in Paris, and later caught in the Saint-Denis apartment of his cousin, Hasna Ait Boulahcen, two days after the November 2015 attacks; or Salah Abdeslam captured in his childhood Molenbeek neighbourhood in Brussels where he hid for weeks after the Paris November 2015 attacks in which he was involved).

France's IS back-to-the-colonial-future experience of this new sort is visible in two cinematic illustrations that capture both the slow-motion emergence of the phenomenon and its subsequent dramatic acceleration. The first one is Michael Haneke's 2005 film *Caché* (*Hidden*). Ostensibly, the film is a psychological thriller about a Parisian couple (played by Daniel Auteuil and Juliette Binoche) whose bourgeois routine is disrupted by a series of creepy videotapes they receive anonymously, showing their home filmed from outside, all in the context of a childhood episode of the husband and his resentment towards the orphaned son of an Algerian family who had been adopted by the man's parents. The evasive whodunit nature of the plot hides a deeper (hidden) dimension in which the colonial past resurfaces to terrorise the lives of the French couple and the now-adult Algerian immigrant by way of their children. As the Algerian man's son confronts the husband (Auteuil), blaming him for his father's suicide, it becomes clear that the repressed memory of the 1960s events and their seeming unrelatedness to the present malaise was misleading – more so, in a further twist, as the couple's son is shown in the last shot meeting with the Algerian man's son (for what purpose it is not clear). Mid-1990s fictions of this sort – foreshadowing everything to come from IS, from culturally mixed foreign fighters to threatening video imagery to psycho-cultural violence in the heart of the über-tribalised post-colonial metropolis city (as they come out of a police station, the couple has a violent argument with a young man of West African origin with the same subtext of post-colonial ethnic tension) – were already indicative of the materialisation of a 'problem' that French society had with that segment of its population, then shapelessly representing an unspoken cultural threat. The second illustration of France's inescapable colonial past and its current reconnection with the IS story comes unsurprisingly from Gillo Pontecorvo's *The Battle of Algiers* (1966). As the 1957–8 events depicted in the film spiralled into violence, and as the Algerian militants' terrorism and the French army's repression symmetrically increased, a scene towards the end of the film shows two Algerian youths at the dead end of their radicalisation driving a van at full speed in the boulevards of Algiers, indiscriminately machine-gunning French passers-by and others sitting at cafés, before eventually ploughing the van into a crowd of Frenchmen and women. Such paroxysm, the *modus operandi*, the identity of the perpetrators and that of the victims, eerily foreshadowed precisely what took place in Paris on 13 November 2015 and in Nice on 14 July 2016 at the hands of IS-inspired attackers.

Beyond the choice he makes to turn to terroristic violence, the post-modern insurgent is also a pathology of empire; a phenomenon that is the hybrid child of a century of colonial experience that has morphed into an imperial one, today begetting forward-looking modern terrorism that is all the time looking in the rear-view mirror. This brings us back full circle to the question of racism and international relations (see the Introduction), and to the blurring of the boundary between opposition and terrorism. As Aziz al Azmeh noted early on, observing the specific French case: 'Primary importance must be attributed to the impossibility of socio-economic assimilation experienced by second-generation immigrants born in situations of urban degradation and into marginal, declining and unskilled industry, at a time of increased state indifference and hostility coupled with racism in the very capillaries of the "host society".[29] The children of post-colonialism falling into such extreme violence are also faced with an environment of this nature in which modernity and liberalism proclaim colour-blindness and equal opportunity while practising exclusion and beaming dispossession:

> So the irony of modernity, the liberal paradox comes down to this: As modernity commits itself progressively to idealised principles of liberty, equality and fraternity, as it increasingly insists upon the moral irrelevance of race, there is a multiplication of racial identities and the sets of exclusion they prompt and rationalise, enable and sustain. Race is irrelevant but all is race. The more abstract modernity's universal identity, the more it has to be insisted upon, the more it needs to be *imposed*. The more ideologically-hegemonic liberal values seem and the more open to difference liberal modernity declares itself, the more dismissive of difference it becomes and the more closed it seeks to make the circle of acceptability ... Liberal modernity denies its racialised history and the attendant histories of racist exclusions, hiding them behind some idealised, self-promoting, yet practically ineffectual dismissal of race as a morally-irrelevant category.[30]

The halogen-like insistence on *laïcité* as a reaction to IS's attacks in France in the mid-2010s was an illustration of this self-generated, historically blind tension in which the violence remained immersed, politics unnamed and race unspoken. As a conflation of different forms of violence, IS circa 2016 in France and Europe is in that sense terrorism by a radical Islamist group born in Iraq but *also* a Westernised rejection of Westernisation, which the Western dweller-perpetrator is only acting out for reasons notionally beyond the West. Abandonment and disarticulation as responses to hegemony are then, as the French context tells us, widening the nature of the sociological base of this 'from-there-but-really-here' political violence. The question at the core of this process is ultimately threefold and concerns the authenticity of agency, the dynamic of cultural borrowing and the structure and technique of (violence) improvisation. As Talal Asad noted:

When a project is translated from one site to another, from one agent to another, *versions of power are produced*. As with translations of a text, one does not simply get a reproduction of identity. The acquisition of new forms of language ... – whether by forcible imposition, insidious insertion or voluntary borrowing – is part of what makes for new possibilities of action in non-Western societies. Yet, although the outcome of these possibilities is never fully predictable, the language in which the possibilities are formulated is shared increasingly by Western and non-Western societies. And so too, the specific forms of power and subjection.[31]

Amid denial, exclusion and radicalisation, it seemed as if French society since the 1960s had been building up slowly and inevitably to the events of 2014–17 by nurturing the production of such versions of violent counter-power. In France,

the fiction of a French society less racialised as compared to the United States and the United Kingdom works on a twofold denial. Historically, this is based on an arbitrary separation between the metropolis and the colonial empire whereby racialisation was not only a matter of representation but of legal and administrative status. [...] The second denial is contemporary as it pretends to ignore that, for the first time in its history, the racialised population of the former colonial empire lives nowadays on the metropolitan territory, thus *de facto* establishing a post-colonial situation.[32]

Indeed, as the socio-economic Third Worldisation of France proceeded,[33] with leading French news magazines (notably *Le Point*, *L'Express* and *Valeurs Actuelles*) multiplying sensationalistic covers against Islam, and as IS attacks augmented, the *banlieues* became militarised and seen by many as occupied territory in effect foreign to France. In a book published in the fall of 2016, one commentator maintained that the French police had contingency plans for an operation dubbed *Opération Ronces* (brambles) to 'reconquer' the *banlieues*, declaring that the plan had allegedly been developed by the French authorities in cooperation with Israeli officers who shared their experience in Gaza. (The French authorities denied that information.[34])

The last part of Al Qaeda's story had been its incipient Europeanisation (the Madrid 2004 and London 2005 operations) and Americanisation

Militarised state-building

Figure 4.1   The biformity of the Islamic State

Transnationalised sleeper agent

Source: Islamic State publications; *Al Naba*, May 2016 and poster on Twitter account, June 2016

(Adam Gadahn, Samir Khan, Anwar al ʿAwlaqi), as well as the rise of its different franchises. The homogenisation that Bin Laden had sought disappeared slowly and he embraced that. In the combined aftermath of the Iraq and Syrian conflicts, and IS operators joining hands from Mosul to Manchester, the violence produced in the metropolis was now on its way to transforming those Western states and societies involved in this process (the United States, the United Kingdom and France, primarily). Rising methods of control of citizens, securitisation, big-brother Orwellian meta-logics, racial and religious discrimination against Arabs and Muslims, lawfare and weaponisation of legislation and military urbanism were the result of the series of military adventures from Afghanistan to Iraq by way of the Sahel, Somalia and Yemen. IS emerged from these ashes to pursue its Al Qaeda-transcending plan, but also to produce and orchestrate something new, namely *boomerang violence* on the West. This transformed the landscape, and its distinct, simultaneous relationship between different causalities and places had echoes of an earlier era of violence and transnationalism in the West.

The 1970s Redux

As IS's post-Mosul international campaign proceeded, and as the do-it-yourself violence it exported from Iraq and Syria into the Western hinterlands increased dramatically in 2015–17, the global context of this situation – while denoting novelty – increasingly resembled an earlier decade during which international conflict, societal malaise and ethnic tensions had featured prominently alongside waves of terrorism and insecurity, namely the 1970s. In reviving the memory of those forgotten 'days of rage',[35] the new 2010s context was revealing another dimension of transnationality that had played out mostly in Europe and in the United States around several radicalised groups. At the point when the new globalised insurgency originated, we therefore find a number of historical currents which merged to inform the violence in different ways. Combined with Al Qaeda's founding matrix (as seen in Chapter 1), these traditions also partake of the new IS operator's trajectory, endowed as it is with a shared transnational consciousness, albeit an eclectic one. Among these few-and-far-between influences, two in particular were important in the deep and almost imperceptible legacy they left on the new story-in-the-making: the Palestinian 'global offensive' noted in Chapter 3,[36] which connected Palestinians and Europeans; and a so-called 'Muslim international', which connected African American domestic issues in the United States with larger international Islamic questions in the Middle East and North Africa. Importantly, neither of these movements was radical Islamist in nature.

During the 1970s – a period more accurately spanning the years 1967 to 1984 – large parts of the Western world came under attack from several movements advocating political violence. In the United States, the Weather Underground Organisation (also known as Weatherman) started a significant underground radical violence tradition in 1969, opening the gates for the Black Liberation Army, the Symbionese Liberation Army, the Fuerzas Armadas de Liberación Nacional, the Pan-Radical Alliance, The Family and the United Freedom Front. Amid years of strife, assassination, war and terror, societal change itself came to the United States through the tumult of the 1970s with a vivid and violent sense of rupture.[37] The terrorism of these groups on their own society adopted the absolutist language of war and punishment of the government. Just as Al Qaeda would in 1996 and 1998, the Weather Underground 'declared war' on the United States in 1970 in its own way, and for six years went on to detonate bombs across the country in New York, San Francisco, Chicago, Boston, Pittsburgh and Washington, DC. A militant from one these 1970s underground movements in the United States later noted: 'People always ask why I did what I did and I tell them I was a soldier in a war.'[38]

Some eras, noted Philip Jenkins, stand out because of the unusual rapidity of change and the transformation of values and ideals in a very short time.[39] The 2010s were indeed similar in that regard, replaying the 1970s in reinvented ways. Particularly in the United States, the echo patterns were visible. Stories of that decade's terrorists were being retold.[40] Racial tension between Whites and Blacks resurfaced, reaching dramatic new heights and indicating that the previous 30 years – the Reagan-driven consumerism of the 1980s, the Clinton-led nonchalance of the 1990s and the Bush-forged aggressive patriotism of the 2000s – were seemingly but an interlude from the unresolved tensions of the 1960s and the 1970s.[41] Wars had then been taken to Vietnam, others were now brought back from Iraq and Afghanistan. The deeper societal meaning of the calls for retaliatory defensive violence that the likes of Malcolm X, and those movements he influenced such as the Black Panthers, had advocated was re-examined, as were the 1965 (Watts), 1967 (Detroit) and 1992 (Los Angeles) riots amid new ones in 2014–16 in Baltimore, Ferguson, Milwaukee and Charlotte. These were but tell-tale signs of another back-to-the-future moment in which the IS story played out elusively for the most part. In the meantime, things had evolved and the Iraq wars, Al Qaeda and IS were now *also* at the unseen centre of this evolution of American society. Whereas it had taken Al Qaeda a few years to attract US-based operators (such as baptised Catholic John Walker Lindh or Queens-born Latino Bryant Neal Vinas), IS mobilised sympathisers in the United States almost at once. Indeed, IS incited US militants at a rate four times higher than Al Qaeda, with 83 per cent of those fighters that joined it from America being US citizens, and 65 per cent born in the United States.[42] That quicker connection was due to the IS approach of 'striking the minds' globally, but it was also informed by an earlier connection between political Islam and African American history, one that re-emerged in the 2010s in film and television series (e.g. *American Crime*).

The relationship between the dispossession of African Americans in the United States and the decolonisation wars had been substantial in the 1960s. Although it never became fully explicit, except in Malcolm X's pronouncements and militancy, and later on in Stokely Carmichael's, the issue had arisen during that decade. For instance, on 3 October 1962, an editorial in the *New York Times* noted that: 'The United States is experiencing in Mississippi what is tantamount to its own form of decolonisation. For our colonialism, sociologically-speaking has been within the USA and not abroad.'[43] From the 1930s to the 1970s, different African American movements in the United States had displayed generic influence by Islam, which was reinterpreted and merged with local American folklore. These semi-political, semi-religious, part-cult, part-business movements included the Temple of Islam (also known as the Allah Temple of Islam, which had opened in 1930 in Detroit), the Moorish Science Temple of America (MSTA, established in Chicago in 1931), the Holy Temple of Islam (an offshoot of the MSTA) and, on a much larger and more visible scale, the Nation of Islam (founded in 1930). Although secular, later on the Black Panthers were partly influenced by that same legacy, but more directly through the more distinctly socio-political, no sell-out approach of Malcolm X and his teachings (at the specific origin of the new disposition was indeed the rebellion conceptualised by Malcolm X in the period between his pilgrimage and his assassination).[44] Sohail Daulatzai has documented that international solidarity moment where radical politics about race inequality in the United States connected with the resistance fight against imperialism and colonialism in the Middle

East and in Africa.[45] The tapestry connecting Malcolm X and his legacy (Stokely Carmichael, Huey Newton, Eldridge Cleaver) with, earlier, *The Battle of Algiers* and, later, the battles of Fallujah (2006 and 2016), is an important, as-yet unexamined scene, which plays out in the background of the radicalisation process of US-based IS militants. 'They think of you as they think of us; they despise us equally' says an Iraqi nationalist to an African American US agent posted in Baghdad about his American colleagues in the novel *Baghdad Blues* – a book written in the 1970s.[46] The most explicit ideological connection between these two different strands materialised when, on 5 May 2007, Al Qaeda released a video message in which its number two, al Dhawahiri, included imagery and speeches of Malcolm X, presenting him as a model to emulate. A year later, on 19 November 2008, another video of al Dhawahiri discussing the actions of Malcolm X was released, again interspersed with footage of the 1960s militant's speeches, notably his 10 November 1963 'Message to the Grass Roots' talk, in which he used the 'house Negro and field Negro' metaphor, which al Dhawahiri proceeded to quote and link to the election of President Obama.

As the 2010s proceeded, as the backlash against African Americans gained ascendancy in pre-Trump America and as police violence on them increased – according to data compiled by the Mapping Police Violence project,[47] 303 African Americans were killed by the police in 2016 and 346 in 2015 (30 per cent unarmed) – the same malaise that had presided over the 1970s made a comeback, and lurking behind it was the spectre of Iraq, Afghanistan and IS. Never explicitly, never too clearly, the issue was there nonetheless, and it is in that sense that the experience of the new Western metropolis insurgent borrowed from or was influenced by what al Baghdadi and his cohorts started in 2014, when they beamed their message calling for international attacks and in time reached an audience. Micah Xavier Johnson, who killed five police officers in Dallas, Texas on 9 July 2016, was a member of the US Army Reserve and served in Afghanistan, where he was awarded the Afghanistan Campaign Medal, an Army Service Ribbon and an Armed Forces Reserve Medal. Similarly, Gavin Long, who a week later killed three policemen in Baton Rouge, Louisiana, was an ex-Marine who served in Iraq in 2008–9. In a video, he spoke of 'fighting back' in the name of 'justice' in reaction to the 'treatment of African Americans'. In March that year, a young African American Mississippi woman, Jaelyn Young, a former honour student, pleaded guilty to conspiring to support IS after trying to travel to Syria with a companion. A year later, on 18 April 2017, Kori Ali Muhammad – a homeless African American Muslim who been associated with gangs, released two hip hop albums under the name B-God MacSun and expressed support for Black nationalism on his Facebook page – killed three people in Fresno, California, declaring his hatred for white people and shouting 'Allahu Akbar' (God is great) during the shootings. Sign-of-the-times episodes such as these were affecting the very manner in which the United States was dealing with the recurring racial question in the country and with terrorism. Indeed, in the aftermath of the 9/11 attacks, the city of Washington had been terrorised during three weeks in October 2002 by a series of sniper attacks that had killed a total of 17 people and which had been perpetrated by John Allen Muhammad and Lee Boyd Malvo. A member of the Nation of Islam, Muhammad declared his admiration for Osama Bin Laden and for Al Qaeda, and, later in jail, Malvo drew pictures of Bin Laden and of characters from the film *The Matrix* (1999).[48]

Re-examination of the years of rage, which in the 1970s had produced deep rifts in American society, only partly revealed the nature of that indirect influence of the 'far-away' conflicts in the Middle East. Because the interventionist violence notionally operated at a distance, and because many African Americans were historically located in a separate, segregated social space,[49] the US's relationship with this new violence was not readily recognised, much less linked to the wars in Iraq and Afghanistan and to the struggle against discrimination in the US. Yet just as Vietnam found its ways into the Bronx and Compton in the 1970s, giving resonance physically and domestically to the violence the United States was enmeshed in abroad, the post-9/11 wars in Iraq and Afghanistan were repatriated and they awakened American radicalism and the social tensions of the 1970s. For the profiled African American Muslim in particular, the problem was especially vivid. A 2015 investigation by the *Guardian* newspaper, for instance, suggested an explicit continuum between police abuses in urban America and the wartime detention scandals, as it uncovered a pattern of brutality to elicit murder confessions from minority Americans at the hands of a Chicago detective, Richard Zuley, from 1977 to 2007, and his assignment at Guantánamo Bay to conduct the interrogation of high-profile detainees.[50] As one commentator noted months into the Trump presidency:

To be a black Muslim today is to be part of wide cross-section of US Muslims of African descent, US-born and immigrants, who are subjected to a double burden of state violence: as black people and as Muslims. They are subjected to the war on crime and the War on Terror, to surveillance, aggressive policing and systematic civil rights violations. ... While the security state renders black Muslims hyper-visible, the multicultural state operates as if they do not exist.[51]

Reflecting on the contemporary situation of African Americans, Melina Abdullah of California State University summed it up: 'The communities in which Black people live really become *occupied territories* and Black people have become seen as *enemy combatants*.'[52] Violence (symbolic or real) turning within came to the United States because of external actions and external pressure, and this fed domestic radicalisation across social lines. Addressing students at Trinity College, Dublin in January 2017, the filmmaker Martin Scorsese remarked that the aftermath of the 2003 war in Iraq 'had created thousands and thousands of Travis Bickles who say they have nothing to lose', referring to the depressed loner vigilante character at the heart of his 1976 film *Taxi Driver*.[53] The same reverse transplantation process was witnessed in the case of members of the Somali community in the twin cities of Minneapolis and St Paul in Minnesota. Initially, the radicalised members of that community were concerned mostly with religious issues, and with Somali questions per se in the context of the Al Shabaab insurgency in the mid-2000s in their country of origin.

As [Al Shabaab] joined Al Qaeda and ISIS, gradually the message widened to encompass questions related to African-Americans. In response, Al Shabaab broadened the pool of Americans to which it [was] appealing. [An IS video] *Pathway to Paradise* ... explicitly appealed to African-Americans through surveying institutional racism throughout the United States. It provides statistics about the mass incarceration of African-Americans, while highlighting racist organisations throughout the country. The video offers Islam as an accepting alternative to the discrimination faced in America. While the narrative is superficially consistent with past Al Shabaab recruitment techniques, the video marks the most explicit incorporation of racial issues into Jihadist messaging.[54]

The new globalised insurgents are, however, only partly political and only distantly shaped by these antebellum feuds, whether in the US or elsewhere. Removed from the 1970s actors' ideologised socio-political grievances, the new operators are driven by a more aggressive political economy of terrorism and are intimately linked to the urban landscape and to the martial use of technology. One reason for this is that they are paradoxically much more shaped by the increasingly militarised police they are facing. That particular police tradition had also been born earlier, again in a symbiotic connection with racial tension in the US in the late 1960s and early 1970s. The August 1965 Watts Riots in Los Angeles allowed the Los Angeles Police Department (LAPD) to introduce, two years later, special forces – the Special Weapons and Tactics (SWAT) unit – departing from classical police methods and borrowing from military methods and gear. Within a few years, amid the Vietnam War and as the militarisation of that department became a recognisable matrix – indeed a romanticised one when, in 1975, Hollywood introduced the fictional television series *S.W.A.T.*, glamourising one such unit[55] – the LAPD's approach to policing gained ascendancy. Specific episodes, such as the 17 May 1974 violent raid on the Symbionese Liberation Army in Compton (hundreds of LAPD officers laid siege to a residential house where Symbionese Liberation Army members were hiding for several hours, shooting an estimated 1,200 rounds of ammunition and killing six members of the group), covered live on television channels, cemented that dynamic. Over the next 40 years, and particularly after 9/11, the methods pioneered by the LAPD kept expanding in a globalising back and forth (the relationship between Compton and Bel-Air, redefined as colonial-colonised spaces,[56] arguably informed the conceptualisation of the Green Zone of Baghdad circa 2003, which then impacted those Western cities in turn as the violence travelled back from Iraq to the US). In the early 1990s, the US Congress had created the military transfer programme, blurring the lines between soldier and peace officer.[57] By 2017, the Department of Defense had transferred more than five billion US dollars in army military hardware to local law enforcement. Further militarised by the wars in Iraq and Afghanistan, and accompanied by privacy violations and a 'top secret America' born out of fear and panic,[58] which yielded an octopus of close to a million people with top security clearance and hundreds of secret governmental organisations – the militarisation of American cities had become the perfect paranoid and inwardly violent terrain for a group like IS to ship its hybrid, do-it-yourself post-modern terrorism.

The post-modernism of IS was illustrated by its multiple referential motifs, the ambiguity it efficiently and purposefully orchestrated and the interpretative space it left for its militant-to-be to use and reuse according to their own specific grievances. Acting through symbolic signs as much as physical acts, it mimicked the violence that had been inserted in its midst as a result of unceasing intervention and shipped it back to the metropolis. In turn, that violence was seized upon variously by disenfranchised youth in France, the United States and elsewhere in the West to give violent voice to their variegated and buried issues – harkening back to the 1960s and 1970s and unresolved post-colonial or racial questions. Such reproduction of the IS message was not a revendication of its agenda – certainly not in the case of the African American story or even the immigrant one in France. Rather, the violent performance influenced by IS was propaganda of the deed 2.0, and such digitalisation of combined counter-narrative, counter-message and counter-action was where the IS story had landed powerfully and unexpectedly. When discussion of IS picked up in the summer of 2014, the world had been introduced to a new term, *foreign* fighter. The phrase could not have been more misleading, for these storm riders were indeed travellers, but they were more than anything else *domestic* fighters.

Conclusion
Colonialism Boomerang

How long can we keep on kidding these people? How long before they turn their guns in the other direction?

George Orwell, *Marrakech* (1939)

To begin with, I turn back time.

Tennessee Williams, *The Glass Menagerie* (1945)

Where was the violence of IS born, what meaning did it carry and where did it head? In inquiring as to the genesis, nature and trajectory of IS and attempting to conceptualise it, this book has argued that the entity which seismically stormed the world stage in the summer of 2014 was a hybrid meta-puzzle and an influential armed group, which, beyond its specific regional Middle Eastern history and radical Islamist nature, repurposed the larger meaning of contemporary violence, birthing a do-it-yourself wave of terrorism. IS, it was submitted, is anchored in an interrelated set of far-reaching and conflict-ridden histories between the Middle East and the West; it is the expression of a multilayered purposive terrorising force directed at local power struggles and societal dystrophies; and it has evolved rapidly towards an evanescent and individualised form of physical and symbolic violence that has been unpacked globally. That group displaced what had emerged 15 years earlier as the most powerful terrorist group in history, namely Osama Bin Laden's Al Qaeda, and it went on to write its own wider and more complex story – one that is open-ended, will increasingly play out in the heart of the West and has escaped the group's initial definition and control.

It was offered that the dominant discourse in policy, journalism and academe about IS has so far been problematic in a number of ways. This is primarily because it has concentrated too much on the micro-narrative of the group's immediate operational actions to the detriment of deeper historical and political issues; has given excessive explanatory weight to the organisation's religious pronouncements; and has exceptionalised IS's violence in the sole purview of the Middle Eastern or Islamic context.

In so doing, such examinations have stood in the way of historicised and comparative analyses of the contemporary meaning of the violence produced, performed and projected by IS domestically, regionally and transnationally. Martial policy and sensationalist media accounts dictated a pace that academia followed too complacently, substituting instant and short-term terrorism expertise for lasting comparative knowledge on political violence. As a result, dominant scholarship about IS has been lacking in sophistication – as earlier work on Al Qaeda had a decade ago – beholden as it is to narratives that one-dimensionally portray a sense of things gone wrong overnight or inevitably turned violent due to the nature of the culture and religion of the people involved. Ultimately and contradictorily, IS under these perspectives was looked upon as either obvious or inscrutable.[1] It is to be either read linearly (as apocalyptic Islamist terrorism) or apprehended as being too complex to be deciphered meaningfully at all. What have been missing are several meta-arguments to help account critically for IS in conceptual ways that go beyond the rehearsed arguments about the group's irrationality, apocalypticism or barbarity. Furthermore, the arguments put forth about IS are not persuasive. The group's religiosity is most certainly front and centre, but arguably it is mere theatrics. The organisation's violence is clearly extreme but, clinically, that is but a manifestation of a terrorising use of force, and stressing that single aspect eschews the socio-genesis and the opportunistic political calculations behind it. IS's terrorism is obvious, and yet one-dimensional discussion of it hardly tells us anything about what its strategic logic conceals. 'How much of a state is ISIS?' 'How Islamic is ISIS?' 'What does ISIS really want?' Such incessant second-guessing of nominal aspects – and in effect uncritical acceptance of the group's discourse at its most basic, declamatory and superficial level – has for too long been characteristic of analyses that lack persuasiveness, particularly so as certain political questions were wittingly or unwittingly kept at bay.

A recontextualisation of IS's regenerational dynamics means connecting several strands of history and geography. These, this work contends, play across three linked temporalities. Historically, IS – as it coalesced in 2012–13 and emerged publicly in mid-2014 – is, first, the manifestation of the reformation of the Iraqi branch of Al Qaeda; an entity itself moulded in several other layers of lineal depth through Al Qaeda's own history since the mid to late 1980s and the Jordanian Abu Mus'ab al Zarqawi's organisation Jama'at al Tawhid wal Jihad between 1999 and 2003. IS is, second, the embodiment of two national insurgencies, in Iraq since 2003 in the aftermath of the US invasion and in Syria since 2011 after the start of the civil war in that country. Thirdly, IS is the expression of a transnational rebellion born in the Western metropolis that expresses itself both in the so-called foreign fighters phenomenon – men and women travelling from around the world to Iraq and Syria to take part in the state-building project of IS – and the domestic operators visiting violence on their own societies, notably in France, the United States, the United Kingdom and Germany. Such three-tiered identity, it is claimed, is inscribed in three different experiences that cumulatively account for the hybrid nature of the movement. IS's story is thus anchored in the colonial story linking the Middle East and North Africa with the West, with specifically earlier patterns of violent interaction in the Levant with the United Kingdom (and to a lesser degree in Asia) and in the central Maghreb with France echoed in the current clashes – a colonial history further made relevant through the manner in which the United States' neo-colonial policies in Iraq after 2003 enabled this dimension to inform the materialisation of IS. The group's trajectory and configuration are similarly inscribed in a globalisation moment, which determined the fluidity, density and intensity of the organisation's usage of violence, and facilitated the global beaming of its action as well as the interpenetration of its cross-currents. Finally, IS is firmly ingrained in post-modernity, as its natural and efficient use and reuse of media, technology, arts, communication techniques and language vividly illustrates – all in the transformative context of urban aesthetics, commercial individualism and societal alienation. The dialectical relationship between these lineages and temporalities thus invite a reading of IS as the sum total of these different layers (see Figure 5.1).

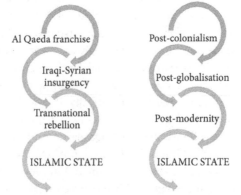

Figure 5.1   Lineages and temporalities of IS

In lieu of a plural IS, however, we have, in the historiography of IS, been treated to the singularity of a religious terrorist group. That dominant storytelling representation of IS and these non-conceptualisations are, it was also argued, situated in a larger incomplete discussion about terrorism, which is itself immersed in a specific construct of international relations – an architecture that conceals not merely familiar Eurocentrism but racism itself, which was present at the inception of 'international relations' (in its modern guise) in the 1910s and continued traversing it for the next hundred years; an 'epistemic racism [that]crosses the lines of social and institutional spheres ... hidden beneath the naturalisation of certain ways of thinking and producing knowledge'.[2] Specifically, that still-dominant configuration of international relations – statist, power-defined, Western-spoken and derivative of colonial and imperial histories – was the platform from which descriptive and prescriptive storytelling about IS proceeded. Such a disposition then logically boxed intellectual work on Al Qaeda, IS and more generally contemporary terrorism as an exercise confined to the revelation of Middle East and North Africa dystrophies or the identification of crazed Islamists. The analytical, historical importance of IS lies, however, neither in its brutal lethality nor indeed in its undeniable efficiency, or even its consequential short-circuiting of Al Qaeda. It lies rather in an original development happening both at its hands (that is, behaviourally) and as the result of the sum total of its hybrid dynamics (that is, objectively), namely *the mutation of violence which the group generated in the very midst of its enemy.* As discussed, Al Qaeda took the battle to the enemy ('from the near to the far enemy') then began shipping it back ('from to the near to the far enemy' ... and back, as it were) without fully closing that sequence. IS emerged, tentacle-like, in that last phase, initially amid eminently local dynamics (Iraq post-2003 and Syria post-2011) but only to use that dual base as a reinforced and better-controlled springboard to redeploy its efforts externally. Only this time, it was done with greater ease within an enabling environment of social sectors from the West migrating to it (the foreign fighters), others emulating its violence in the heart of the Western metropolis (the Kouachi brothers, the Tsarnaevs and similar actors), as well as Muslim and Western states increasingly displaying authoritarianism towards their populations in the name of opposing the new IS threat. Such circularity of the transnational terrorism pioneered by Al Qaeda and upgraded by IS ushered in a new dimension of this discussion, where post-colonialism meshes with post-globalisation revealing what post-modern violence is beginning to mean. Simply put, at this stage the meaning of dominant contemporary political violence is violence shipped back to its exporter. Al Qaeda, IS and their avatars-in-the-making are but post-modern symptoms of a larger post-colonial dynamic that has been transformed by the refund patterns offered by globalisation.

Return to Sender

When Al Qaeda crashed the world stage of global politics on that fateful Tuesday in September 2001, unleashing its terrorism in New York and Washington, the world embarked on a decade during which it was systematically treated to explanations of that group which highlighted its irrationality, religious fundamentalism and barbarity. In the context of a mental horizon dominated by the accretion of emotional commentary and ideological amplification, the study of Al Qaeda remained for a long time confined to the boundaries of journalistic accounts and policy planning. When academe fought its way in, it also erred by going down the road of Islamic theology and neo-Orientalist readings of a group whose instrumentalisation of Islam always ranked secondarily to its political and martial agenda. Lost in that translation were the functional innovations and behavioural displacements introduced by the first transnational non-state armed group in history, its offsetting reinventing of political violence, its influence on both a new generation of privatised terrorism (from the Islamophobe Anders Breivik to the Kouachi brothers by way of US Sergeant Malik Nidal Hassan and the Tsarnaev schoolboys) and a novel type of self-empowered armed group which would come to control vast territories in Iraq, Afghanistan, Syria, Libya, Mali, Somalia, Nigeria and Yemen. The Salafist ideology of IS was endlessly dissected, while the group's *modus operandi* was neglected analytically, and proceeded to alter the parameters of early twenty-first-century international relations. Logics of 'eradication' and 'termination' dominated such journalistic, policy and scholarly discourse, and at the occasion of Bin Laden's anticlimactic disappearance (following the largest manhunt in history; his number two is still on the run), Al Qaeda was decreed defeated, decimated and finished. Seldom had a narrative of closure been so misleading.

When, three years later, IS announced that it was becoming the Caliphate, that same sequence of analysis was reopened. Familiar 2000s arguments reappeared in the 2010s, again advancing savant theses about the motivations of this new entity and gauging the levels of its 'Islamicity' and its violence. It was no small paradox that after years of planetary discussion of Al Qaeda and dozens of explicit discourses by their respective leaders, we were now asking the very same set of questions about IS. In truth, the reification of a documented story of the predictable maturation of a promethean Al Qaeda franchise-gone-local-and-moving-to-surpass-its-begetter into an inscrutable Islamic group driven solely by blind violence, partakes of a logic of avoidance of the political. To be certain, Al Qaeda spoke repeatedly of the Caliphate as an aspiration, and IS formally pursued it in statements and deeds. Yet even if both were 'religious' groups, there were many other irredentist entities of which the same could be said, because religion per se (more generally and beyond the Middle East and North Africa) has come to occupy a central place in the new conflicts, with one-third of countries experiencing a 'religious conflict' of one form or another. Furthermore, such an intensified interface between religion and global politics is a historical phase resulting from specific interlinked episodes over the past decades, namely the slowing down and eventual end of the Cold War, the 1979 revolution in Iran, the Soviet invasion of Afghanistan and the related rise of transnational Islamism, 9/11 and its international impact, the United States' invasion of Iraq and the opening of the Pandora's box between Sunna and Shi'a. If the readability of IS as a religious actor is warranted, it is primarily because there is a universal background of increased, religion-driven and religion-dominated conflicts, rather than because it has a unique *modus essendi*.

The importance of IS rests elsewhere, in three impactful and challenging dimensions very much of this world. First of all, the degenerated consequences of an Iraqi society preoccupied with and occupied by war for three decades since September 1980. The combined aftermath of Saddam Hussein's devastating wars in the 1980s, the UN's cruel 1990s embargo and the United States' cancerous invasion and occupation in the 2000s have cumulatively monstered an Iraqi generation bent on destruction and self-destruction, with lasting societal dystrophies. Second, the accelerated statisation of the armed group which IS has become has inspired other groups (such as Boko Haram and Ansar Beit al Maqdis), and the concomitant destatisation of states (in Iraq, Syria, Libya and Yemen) has yielded a fluid state-society grammar to which the international community has so far primarily responded with problematic interventions that have made matters worse. Finally, the ability of what once was, successively, Jama'at al Tawhid wal Jihad

(1999–2004), AQI (2004–6) and ISI (2006–13) to invoke and revoke Al Qaeda and be reborn as ISIL (2013–14) and then as IS (2014–), with an ambition to re-establish an Islamic Caliphate defunct since 1924, has ushered in a second stage in the transnationalism pioneered by Al Qaeda. The paradoxical, simultaneous pursuit of a territorial ambition (in the Levant) and a globalised influence (40 pledges of allegiance and/ or support in the two years between June 2014 and June 2016) reveals a hybrid entity-in-the-making; one that is internally transformed by an open-ended interface between radical Islamists, thousands of über-ideologised and disenfranchised youth coming from around the world, Syrian militants bent on bringing down Bashar al Assad, former Ba'athist officers driven by Tikriti revenge and Baghdadi hoodlums tortured in US and Shi'a prisons, all sporadically allied with Arab tribesmen with financial rewards and community control on their mind. Problematically, such complexity is reduced to musings on the religiosity of the group, non-consequential debates about the group's appellation, conspiratorial thinking about its genesis and premature announcements of its defeat. A more textured understanding of IS takes us into post-colonialism, with a critique directed at the lack of recognition of the political and historical nature of the movements observed – as well as the 'deadly configuration of humans and technology external to the state' that such groups represent.[3] However, the classical post-colonial perspective can itself be of limited use in trying to make sense of the IS phenomenon, since it carries an anchoring in peripherality,[4] whereas IS as discussed in Chapter 4 is a manifestation that equally proceeded from the centre. IS fundamentally calls, therefore, for an additional forward-looking reading, as it is undergirded by modernity. In that sense, its creative use of communication technologies should not come as a surprise:

Indeed, marginality can produce an extraordinary degree of intelligence, not to speak of organising ability. These processes do not apply only to industrial countries. … Whole countries are more marginal today than they were at independence from colonialism. Such situations provide the raw materials, and in abundance, for the recounting of loss, of specifying grievances, of deprivation of life and liberty, the stuff of storytelling, the playgrounds for cosmocrats and prophets and the mytho-logics on which violence depends.[5]

The incubation of the IS feedback loop is then an affair of long standing. Upon close examination, there is a longer history of violence imported back to the metropolis, of which the IS saga is arguably just the most recent and transformed episode – the novelty being that this latest phase of the process is done at the hands of the subaltern. World War I was, for instance, linked directly to the colonial wars which immediately preceded it. After World War II, colonial hegemony was 'silently' repackaged. As Frank Furedi argued[6] – examining diplomatic and newspaper correspondence during the 1930s to 1950s – the relaxation of racist disposition during that phase was linked to the restlessness of the colonies. Subsequently, the 'emergencies' in Malaysia, Kenya, Aden and Indonesia served as the matrix for Northern Ireland, and the methods which the British had used in their colonies in the 1950s – in Kenya[7] and Malaysia – to put down the Mau Mau Uprising and the Malayan Emergency rebellions against their rule were used in counter-terrorism measures in Ireland in the 1970s. Both Great Britain's response to the intensification of the Irish Republican Army actions in the 1970s and France's reaction to terrorism on its soil from the 1980s onwards, were influenced by these two countries' respective colonial histories. Whether from the 1920s to the 2000s in Iraq, or from the British Mandate in Palestine in the 1940s to the trouble in Ireland, the British military experience – internment, indefinite detention without trial and blunt use of force – has been mirroring itself regularly in these conflicts,[8] as was the case with the road from Vietnam to Iraq for the United States. Preoccupied for 50 years with the Cold War, the West dealt with the Global South in a way that maintained the status quo. With the end of the Cold War, a new dynamic was unleashed. Saddam Hussein solved the riddle for George H. W. Bush, as the coincidence of his invasion of Kuwait in August 1990 with the fall of the Berlin Wall nine months earlier pre-emptively filled a strategic post-Communism void-in-the-making. The larger identity behind 'Saddam' was then available to further build the narrative from the Red to the Green menace – and that in turn fuelled Bin Laden's project, as he himself stated in his 1996 and 1998 declarations of war against the United States that set the stage for IS.

From this perspective, it becomes clear that the Al Qaeda-initiated and IS-perpetuated terrorism from the periphery played out against a deeper historical and political background. Awareness of the colonial past, bitterness as to post-colonial dynamics and resentment towards the local repressive regimes were carried over and linked to contemporary situations – notably in Iraq – wherein the notion of revenging occupation and manipulation was featured regularly in the pronouncements of almost all the actors associated with Al Qaeda and IS. Such *lex talionis* logic was expressed in the titles of the video messages released by IS in 2014–17 (e.g. *Punish Them with an Equal Punishment*; *If You Return, We Shall Return*; *If You Punish, Punish as You were Punished*; *An Appropriate Reward*) just as it was heard in Bin Laden's speeches delivered between 2002 and 2006 ('Reciprocal treatment is part of justice', 'Just as you kill, you will be killed. Just as you bomb, you will be bombed', 'Our actions are but reactions to your acts', 'Just as you lay waste to our nation, so we shall lay waste to yours', 'For every action, there is a reaction'). In time, this logic travelled to the transnational agents of IS per the group's biformity (see Figure 4.1). A revealing, initially unaired exchange between one of the Kouachi brothers, Chérif, and a journalist of the French television news channel BFM illustrates this mindset. On the morning of 9 January 2015 – two days after he and his brother had conducted the attack on the *Charlie Hebdo* magazine offices, and as they were hiding in a factory near Paris – Chérif Kouachi answered a telephone call placed to the warehouse by Igor Sahiri, a member of the French news station's editorial team, who then had the following conversation with him:

> *Chérif Kouachi*: We just tell you that we are the defenders of the Prophet and that I was sent – I, Chérif Kouachi, by Al Qaeda in Yemen.
>
> *BFM Journalist*: OK.
>
> *Kouachi*: I went over there and I was financed by Sheikh Anwar al 'Awlaqi.
>
> *Journalist*: OK. When was this, roughly?
>
> *Kouachi*: A while ago. Before he was killed [on 30 September 2011].
>
> *Journalist*: OK, so you came back to France recently?
>
> *Kouachi*: No, a long time ago. Don't worry. I know how to do things properly.
>
> *Journalist*: OK, and now there's only the two of you, you and your brother?
>
> *Kouachi*: That's not your problem.
>
> *Journalist*: Do you have other people there with you?
>
> *Kouachi*: That is not your problem.
>
> *Journalist*: OK. And you intend to kill again in the name of Allah? Or not?

Kouachi: Kill whom?

Journalist: I don't know. It's a question I'm asking you.

Kouachi: Did we kill civilians during these two days that you have been looking for us?

Journalist: You killed journalists.

Kouachi: No, but did we kill civilians or people? Were we bloodthirsty during these two days that you were looking for us? Do you hear me?

Journalist: Wait Chérif, have you killed anyone this morning?

Kouachi: But we are not killers ... We are defenders of the Prophet. We do not kill women. We kill no one. We defend the Prophet. Those who offend him, there's no problem we can kill them. But we don't kill women. We are not like you. We are not like you. It is you that kill the children of Muslims in Iraq, in Syria, in Afghanistan. That's you. That's not us. We have codes of honour, us, in Islam.

Journalist: But you took vengeance nonetheless ... You killed twelve people.

Kouachi: That's right. Because we took vengeance. That's it. You said it all. We took vengeance. Exactly. There you go, you said it yourself; because we took vengeance.

The shipping back of colonial and interventionist violence is an unfinished and open-ended process. Echoes of that interfaced and deforming experience are still ringing, distilling a legacy in ways that are societally, socially and humanely unexpected. Reflecting on the newly empowered US immigration officers enforcing the 2017 discriminating 'Muslim ban' under the Donald Trump administration, one analyst noted:

For people who witnessed the American wars in Afghanistan and Iraq, such an aggressive stance is all too familiar ... All this reminds me eerily of the words and actions by United States military officers who helped create the conditions that led to the abuses of Iraqi detainees at the notorious Abu Ghraib prison ... Even the language is similar. On 14 August 2003, as the Iraqi insurgency was mushrooming, an Army officer in the Human Intelligence Effects Coordination Cell at American military headquarters in Iraq sent out a directive saying that 'the gloves are coming off regarding these detainees'. In case that wording left any doubts, he added, 'We want these individuals broken.'[9]

Such domestic imperialisation of the republic, as witnessed in the case of the rise of American authoritarianism, is arguably a by-product of the proto-colonial administration of Iraq a decade earlier. The more the US behaved in a colonial way, the more the colonised adopted violent reactions reminiscent of the colonial era and influenced others around the world, but also provided a narrative that could be picked up by the likes of Michael Adebolajo in London and Chérif Kouachi in Paris. In opposing the West so brutally and so radically – with professionally planned, take-no-prisoner, ultra-violent terrorism – IS furthered this sequence and repurposed it according to its specific state-building design. In the event, the notion of empire can no longer be seen euphemistically as a distant memory – merely in a sanitised logic of ornament – and the fundamentally dichotomising nature of colonialism, as Frantz Fanon identified it long ago, starts being replayed in remixed ways.[10] And so, if well into the twentieth century and more so as this new century started, the West continued to think imperially,[11] today the counter-imperial thinking of an insurgent, terrorising and militarised type has materialised, thickening the plot.

In the name of anti-terrorism, after 9/11 the United States launched a process of renewed imperialism under the guise of the GWOT, which came back to haunt and endanger it and a large segment of the West with it. Besides IS's own Al Qaeda-forged and independently produced ambition to terrorise the West, as seen in Chapter 1, the path chosen to face the problem of terrorism was constitutive of a strategic entrapment that had culminated a decade after 9/11 in imperial hubris amid IS's rise. The fetishisation of killing itself – as a way to rid oneself from terrorism – had been on display since the early days of the 9/11 aftermath and has continued ever since, with presidents boasting in that regard. 'I am a war president', declared President George W. Bush in February 2004, to which President Barack Obama added, in September 2011, that he was 'good at killing', while President Donald Trump declared enthusiastically in February 2016 that he would 'approve torture in a heartbeat' and 'bring back waterboarding and a hell of a lot worse', and in January 2017 added that 'torture works'. With the War on Terror reported in a way that emphasised national security over civil liberties, that process forged ahead, facilitated by ethical disconnect. An army veteran who was a contract interrogator in Iraq in 2004, and who admitted torturing prisoners in Abu Ghraib, noted the apathy he faced when talking about the things American soldiers carried out in Iraq: 'It was my first encounter with a generation that d[id] not consider the release of the Abu Ghraib photographs to be a critical moment in their lives ... Abu Ghraib will fade. My transgressions will be forgotten.'[12] In effect, the two most important events in the historical socio-genesis of IS – the torture at Abu Ghraib and the hanging of Saddam Hussein – are absent from mainstream Western public memory today. Indeed, they are arguably, psychologically speaking, repressed memories among IS itself. Their imprint is, however, most visible in the manner in which the group performed its violence. Orange jumpsuit there, orange jumpsuit here. The beamed message of reciprocal treatment was made more obvious as IS captors waterboarded four Western hostages in August 2014, which they explicitly staged in video messages. As IS pursued its terrorism campaign, it further influenced the cementing, rationalisation and normalisation of the garrison state in the West. From Archibald Paton Thornton's *The Imperial Idea and its Enemies*, published after the Suez affair in 1956, to Niall Ferguson's *Empire*, released after 9/11,[13] enthusiasm for imperial order has often been manifested in the aftermath of political setbacks lived through by the metropolis. In 1993, in an article entitled 'Colonialism's Back and Not A Moment Too Soon', Paul Johnson wrote in the *New York Times Magazine* that: 'There simply is no alternative in nations where governments have crumbled and the most basic conditions for civilised life have disappeared.' In 2015, Robert Kaplan maintained in *Foreign Policy*, that 'imperialism bestowed order ... The challenge now is less to establish democracy than to re-establish order.'[14]

In such a context, where history so consequentially and multifacet-edly determines their interface, IS and the West can be seen as caught in a dance of mutual implication and rejection, which Elizabeth Povinelli captured indirectly when discussing what she termed the 'governance of the prior':

From the point of view of the governance of the prior – the priority of the prior across political, market and social relations – the indigenous does not confront the state, nor does the state confront the indigenous. Both are caught in *strategic manoeuvres of temporalisation and territorialisation* around this problematic because the nation-state and the indigenous share a set of vital organs originating in a history that pre-dates their emergence even as this history of the present, and in the present, continually foregrounds that these organic transplants are subject to an intense and complex immunity crisis.[15]

The past is here not merely a prologue to such hubris and counter-hubris. The incessant mechanisation of death and its staging are going hand in hand with the dehumanising techniques of the past, allowing for their reintroduction in an updated terrorism format. In expanding its dominion, the West has created the conditions of an improvised, updated and mutated use of technology by its enemies, which today take the form of self-empowered non-state armed groups present abroad and increasingly in the West itself. The texturing of the new violence has moved beyond the Norman Rockwellisation of the colonial distant to the Instagramisation of the metropolitan local. The multiplicity of interlocking conflicts that presided over IS's birth were ultimately transcended by the consequences of that violence. The stage was set for the next wave of terrorism, one in which past and present would meet in original ways.

Future Pasts of IS

In the face of the resilience of IS, in 2015 analysts started considering the possibility of its victory and entertaining the idea of affording it diplomatic recognition.[16] Such assessments were as hasty as the earlier dismissals had been – for example, in January 2014 President Obama assessed the rising IS group as 'a jay-vee [junior varsity] team' not on the level of Al Qaeda.[17] IS cannot win in a classical military sense and granting it diplomatic recognition is impossible. More important was the historical sequence that had played out, framing the global interaction and leading to such assessments of what ultimately is but an armed group. By the end of the 2010s, the world had lived two full decades dominated by the theme of terrorism. Al Qaeda in the 2000s and IS in the 2010s were the lead actors of this period. The global scene had *de facto* been coloured 'terrorism' for almost 30 uninterrupted years. During this time, the movements themselves, as discussed, experienced important and accelerated transformations. The Arab Afghans gave birth to Al Qaeda, which mutated into a second version that launched regional versions, which in turn allowed one of these offshoots, IS, to rise and transcend the two initial structures. That entity, IS, then stood complex, multifaceted and multilayered, in turn harbouring several different identities (see Table 3.3). With none of the different dimensions of IS overtaking the others – the local Iraqi and Syrian insurgents and the incoming foreign fighters pursued a set of goals, each ascribing priority to different aspects of their struggle – it emerged that the mix of that sort of loose terrorist vortex was becoming cemented as a form of violence in and of itself. A type of terrorism building and gathering momentum in the periphery, but not remaining there and all the time moving back and forth on the centre–periphery continuum. As Paul Rogers noted, IS is a window into the future:

[W]e are moving into an era of revolt from the margins ... In this global context, we should not see ISIS as a specific movement that must be confronted and destroyed, believing that, once this is achieved, all will be well. This view misses the point. Rather, the way in which ISIS has spread and evolved into a transnational movement should be seen as an instance of a phenomenon that is likely to be repeated in the future, perhaps in very different circumstances that stretch far beyond the Middle East ... This means that understanding the process of evolution as it applies to ISIS has a more general relevance.[18]

At the core of that geo-spatial evolution stood another determinant back and forth, namely the historical relationship between these Western and Southern worlds, and the double genesis of the now-merging violence. From the Arabian Peninsula's Ikhwan in the 1910s to the Levantine Jabhat al Shaam in the 2010s, armed non-state groups have remained a feature of Middle Eastern and North African politics and conflicts for a century. Similarly, Islamists have long had a networked presence in the West, notably in Europe.[19] However, the 40-year Al Qaeda-IS saga was really set in motion as interventionism – first in Afghanistan by the Soviets in the 1980s, then in Iraq by the US in the 1990s and 2000s, then in Syria by the US and Russia in the 2010s – came of age and became a contemporary, unrestrained practice. The first part of that exercise ended with 9/11 – a momentous event itself constituting a culmination and a beginning. The second act was filled with reactions to that attack. We are today at the end of a long, convoluted and plot-thickening third act. The circulation of that violence produced an inner sequence whereby Afghanistan (1979) led to Al Qaeda, Iraq (2003) led to IS – which led to the home-grown do-it-yourself Western terrorist. Logically, the trend of boomeranged terrorism is bound to increase in the next phase. The unceasing conflicts abroad and the deepening alienation at home are continuously fuelling rebellious violence, and the inventiveness that comes with the current generation will provide further possibilities for its constant reimagination, but one that also borrows from the past and is influenced by it (as attested to by the recurrence of vehicles ploughing into civilians in 2016–17). The back and forth of the metropolis–periphery interface is, in effect, where these actors have clashed and met. The global circulation of violence was also present in earlier eras, and cases of Southern influence had certainly materialised before. For instance, the asymmetrical methods which inspired the extreme-left European groups of the 1970s, as a result of the writings and actions of the Vietnamese, Chinese and Argentinian leaders Ho Chi Minh, Mao Zedong and Che Guevara, had been pioneered earlier in northern Morocco by Abdelkrim al Khattabi in 1921 during his insurgency against the Spanish occupation.[20] Similarly, by looking at the 1960s and 1970s as long-gone eras whose violence is not relevant to current processes, we miss the sense in which they were the first terrain of internationalised, post-colonial violence. The 2010s are a follow-up to these ignored, suppressed and marginalised historical memories.[21] As the United States started 'monstering' people in Iraq in 2003, it opened the door to the political travesty that would come to fruition 15 years later and acquire lethal agency, with IS acting against these histories and in turn empowering operators around the world, notably in the heart of Western countries.

IS is characterised by extreme violence, performed at levels that Al Qaeda had never attempted – with the exception of al Zarqawi, who unsurprisingly is the historical leader IS most often refers to. Beheadings and other atrocities were regularly committed by the group. Among many extreme acts throughout those years, a paroxysm of sorts was reached in February 2015 when a video (*A Message Signed with Blood to the Nations of the Cross*) showed the decapitation of 21 Coptic Christians on the shores of Libya, and another (*Healing the Believers' Chests*) showed a Jordanian air force pilot, Muath al Kasasbeh, whose plane had crashed near Raqqa, caged and burned alive. On the Western side, the new/old violence features *Rambo*-like returning soldiers carrying trauma and violence from the wars in Iraq and Afghanistan, but it also features novel profiles of the urban insurgent and the corporate military contractor doubling-up the constantly expanding militarisation of security. A declassified 2009 report by the United States Department of Homeland Security noted the potential terrorist threat represented by some returning war veterans, highlighting their combat skills: 'These skills and knowledge have the potential to boost the capabilities of extremists – including lone wolves or small terrorist cells – to carry out violence. The willingness of a small percentage of military personnel to join extremist groups during the 1990s because they were disgruntled, disillusioned or suffering from the psychological effects of war is being replicated today.'[22] In between, regionally, IS influenced the rise of armed groups and confirmed the destatisation playing out across the Arab world. In Iraq, a coalition of militias known as Al Hashd al Sha'abi (the Popular Mobilisation Forces), comprising 120,000 men, was set up in July 2014 to battle the organisation. In Syria, al Baghdadi's group squared off with Hezbollah (in Lebanon itself in the Bekaa Valley in May 2015) and several other new Syrian groups that had emerged after 2011 in opposition to Bashar al Assad's regime. In Libya it spawned offshoots, notably Ansar al Shari'a. And in Yemen, the Houthis rode the Iraqi-Syrian group's geostrategic moment according to their own mode and for their own purposes as they reactivated their local irredentist struggle in August 2014, leading within months to a full-scale war with Saudi Arabia (which had conducted a first incursion against the Houthis in November 2009). Beyond, in West Africa, groups like Boko Haram became attracted to IS, carrying their own unresolved colonial history that was now being turned on to their own societies.

What has been the overarching net effect of this sequence, and how has this political violence transformed the global order? As regards the West, this has poisoned the daily life of many Westerners now living amid normalised fear and routinised conflict, with an augmented segment succumbing to explicit and unapologetic racism towards Muslims, including fellow nationals of their countries reflexively associated with terrorism. The effects of this siege mentality and of this militarisation of life are insidious, and are bound to colour the next phase of modernity, as captured by Stephen Graham:

The crossover between the military and the civilian applications of advanced technology – between the surveillance and control of everyday life in Western cities and the prosecution of aggressive colonial and resource wars – is at the heart of a much broader set of trends ... Of course, the effects observed in the urban Western setting differ wildly from those seen in the war-zone. But, crucially, whatever the environment, these hi-tech acts of violence are predicated on a set of shared ideas. Fundamental to the new military urbanism is the *paradigmatic shift* that renders cities' communal and private spaces, as well as their infrastructure – along with their civilian population – a source of targets and threats. This is manifest in the *widespread use of war as the dominant metaphor in describing the perpetual and boundless condition of urban societies* – at war against drugs, against crime, against terror, against insecurity itself. This development incorporates the stealthy militarisation of a wide range of policy debates, urban landscapes and circuits of urban infrastructure, as well as whole realms of popular and urban culture. It leads to the *creepy and insidious diffusion of militarised debates about 'security' in every walk of life.* Together, once again, these work to bring essentially military ideas of the prosecution of, and preparation for, war into the heart of ordinary, day-to-day life.[23]

New discourses about terrorism and practices of war and securitisation work today to problematise (urban) life per se. Crucially, this occurs in telescopic ways that intimately link cities in the metropolitan and capitalist heartlands with those on colonial frontiers and peripheries.[24] A permanent narrative about terrorism and an unrestrained practice of war have taken over culturally, socially and politically across the globe. IS thus came to occupy a logical place in such a new world, choreographed here and there since 9/11 in a way that has the terrorist play the role of permanent threat to the megapolis (a role, we should recall, IS assigned itself), with surveillance, vigilantism and terrorism interlocked. Again, Al Qaeda had influenced that process in real life and in fiction – for instance, in the Christopher Nolan-directed *The Dark Knight* (2008) instalment of the popular Batman film series, the Joker character was an obvious metaphor for Osama Bin Laden issuing ultimata to the people and authorities of Gotham/New York forcing them to make existential choices about survival,[25] while foreshadowing the more militarised, hybrid and post-modern local/foreign terrorism of the Bane character in the sequel *The Dark Knight Rises* (2012). Indeed, just as 'the battlegrounds of colonial order lay as much on African soil as in the publications written by the participants in the war once they have returned home',[26] the contemporary dynamics of post-colonial terrorism are equally shaped by the representations in books and films produced upon 'return'. In effect, the terrorist of the future will increasingly blend fiction and reality and be himself or herself the product of the difficulty to distinguish real life from its representation. Not merely finding inspiration in it, the future terrorist will come to regard fiction as the very terrain to produce his or her violence. (On 20 July 2012, a gunman, James Eagan Holmes, dressed in military clothing, conducted an attack on a film theatre in Aurora, Colorado screening *The Dark Knight Rises*, detonating grenades and using multiple firearms, killing twelve people.)[27] Paradoxically, violence is thus celebrated artistically and metaphorically, and denounced and feared when displayed too close for comfort. *Star Wars* filmgoers cheer the destruction of the Death Star battle station by a group of rogue ragtag insurgent Alliance Rebels led by ancient warriors believing in a mystical religion and fighting an asymmetrical war, not seeing the irony that in effect the Death Star is the Pentagon, Coruscant is New York, Senator Palpatine is Bush and Bin Laden is reminiscent enough of the old and reclusive Obi-Wan Ben Kenobi hiding in the desert. The public is in effect cheering for the very fictionalised terrorists they will fear upon exiting the movieplex – or indeed *in* popcorn *situ*, as did a woman in Italy who called the police after seeing a veiled Muslim woman filmgoer texting 'suspiciously' during a screening.

The imperial vision has produced its terrorism antidote. The emergence of a non-state actor's absolutist and violently extremist opposition, such as the one displayed by IS, took place in the context of the consolidation of the early twenty-first century neo-imperial national security state. Self-focused linear writing of history has combined with state-centred perspectives to render the mapping of the elusive IS political phenomenon very difficult. The trends prevalent in *non*-understanding the group – except in terms of its violence (not the interventionist or torturing ones that partially birthed it) or in terms of identify and faith (rather than politics) is indicative of an intellectual dead end, reached well before the organisation materialised. *End of History* and *Coming Anarchy* narratives holding hands in the 1990s came to frame logically the *Road Warrior*-flavoured imagery discussion on IS 20 years later. In this context, the argument about empires advancing in fits of absent-mindedness is misleading. In infusing civilian life with military logic and artefacts – starting off when the 1991 Gulf War's Humvee became a fashion and status statement as the civilian Hummer car marketed by AM General – the US military in effect opened a gate that could be 'reversed', literally, with the hacking by IS of Centcom's Twitter account in January 2016. The increasingly incestuous relationship between the elements of war and those of peace and the incorporation of the former into the private lives of citizens – a zeitgeist Nick Turse captured as the militarisation of MySpace in the context of a Dolce Vita War on Terror with Starbucks in Gitmo and iPods in iRaq[28] – facilitated what the so-called lone wolves would come to embody. As Karen Dawisha notes:

Such an [imperial] expansion may, in the fullness of time, prove to have been irrational or unwise, but the original impulse to expand has to have been a conscious one on the part of the elites designed to serve what elites perceive to be state interests. Moreover, a policy of imperialism pursued by the centre is, of course, unlikely to be advertised as such, but it is important nevertheless to include in one's conceptualisation of imperialism the effort by one country to wrest formal sovereignty by another.

As Dawisha adds: 'Discerning intent is particularly important in the case of those states which have a heritage of imperial behaviour or which are geographically large and economically powerful. Failure to consider the motivation of elites in the metropole, therefore, would lead one to blur the conceptual distinction between, for example, French policies in Algeria before and after independence.'[29] To not do this, and link it to an understanding of IS, is to continue to foster conceptual limitations as we go into the next phase of these issues.

The new terrorism will be fuelled by the apathetic tolerance and acceptance of the securitisation logic, as it became cemented in the first 20 years of this century under the pretext of putting down the terrorism performed successively by Al Qaeda and IS. As surveillance has become glamorised and the militarised state popularised through skilful control, futuristic fictions with fascist imagery – such as the science-fiction film *Starship Troopers* (1997), featuring soldiers fighting giant bugs in desert campaigns – become a narrative whose iconography can now be understood at face value, and its second degree lost. The new terrorism will thus want to punish its own society – echoing its Anarchist ancestor – while equally seeking publicity and one's Warholesque 15 minutes of fame. If Al Qaeda ever resurfaces it will be under the leadership of Bin Laden's son, Hamza (born in 1989) – who has already issued five statements since 2015 (on 13 August 2015, on 11 May and 12 July 2016 and on 13 and 20 May 2017) threatening the West – or someone claiming a direct nominal legacy. (Entitled 'We Are All Osama', Hamza Bin Laden's July 2016 message gave an indication of the anchoring of his project into the father figure of the movement and the importance attached to lineage.) If, for its part, IS re-emerges in the future, it will be under a logic of reappropriation and reinterpretation, with groups possibly leading it from anywhere in the world, featuring potential names such as the New Islamic State, the Real Islamic State or indeed Islamic State in the United States.

Pensamiento Nuevo on Terrorism

Paradoxes abounded as IS pursued its project, apparently dictating the terms of engagement but gradually losing control of its destiny by virtue of its actions – just as Al Qaeda had. It can be maintained that in effect IS lost control of its own story the moment it called upon those in the West to rise up – that is, at its formal birth on 29 June 2014. The willed incorporation of that dimension was not merely about numbers or soldiery; it brought with it another, different and unexpected story. The coexistence of the middle aged former Ba'athist officer with the youngster from the French suburbs could not remain steady and cogent in the coproduction of violence, and carried with it the seeds of an inevitable transformation of the IS entity – an evolution which would, more importantly, play on the international dimension. In that sense, IS was intimately and inherently hybrid and Western as much as Oriental, and its statist architecture – for all its anchoring in colourful Islamic history – more modern and Western.

Above and beyond its specific history, or the complexity, mutation and novelty it has displayed, IS has raised the deeper question of understanding terrorism contemporaneously. Slowly, throughout the 1990s and in accelerated fashion in the wake of the 9/11 attacks, an internationalised 'politicisation of expertise'[30] around terrorism has come to frame thinking on terrorism in increasingly dogmatic, taboo-filled and self-referential terms preventing a proper, clinical social sciences discussion of what has been developing as a consequential remaking of international affairs. The resulting discussion on terrorism, and the misleading safety of the familiar which this debate carries, are the products of a specific historical moment and the continuation of an earlier, conceptually incomplete construct of international relations. In either mode, this does not help the social scientist grasp the meaning of what new violence is playing out, and indeed how past violence shaped it. More insidiously, the previous offerings prevent that search by avoiding the obvious political questions raised by political violence. The discussion on terrorism is similarly stuck in a dynamic whereby positions and assumptions confine most analysts to Manichean logics of bipolarity; attack and defence, rise and fall, emergence and disappearance, us and them. Alongside one-dimensional official pronouncements and sensationalistic journalistic stories, the dominant, think tank analyses function on a mode that principally documents the dangerousness of the terrorists and offers advice as how to combat and defeat them. Primarily as a result of such heavy-handed push, another group of analysts, while bringing more context, flesh out the complexity of the environments in which these terrorists operate or came into being, but also end up discussing the groups themselves atomistically and the ways to neutralise them. In either mode, the discussion is excessively actor-led (us or them), immediate (the urgency of the policy questions) and driven by a desire to close the problem (by terminating, one way or the other, the trouble-maker). A third difficulty, noticed earlier in the cases of both the nationalist terrorism of the 1950s and the transnational Islamist terrorism of the 2000s, is the manner in which the terms of the discussion proceed top-down, North-South and centre-periphery, with terrorism qualitatively identified as a threat to the former set of (developed and democratic) nations proceeding from the (underdeveloped and dangerous) lands of the latter. If, in recent years, many in the South – among both state and civil society actors – have displayed a discourse about terrorism close enough to their partners in the North, it remains the fact that terrorism is overwhelmingly associated with the 'troubled spots' of the South, and specifically with the most recent phase in the Middle East and with Islam. In effect, any thinking on what terrorism is and what it is today is paralysed by these three anchors.

Such analytical self-limitation is no longer tenable. Its cementing in recent years, as IS vigorously pursued its design and as counter-terrorism increasingly turned authoritarian, risks producing a new generation of researchers that do not even see or entertain the possibility of thinking beyond those specific configurations of the discussion. Breaking through the current dumbed-down, formulaic, actor-specific, politically sanitised, culturalist, commercial, Manichean, racialised and a-historical representation of terrorism is an urgent intellectual project. Building on the Argentinian philosopher Rodolfo Kusch's concept and the discussion of his work by Walter Mignolo,[31] what must be embarked on, in such a context, is a form of *pensamiento proprio* on terrorism – that is, independent and comparative critical thinking on political violence derived from full, non-culturalised intellectual agency and away from the ambient politicisation and securitisation of the topic. Such a project would not be a subjective and reactive interpretative framework, but rather an attempt at deciphering what terrorism – beyond the sterile and ultimately circular debates on its definition or subjectivity – has come to encompass two decades into the twenty-first century and several generations after the Russian Anarchists linked that violence with modernity. Elaborating this new matrix, a *pensamiento* – not merely *proprio* but also *nuevo* –

on terrorism implies the articulation of a new 'regime of knowledge', to use another related concept developed by Hamid Dabashi.[32] At the heart of this exercise stand the twin challenges of coming to terms with the political power of the term itself and the tensions of the dominant articulations of 'terrorism' and 'counter-terrorism'.[33] The violence of IS lays at our feet the responsibility of deciphering and attempting *an enabling delinking* of this sort to help further thinking on violence as it mutates before our eyes in the North and in the South. The dominant conceptual framework that exists about terrorism is not easy to engage with in such a project, as it is resistant, protected by policy, convenient for media representations and further anchored in a deeper and more problematic construct of international relations. The latter aspect is where the intellectual battle must be fought. International affairs, as they are taught today, do not adequately take account of their own historical lineage and eschew that interrogation as a non-issue, which prevents us from identifying newcomers such as IS. Specifically, the spatio-temporalities that international relations established historically are Eurocentric and, as such, do not allow for a proper representation of time and space as they are conceived – particularly as regards conflict – and as they are occupied by actors from elsewhere.[34] Similarly, the disappearing and erasing of colonialism from the contemporary international affairs discussion prevents a granular mapping of violence, new and old. The question of colonial domination has, for instance, shifted from the moral and political field to the study of its diversity and its administrative practices. Current developments make it imperative to reintroduce discussion about the former, namely the history and ethics behind current policies of the great powers and the political dynamics underscoring them, inasmuch as they generate counter-violence that is now taking the form of transnational militarised terrorism. The mutation of the conflict scene and of terrorism itself also explains, in a historicised way, the so-called 'nexus' question, because the increased interface between terrorism and criminality in recent years also has a deeper history. Where terrorism went up in the post-9/11 period, the interface similarly increased, notably in the Sahel and in the Middle East, with more and more influence on the cartels' *modus operandi*, as witnessed from Ciudad Juárez to Raqqa by way of Marseilles and Kidal.[35]

Such a proposed episteme is not about (Southern) emancipation or independence, it is about inquiry proper and laying an objective claim on conceptualisation and codification – an inquiry into terrorism that would seek to decipher its nature, not remain indexical, derivative and ultimately compromised by the politics it is meant to study. What, in effect, can we ultimately say about the political violence in the South beyond its *anti*-nature? What silences or unexplored knowledges are still beyond the reach of the analyst as he or she looks into Algiers circa 1957, Munich 1972, New York 2001, Paris 2015 or London 2017, beyond the desire to punish through killing? What dwells into those clashes? Can a *post*-post-colonial frame be built beyond the confines of an identity and finger-pointing critique, standing on its own? Structural racism constitutive of international relations, which also presided over the birth of international law,[36] had provided context for the discussion of the emerging challenge posed by radical violent Islamism since the 1980s. In such a context, where critical thought is regarded suspiciously – particularly as regards security issues – the mapping has proceeded according to a combination of amnesia and absence of accountability.[37] These two aspects cannot be overstated – and are indeed understated, if not invisibilised in technocratic terrorology and a-historicised security studies more broadly. In truth, when it comes to terrorism generally and IS more specifically, metropolis-centric standards remain largely unquestioned. They suffuse this discussion, as interaction is still considered to be one way. The travails of Western societies, put under pressure by the terrorist violence and by hordes of migrants, are carefully considered in analyses that discuss the limits of cosmopolitanism, economic imperatives and the evolving rights of a citizenry in a democracy – but seldom is attention given to the original non-Southern human security impulse of that migration or the deeper political sources of that violence. However, in and of itself, and for all its urgent need, critique of these problematic limits remains inevitably derivative, taking its cue on that most elusive 'T' thing from imperial politics and securitisation. The fullness of the conceptualisation of the terrorism issue and the panorama of its overarching performance must lie elsewhere and cannot be limited to their – admittedly legitimate, as one prerogative – interpretation by the Western metropolis; or indeed confined to a Southern reactive critique of that interpretation (equally legitimate, as another's prerogative). Beyond hubris and paraphernalia, the greener pastures of intellectual penetration that comparatively map a new socio-historical topography of the political violence conundrum lie ahead for the social sciences. Theorising IS, rather than storytelling or merely documenting its obvious terrorising violence, can help us make sense of these larger and more important issues. Such efforts can lead us beyond, to question the dominant gaze on this group and see in it signs of our times, whereby violence moves back and forth, power is uncertain, discourse is virtual, meaning is evanescent, strategy is elusive and trajectories are uncontrollable. These larger issues stand at the heart of the discussion on terrorism and possible ways to understand IS.

Glossary

ansar	companions
'asabiyya	social solidarity, cohesion, consciousness
ba'ath	renaissance
bay'a	oath of allegiance to a leader
caliph	head of Muslim community; used in the succession after the Prophet
da'wa	Islamic proselytising
dawla	state
din	religion
diwan, dawawin	department(s)
emir	leader, commander, ruler
fard	religious obligation
fatwa	religious ruling
fedai, fedayeen	combatant(s), usually associated with Palestinians in the 1970s
fitna	dispute; antagonism between Muslims at beginning of Islam
hijra	migration, journey
idara	administration
imam (Sunni)	worship leader or scholar; no clergy status
imam (Shi'a)	political and religious leader of the community; leading status
istikhbarat	intelligence services
jazeera	island
jihad	struggle
jizya	religious taxation
junud	soldiers
kaffir, kuffar	unbeliever(s)
kataeb	brigades
khilafa	caliphate
madrassa	school; often associated with religious or Qur'anic schools
maghreb	western part of the Arab world; the North African states
mashreq	eastern part of the Arab world; Nile Valley, the Gulf and the Levant
minbar	pulpit
muhajir	migrant fighter

mujahid	Muslim holy warrior
mukhabarat	intelligence services
munadhil	fighter, combatant
muqawama	resistance
murtad	apostate
nahda	awakening
nasheed	anthem
nidham	regime, system
qabila	tribe
qaeda	base
qawma	rising
qutriya	regionalism
salab	path
salafism	conservative reform branch in Sunni Islam
shaqi	toughman
shari'a	Islamic religious law from the Qur'an and the Prophet's sayings
sharif, shurafa	nobleman/men usually associated with descendants of the Prophet
shaykh	elder, leader, governor; connoting age, wisdom and leadership
Shi'a	second-largest denomination of Islam
sulta	power
Sunna	largest denomination of Islam
taghout, tawagheet	religiously illegitimate ruler(s)
takfir	excommunication
tareeq	way, avenue
tawahoush	savagery
tawhid	effort at religious unity
thawra	revolution
'ulama	Muslim scholars
umma	Islamic nation or collective community
'unf	violence
'uruba	Arabhood
watan	country, homeland
wataniya	patriotism
zakat	alms

Chronology

1979

24 December   The Soviet Union invades Afghanistan.

1984

Abdallah Yusuf al 'Azzam, later joined by Ayman al Dhawahiri and Osama
Bin Laden, establishes the Maktab al Khadamat in Peshawar, Pakistan,
to raise funds and recruit foreign *mujahedeen* to fight against the Soviet
Union in Afghanistan.

1988

11 August   Osama bin Laden and associates set up Al Qaeda during a
              meeting in Peshawar, Pakistan, with Ayman al Dhawahiri,
              Abdullah al 'Azzam and Sayyed Imam al Sharif. The stated
              ambition of the group is to keep *jihad* alive after the defeat
              of the Soviet Union in Afghanistan.

1989

15 February   The last Soviet Union troops withdraw from Afghanistan.

December   Abu Mus'ab al Zarqawi travels to Afghanistan to join the
              mujahedeen. He works initially for an Islamist newspaper,
              Al Bunyan al Marsous, and later receives training at the Sada
              camp, in eastern Afghanistan, run by Mohamed Atef, Al
              Qaeda's military chief.

1993

January   Abu Mus'ab al Zarqawi returns to Jordan.

Autumn   Abu Mus'ab al Zarqawi, along with cleric Abu Mohammad
              al Maqdisi, establish the militant group Bay'at al Imam in
              Jordan.

1994

29 March   Jordanian Security Services arrest Abu Mus'ab al Zarqawi
              for his participation in Bay'at al Imam and for possession of
              explosives and weapons.

1996

27 November   A Jordanian court sentences Abu Mus'ab al Zarqawi to 15
              years in prison.

1999

18 March King Abdullah II of Jordan releases Abu Mus'ab al Zarqawi from prison as part of a general amnesty for political prisoners.

Summer Abu Mus'ab al Zarqawi travels to Pakistan where he is briefly imprisoned by the Pakistani authorities and has his visa revoked.

October Abu Mus'ab al Zarqawi moves to Kabul, Afghanistan, following his release from prison.

12 December Jordanian police arrest 16 Al Qaeda militants planning to bomb four tourist locations in Jordan around the time of the millennium. Abu Mus'ab al Zarqawi is involved in planning the attacks.

Late Abu Mus'ab al Zarqawi establishes a militant training camp in Herat, Afghanistan, reportedly with US$200,000 of seed money given by Osama bin Laden. The camp allegedly trained fighters for his new militant group Jama'at al Tawhid wal Jihad (Organisation of Monotheism and Jihad).

2001

11 September In an Al Qaeda-organised operation conducted by 19 kamikazes, two hijacked planes destroy New York's World Trade Centre Twin Towers and another plunges into the Pentagon. A fourth hijacked plane crashes in Pennsylvania. Close to 3,000 people are killed.

7 October The United States and the United Kingdom launch military operations in Afghanistan aimed at removing the Taliban from power. Al Jazeera airs a taped message by Osama Bin Laden: 'America will no longer be safe'.

2 December A Sudanese national fires a Stinger missile at a US aeroplane inside the Prince Sultan airbase in Saudi Arabia.

12 December Abu Mus'ab al Zarqawi flees from Afghanistan with a number of his followers and establishes himself in Mashad, Iran by January 2002.

22 December A British national of Sri Lankan origin, Richard C. Reid, attempts to blow up American Airlines flight 63 from Paris to Miami, using C-4 explosives inserted in one of his shoes.

2002

11 February The Jordanian Security Court sentences Abu Mus'ab al Zarqawi to 15 years in prison *in absentia*, for his participation in the failed millennium attacks on four tourist sites in Jordan.

28 March	Abu Zubayda, senior member of Al Qaeda and coordinator of the August 1998 attacks on the US embassies in Nairobi and Dar es Salaam, is arrested in Faisalabad, Afghanistan.
March	Abu Mus'ab al Zarqawi arrives in Baghdad to receive medical treatment and stays for at least two months to fully convalesce.
11 April	A truck bomb attack is conducted by Tunisian Islamist Nizar Naouar against the Al Ghriba synagogue on the island of Jerba in Tunisia, killing 21 individuals, including 14 German tourists.
8 May	In Karachi, Pakistan, a bomb explodes in front of the Sheraton Hotel killing 14 individuals, eleven of whom are French naval construction engineers.
14 June	A bomb explodes in front of the US consulate in Karachi killing twelve people and wounding 45.
5 July	An Egyptian national opens fire on the offices of the Israeli airline El Al at Los Angeles airport killing two individuals.
9 September	Al Jazeera airs a videotape in which Bin Laden details the 11 September 2001 operation and the identity of its 19 perpetrators.
6 October	A bomb attack takes place against a French oil tanker, the Limburg, near Sana'a, Yemen.
8 October	A group of American soldiers is attacked on the island of Failaka near Kuwait City, Kuwait. One US soldier is killed.
12 October	A bomb attack takes place at a nightclub in Bali, Indonesia, killing 202 people, mostly Australian tourists.
28 October	Abu Mus'ab al Zarqawi organises the assassination of Laurence Foley, an American diplomat, outside his home in Amman, Jordan.
12 November	Osama Bin Laden delivers an audio speech in which he declares to Western governments: 'As you kill, you shall be killed'.
21 November	In Kuwait City, a Kuwaiti policeman fires on two US soldiers, gravely wounding them.
28 November	In Mombasa, Kenya, two SAM-7 missiles are fired on a Boeing 757 of the Israeli charter company Arkia. Simultaneously, a car bomb attack takes place outside the Paradise Hotel where several Israeli tourists reside. The assault kills 18 individuals including three Israelis.

30 December	Three US physicians are killed in Jibla, south of Sana'a in Yemen, by a Yemeni university student.

2003

21 January	A US citizen is killed and another wounded during an ambush near Kuwait City.
1 March	Khaled Sheikh Mohammad, planner of the 11 September attacks, is arrested in Rawalpindi, near Islamabad, Pakistan.
5 February	Colin Powell, the US Secretary of State, labels Abu Mus'ab al Zarqawi as a link between Al Qaeda and Iraqi President Saddam Hussein, during a speech before the United Nations Security Council making the case for waging war against Iraq.
20 March	The United States and the United Kingdom invade Iraq.
9 April	Baghdad falls to the US Army.
12 May	In Riyadh, Saudi Arabia, the Al Hamra residential complex, housing Americans and Britons, is the target of three bomb attacks, which kill 39 individuals including twelve US citizens; 149 are wounded.
16 May	In Casablanca, Morocco, 14 suicide bombers conduct five simultaneous attacks on the Belgian Consulate, the Spanish cultural centre (Casa de España), an Italian restaurant (housed in the Hotel Farah-Maghreb) and the Israeli Circle Alliance; 45 people are killed and 100 wounded.
5 August	A car bomb targets the Hotel Marriott in Jakarta, Indonesia, killing 15 and wounding 150.
7 August	Jama'at al Tawhid wal Jihad detonate a truck bomb outside the Jordanian Embassy in Baghdad. Seventeen people die and at least 40 people are injured.
19 August	A Jama'at al Tawhid wal Jihad suicide bomber drives a truck bomb into the headquarters of the United Nations Assistance Mission in Iraq. The United Nations' Special Representative in Iraq Sergio Vieira de Mello is killed in the attack along with 21 others.
29 August	Jama'at al Tawhid wal Jihad detonate two car bombs outside the Shi'a Imam Ali Mosque in Najaf. The attack injures 500 and kills at least 95 people including Ayatollah Mohammad Baqir al Hakim, the leader of the Shi'a political party Supreme Council for the Islamic Revolution in Iraq.
8 November	In Riyadh, Saudi Arabia, a bomb attack targets a residential building housing foreign diplomats; 17 individuals are killed and 120 wounded.

12 November	Jama'at al Tawhid wal Jihad detonates a truck bomb outside the Italian paramilitary police headquarters in Nasiriya, Iraq. Twenty-two people are killed, including 17 Italian soldiers, and more than 100 are injured.
15 November	In Istanbul, Turkey, a truck bomb attack takes place against two synagogues, killing 24 and wounding 300.
20 November	Two car bombs target the British Consulate and the British bank HSBC in Istanbul; 27 people are killed and 400 wounded.

2004

2 March	On the day of 'Ashura, a holy day in Shi'a Islam, nine Jama'at al Tawhid wal Jihad suicide bombers blow themselves up in Karbala, Iraq, killing 120 people. In Baghdad, three Jama'at al Tawhid wal Jihad car bombs are detonated outside the Kadhimiya shrine, killing 58 people. Both attacks are followed by sustained mortar and rocket fire and more than 500 people are injured in the two operations.
6 April	Abu Mus'ab al Zarqawi releases an audiotape online claiming responsibility for a number of attacks, including the United Nations' bombings. A Jordanian court sentences Abu Mus'ab al Zarqawi and six others to death *in absentia*, for the killing of Laurence Foley in October 2002.
11 March	Four simultaneous attacks, claimed by the European wing of Al Qaeda, take place in Madrid. Between 7.39 and 7.55 am, ten bombs planted in four different trains explode at the Atocha, El Pozo, Alcalá de Henares and Santa Eugenia stations killing 190 and wounding 1,434 individuals.
15 April	In an audio message aired by the Arabic satellite channels Al Arabiya and Al Jazeera, Bin Laden renews his commitment to fight the United States and offers to 'cease operations' against those European countries that would stop 'aggressions against Muslims'. The truce proposal is rejected by European leaders.
28 April	The American TV show *60 Minutes* publishes photos of US Army soldiers and CIA personnel committing human rights violations, including torture, sodomy and sexual abuse, against detainees in the Abu Ghraib prison in Iraq.
1 May	An oil refinery in Yanbu, Saudi Arabia, is attacked by gunmen targeting senior executives at the facility, partly owned by Exxon Mobil. Five foreigners are killed, including two Americans.

11 May   The website Muntada al Ansar airs a video titled *Abu Mus'ab al Zarqawi Slaughters an American*. The five-minute video shows al Zarqawi beheading American hostage Nick Berg, a freelance radio-tower repairman, and threatening further deaths as retaliation for the torture at Abu Ghraib prison.

17 May   A Jama'at al Tawhid wal Jihad car bomb kills Ezzedine Salim, the president of the Governing Council of Iraq, in Baghdad.

29 May   In Khobar, Saudi Arabia, gunmen attack a building housing Western companies' offices killing 22 individuals.

18 June   A Jama'at al Tawhid wal Jihad car bomb targets the new Iraqi army recruitment centre in Baghdad. Thirty-five civilians are killed and 145 wounded. US engineer Paul M. Johnson Jr is abducted and beheaded in Jeddah, Saudi Arabia.

22 June   Al Jazeera receives a video showing Jama'at al Tawhid wal Jihad decapitating South Korean hostage Kim Sun-il. The group had kidnapped Sun-il in Fallujah, Iraq on 30 May and demanded that South Korea withdraw its 660 medics from Iraq and cancel plans to send 3,000 more soldiers to Iraq, in return for Sun-il's release.

July   The US government increases the bounty for information leading to Abu Mus'ab al Zarqawi's capture from US$10 million to US$25 million.

1 August   Six Jama'at al Tawhid wal Jihad car bombs target Christian parishioners as they are leaving evening mass at two churches in Mosul and Baghdad. Twelve people are killed and 71 injured.

14 September   A Jama'at al Tawhid wal Jihad car bomb hits a market in Haifa Street, Baghdad, near a police station. The attack kills 47 people and wounds 114.

7 October   Jama'at al Tawhid wal Jihad posts a video online showing the beheading of British hostage Ken Bigley. Jama'at al Tawhid wal Jihad had previously released three videos showing Bigley directly calling on British Prime Minister Tony Blair to intervene and release all Iraqi female prisoners held by the International Coalition.

27 October   Abu Mus'ab al Zarqawi swears a *bay'a* (pledge of allegiance) to Osama bin Laden. Jama'at al Tawhid wal Jihad is renamed Tandhim Qaedat al Jihad fi Bilad al Rafidayn, commonly known as Al Qaeda in Iraq (AQI).

7 November	American and Iraqi troops begin a two-month operation, codenamed Operation Fajr, to take control of Fallujah from AQI and other insurgent groups. A total of 107 American, British and Iraqi soldiers die and 613 are wounded during the battle, while around 1,200 militants are killed and another 1,500 captured.
December	Abu Bakr al Baghdadi is released from Camp Bucca detention centre, where he was held as a civilian detainee for eight months. (A different possible date for al Baghdadi's release is September 2009, see below.)

2005

30 January	Elections are held for the National Assembly of Iraq. AQI launches over 100 attacks on polling stations, killing over 44 people.
2 April	AQI attacks the US-run Abu Ghraib prison with two suicide car bombs and combined grenade and small arms fire. Two American soldiers are killed and approximately 44 are wounded in the attack.
7 July	Coordinated explosions take place in three underground trains and one double-decker bus in central London, killing 56 people and injuring 700. AQI releases a video stating that it had killed Egypt's ambassador to Iraq, Ihab El-Sharif.
9 July	Ayman al Dhawahiri, the deputy leader of Al Qaeda, sends a letter to Abu Mus'ab al Zarqawi encouraging him to stop publicising AQI attacks on the Shi'a and to tone down the group's enforcement of Sharia law.
23 July	Three bombs are detonated in the Egyptian resort city of Sharm el Sheikh, killing 63 people. Two of the bombs target resort hotels housing Western tourists and the third goes off in the city's marketplace.
19 August	Attackers fire Katushka rockets in the Jordanian port city of Aqaba, narrowly missing a US Navy ship, and killing a Jordanian security guard in a dockside warehouse. Two rockets are fired into the nearby Israeli port city of Eliat, causing minor damage.
14 September	Abu Mus'ab al Zarqawi releases an audio tape declaring an 'all-out war' against the Shi'a in Iraq, on the same day that AQI launches a dozen attacks on Baghdad, killing 160 people.
1 October	Three suicide bombers strike tourist restaurants in Bali in Indonesia, killing 20.

9 November	Three AQI suicide bombers detonate themselves at the Radisson SAS, Grand Hyatt and Days Inn hotel in Amman, Jordan. Sixty people die and 115 are injured in the attacks.
29 December	AQI militants fire rockets on Israel, killing five soldiers.

2006

7 January	Al Jazeera airs a message by Ayman al Dhawahiri in which he claims that George W. Bush has lost the war in Iraq.
15 January	The website Hanin.net announces the creation of the Mujahideen Shura Council, a coalition of six Iraqi Sunni insurgent groups, including AQI. Abu Mus'ab al Zarqawi is appointed the leader of the council.
19 January	In an audiotape message aired by Al Jazeera, Osama Bin Laden offers a truce to the United States and threatens new attacks inside the United States.
22 February	AQI detonates two bombs in the al Askari Mosque, the third-holiest site in Shi'a Islam, located in Samarra, Iraq. No one is injured but the bombings spark sectarian clashes, in which over 1,000 people die within the first week after the attack.
30 January	Al Jazeera airs a video message by Ayman al Dhawahiri in which, referring to Bin Laden's 19 January statement, he declares: 'Osama Bin Laden offered you a decent exit from your dilemma but your leaders insist on throwing you in battles'.
25 April	Al Jazeera airs a half-hour videotape recording of Abu Mus'ab al Zarqawi, shown with his men in the Iraqi desert, in which he refers to the truce offer made by Bin Laden to the United States ('our leader Osama Ben Laden may Allah protect him, had offered you a long truce. It would have been better for you and those who are with you if you had accepted, but your arrogance pushed you to refuse'). In the same message, al Zarqawi also indicates plans to establish 'an Islamic State' (*dawla islamiya*) in Iraq.
28 April	Al Jazeera airs a videotape message by Ayman al Dhawahiri, originally posted on a website, in which he claims that AQI has conducted 800 operations in three years and that this effort has 'broken the back of the United States' in Iraq.
20 May	Nouri al Maliki is appointed prime minister of Iraq.
7 June	Abu Mus'ab al Zarqawi and several of his men are killed by a US airstrike on a house near Baquba, Iraq. Abu Hamza

	al Muhajir is appointed the new leader of the Mujahideen Shura Council.
16 June	The Mujahideen Shura Council kidnaps two American soldiers from a checkpoint in Iraq.
1 July	Al Jazeera airs an audiotaped message by Bin Laden in which he calls on Abu Hamza al Muhajir to pursue attacks on Americans.
12 July	The sixth Arab–Israeli war starts. It takes place between the state of Israel and the Lebanese non-state, armed group Hezbollah and lasts 33 days.
September	Thirty Sunni tribes in the Anbar province in Iraq form the Anbar Awakening Council in order to fight the Mujahideen Shura Council. The group is later integrated into the US Army's surge strategy.
11 September	Al Dhawahiri announces that the Algerian Islamist organisation originally set up in 1998 and known as the Salafist Group for Preaching and Combat has joined the ranks of Al Qaeda.
15 October	The Mujahideen Shura Council announces the creation of the Islamic State in Iraq (ISI), with Abu Omar al Baghdadi as its first Emir. Abu Hamza al Muhajir shortly after announces the disbanding of the Mujahideen Shura Council in favour of ISI.
December	ISI declares Baqubah city, in the Diyala province, as its capital.
30 December	Saddam Hussein is executed by hanging in Camp Justice, a joint Iraqi-American base, on Eid al Adha, the holiest celebration day for Sunni Muslims.

2007

10 January	US President George W. Bush announces a new 'surge' strategy in Iraq, providing 20,000 additional US soldiers to Baghdad and Anbar provinces in order to remove Sunni insurgents, including ISI.
11 January	The Salafist Group for Preaching and Combat announces that it is formally changing its name to Al Qaeda in the Islamic Maghreb (AQIM).
18 June	After engagements had started in March, around 8,000 US and Iraqi troops begin Operation Arrowhead Ripper, a five-month operation to rout ISI from Baqubah.

25 June	An ISI suicide bomber attacks a meeting of Anbar tribal leaders at the Mansour Hotel, Baghdad. Thirteen people die in the attack.
14 September	ISI assassinates Sheikh Abdul Satter Abu Risha, the leader of the Anbar Awakening Council, and threatens to kill other tribal leaders who cooperate with US or Iraqi government forces.
22 October	Al Qaeda's media branch, Al Sihab, releases an audio message of Osama Bin Laden addressed to the Iraqi people.

2008

8 January	Multinational forces launch the seven-month Operation Phantom Phoenix in Diyala, Salah al Din, Kirkuk and Nineveh provinces to oust remaining elements of ISI from these areas. During this operation 890 ISI militants are killed and more than 2,500 captured.
13 January	The Iraqi parliament passes legislation allowing former members of Saddam Hussein's Ba'ath Party to be employed by the state and the military.
25 March	Muqtada al Sadr, leader of the Shi'a militia Mahdi Army, launches a nationwide civil disobedience campaign, following a crackdown by Prime Minister al Maliki and the Iraqi security forces.
2 June	Al Qaeda claims the bombing of the Danish embassy in Pakistan in which six people perish. Al Qaeda in Afghanistan and Pakistan leader Mustapha Abu al Yazid issue a statement indicating that the attack was in retaliation for the publishing in Denmark of cartoons negatively depicting the Prophet Mohammad.
29 July	A Pashtu-language Pakistani television channel reports that deputy Al Qaeda leader Ayman al Dhawahiri was killed in a 28 July US airstrike on a *madrassa* in the Pakistani tribal belt along the Afghan border. The information is not confirmed.
1 September	The US hand control of the Sunni-majority Anbar province to the Iraqi government.
17 November	The US and Iraqi governments sign the US-Iraq Status of Forces Agreement, stipulating the withdrawal of US troops from all Iraqi cities by 30 June 2009 and a complete withdrawal of all US troops from Iraq by the end of 2011.
26 November	In a series of coordinated attacks lasting three days across Mumbai, India, Lashkar-e-Taiba militants landing in

speedboats kill 164 people in two hotels, the city's train station, a café, a Jewish centre, a hospital and the port area.

2009

7 January	US Army Major Nidal Malik Hassan, who had been in contact with Al Qaeda in the Arabian Peninsula (AQAP) cleric Anwar al 'Awlaki, kills 13 people at the US Fort Hood military installation in Texas.
19 August	ISI launches three coordinated car bombs and mortar strikes on the Iraqi Foreign and Finance Ministries in Baghdad. At least 101 people die in the attack and 550 are injured.
27 August	A suicide bombing by AQAP targeting Saudi Arabia's Assistant Interior Minister is thwarted in Riyadh.
September	The US releases Abu Bakr al Baghdadi from Camp Bucca prison, when the entire camp is officially closed down. (A different possible date for al Baghdadi's release is December 2004, see above.)
25 December	A Nigerian national, Umar Farouk Abdulmuttalab, with connections with the AQAP, attempts to trigger a bomb on board Delta Flight 253 flying from Amsterdam to Detroit.

2010

18 April	The US launches an airstrike on an ISI safe house near Tikrit, Iraq, killing both Abu Hamza al Muhajir and Abu Omar al Baghdadi.
1 May	A US national and budget analyst of Pakistani origin, Faisal Shahzad, attempts a foiled car bombing in Times Square, New York.
16 May	Abu Bakr al Baghdadi is named as the new leader of ISI.
27 October	Al Jazeera airs a statement attributed to Bin Laden in which he threatens to attack France if French troops do not leave Afghanistan.
29 October	Two mail packages containing explosives are discovered on board cargo planes bound from Yemen to the United States. AQAP claims the foiled operation.
31 October	ISI fighters launch an attack on the Our Lady of Salvation Syriac Catholic Church in Baghdad with explosives and light weapons, killing 58 people and injuring 78. An ISI announcement states that the attack was in revenge for an Egyptian Muslim convert who was being held against her will in a Coptic Christian church in Egypt.

2011

2 March	Arid Uka, a Kosovo Albanian living in Germany, shoots and kills two United States Air Force airmen at Frankfurt airport.
2 May	The United States announces that in Abbottabad, Pakistan, US Navy SEALs have stormed a compound, killing Osama bin Laden and four other people.
3 June	In Hama, Syria, around 50,000 people participate in 'Friday of the Children' protests against the Syrian regime. The protest was sparked by the Syrian army's killing a number of children in Dar'aa for spraying anti-government graffiti on the town's walls.
16 June	Al Qaeda announces formally that Ayman al Dhawahiri has been appointed as its new leader.
August	Abu Bakr al Baghdadi sends a cell of ISI fighters to Syria, led by Abu Mohammad al Jolani, in order to establish a new Syrian branch.
4 October	The US Department of State names Abu Bakr al Baghdadi as a 'specially-designated global terrorist' and offers a reward of US$10 million for information about his location.
18 December	The last 500 US troops leave Iraq, completing the withdrawal of US combat troops. The next day Shi'a Prime Minister Nuri al Maliki issues an arrest warrant for former Sunni Vice President Tariq al Hashemi on charges of running a death squad that killed Shi'a political opponents. The Sunni bloc in parliament begins a boycott that brings the government to a standstill.

2012

23 January	In Syria, Abu Mohammad al Jolani formally announces the creation of his group Jabhat al Nusra li Ahl al Shaam (Support Front for the People of the Levant).
20 March	ISI launches a wave of mortar, improvised explosive device, car bomb and shooting attacks across ten cities in Iraq, including Baghdad, Kirkuk and Ramadi, targeting Shi'a civilians and security institutions. Fifty-two people are killed and over 250 are injured.
21 July	Abu Bakr al Baghdadi announces the launch of ISI's 'Breaking the Walls' campaign, aiming to both target institutions of the Iraqi government and free ISI members from government prisons. Over the course of a year, ISI

conducts six prison breaks and 24 car bomb attacks against government institutions.

28 December   Tens of thousands of Sunni Iraqis participate in 'Friday of Honour' protests across ten cities against the sectarian policies and actions of Shi'a Prime Minister Maliki's government.

2013

8 April   Abu Bakr al Baghdadi releases an audio statement online announcing that Jabhat al Nusra has always been a subsidiary of ISI and that the two groups are merging to form Islamic State in Iraq and Syria (ISIS).

9 April   Abu Mohammad al Jolani rejects the merger and claims that Jabhat al Nusra was created by ISI. Al Jolani reconfirms his pledge of allegiance to Ayman al Dhawahiri and Jabhat al Nusra's loyalty to Al Qaeda.

9 June   Al Jazeera publishes a letter written by Ayman al Dhawahiri to the leaders of Jabhat al Nusra and ISIS. Al Dhawahiri states that Abu Bakr al Baghdadi was wrong to announce the merger without alerting Al Qaeda's leadership and declares the merger between the two groups to be invalid. Al Dhawahiri orders ISIS fighters to return to Iraq and sends Khaled al Suri to act as a mediator between the two groups.

15 June   Abu Bakr al Baghdadi releases an audio statement online rejecting the orders of Ayman al Dhawahiri to break up ISIS and to confine his activities to Iraq, stating that 'I have chosen the command of my lord over the command in that letter which contradicts it'.

9 July   ISIS gunmen assassinate one of the leaders of the Free Syrian Army, Kamal Hamimi, in Lattakia, Syria.

21 July   ISIS launch an attack on Abu Ghraib prison using twelve car bombs, in combination with mortar and rocket fire. ISIS successfully breaches the prison walls, allowing over 800 prisoners to escape. Abu Bakr al Baghdadi announces the end of the 'Breaking the Walls' campaign immediately following this attack.

29 July   ISIS announces the beginning of its new military campaign, 'The Soldiers' Harvest'. This campaign has the twin aims of controlling territory and targeting Iraqi government security forces.

5 August	ISIS fighters overrun government forces and take control of the Menagh Air Base outside of Aleppo, Syria.
September	ISIS takes control of Azaz city, Syria, from Free Syrian Army fighters.
22 November	Seven Sunni Islamist groups, including Jaysh al Islam and Ahrar al Shaam, form a new alliance called the Islamic Front in order to protect themselves from attacks by both ISIS and the Syrian regime.

2014

4 January	ISIS takes control of the majority of Fallujah and kills over 100 people, displacing thousands of residents.
February	ISIS ousts rebel groups from the remaining contested districts of Raqqa, Syria and subsequently designates Raqqa as its capital in Syria.
3 February	Ayman al Dhawahiri publishes a letter stating that Al Qaeda has severed all links with ISIS and that it does not agree with and is not responsible for ISIS's actions.
23 February	ISIS assassinates Khaled al Suri, the cleric sent by Ayman al Dhawahiri to mediate between ISIS and Jabhat al Nusra, in a suicide bomb attack in Aleppo.
April	ISIS launches a mobile application called 'Dawn of Glad Tidings' on the Google Play Store. The application allows ISIS to send tens of thousands of tweets each day from participating Twitter accounts and orchestrate advanced social media campaigns on Twitter.
24 May	Mehdi Nemmouche, a French national of Algerian origin, shoots and kills three people at the Jewish Museum of Belgium in Brussels. Nemmouche spent one year fighting in Syria and recorded a video prior to the attack pledging his allegiance to ISIS.
5 June	ISIS forces in Iraq and Syria begin their northern Iraq offensive by attacking Samarra, in the Salah al din province, and briefly taking control of the university and municipal building, before being repelled by the Iraqi government.
4 June	Approximately 1,500 ISIS fighters launch a seven-day operation to take control of Mosul, Iraq, from around 30,000 government forces stationed in the city.
10 June	ISIS takes full control of Mosul with the capture of Mosul International Airport and the desertion of the last remaining Iraqi security forces. ISIS loots the Mosul Central

Bank and seizes US$429 million. Around 500,000 Mosul residents flee the city during ISIS's offensive.

11 June   ISIS fighters, travelling in around 60 vehicles, continue their advance from Mosul by attacking Tikrit and Baiji simultaneously. In Baiji, ISIS takes control of the majority of the town, except its oil refinery, before retreating the next day. ISIS takes full control of Tikrit, the birthplace of Saddam Hussein and capital of the Salah al din province, and releases 300 prisoners.

12 June   ISIS continues its advance and seizes ten cities in the Salah al din province. ISIS executes 1,500 Shi'a government forces based in Camp Speicher, Tikrit.

23 June   ISIS captures Tal Afar airport and the town itself.

24 June   ISIS seizes control of the Baiji oil refinery, which produces a third of Iraq's oil output, after ten days of fighting with Iraqi security forces and the final desertion of 400 soldiers from the Iraqi army 37th Brigade.

29 June   ISIS posts an audio recording online declaring that it has established an Islamic Caliphate, that Abu Bakr al Baghdadi has been appointed as its first Caliph and that it has changed its name to the Islamic State (IS). The same day, the group releases two videos entitled *Breaking the Borders* and *The End of Sykes–Picot*, which show its fighters destroying several Syrian-Iraqi border posts in Qaim, Waleed and Traybil and declaring 'the end of the colonial 1916 Sykes–Picot agreement'.

3 July   IS takes control of al Omar oilfield, the largest oilfield in Syria, from Jabhat al Nusra.

4 July   IS publishes a video showing Abu Bakr al Baghdadi delivering the sermon at Friday noon prayers in al Nabi mosque, Mosul. Baghdadi introduces himself as Caliph, and calls on all Muslims around the world to join IS and unite behind him as their leader.

5 July   IS releases online the first issue of its English-language magazine, *Dabiq*.

25 July   IS overruns the 17th Syrian Division Military Base near Raqqa, Syria. IS beheads several soldiers and places their bodies in a square in central Raqqa.

3 August   IS conquers large parts of the Nineveh province and takes control of Sinjar city. The group kills over 5,000 Yazidi people during its takeover of Sinjar and takes thousands of

Yazidi women into captivity. Approximately 50,000 Yazidis flee to the Sinjar mountains where they are surrounded by IS fighters.

7 August   US President Barack Obama authorises targeted airstrikes against both IS positions threatening the city of Erbil and IS positions based around Mount Sinjar. President Obama also authorises air operations providing food and water to the Yazidis on Mount Sinjar.

13 August   The US announces that IS's siege of the Yazidis on Mount Sinjar has ended with over 50,000 Yazidis escaping due to the actions of US airstrikes and Kurdish Peshmerga fighters.

16 August   IS massacres 700 members of the Al Shaitat tribe in Deir Ezzor province, Syria, over a dispute about two oilfields.

19 August   IS's Al Hayat Media Centre releases a video showing British IS fighter Mohammed Emwazi, nicknamed 'Jihadi John' in the press, beheading US journalist James Foley in response to US airstrikes in Iraq. Emwazi also states in the video that kidnapped US journalist Steven Sotloff would be executed if the US did not stop its airstrikes against IS.

2 September   IS's Al Furqan Media releases a video showing Mohammed Emwazi beheading Steven Sotloff. The video also shows Emwazi threatening to kill British hostage David Haines if other foreign governments join the US bombing of IS positions.

10 September   US President Obama announces a new international coalition, an expansion of US air strikes in Iraq and the deployment of 475 military advisors to 'degrade and ultimately destroy ISIS'.

13 September   IS releases a video titled *A Message to the Allies of America* showing ISIS militants beheading Steven Sotloff and threatening to execute British hostage Alan Henning next.

14 September   Khaled Abu Suleiman, a leader of AQIM, announces that he is breaking with Al Qaeda and swearing allegiance to Abu Bakr al Baghdadi. He announces the creation of a new group called Junud al Khilafa fi Ard al Jazayer (Soldiers of the Caliphate in the Land of Algeria).

17 September   IS begins a major offensive to capture the Kurdish town of Ayn al Arab/Kobani, Syria.

18 September   Abdul Numan Haider injures two policemen in a knife attack in Melbourne, Australia. Haider would be later profiled in IS's *Dabiq* magazine.

19 September   French President François Hollande authorises airstrikes against IS positions in Iraq.

20 September   Junud al Khilafa fi Ard al Jazayer beheads French tourist Hervé Gourdel, whom they had previously kidnapped from the Djurdjura National Park in Kabylia, Algeria.

21 September   Abu Mohammed al 'Adnani, IS's chief spokesperson, delivers a speech calling on all ISIS supporters to attack non-Muslims in whichever country they live.

22 September   The United States, Bahrain, Jordan, Qatar, Saudi Arabia and the United Arab Emirates begin airstrikes against IS and Jabhat al Nusra positions in Syria.

26 September   The UK Parliament votes to participate in airstrikes against IS positions in Iraq.

3 October   IS publishes a video online showing Mohammed Emwazi beheading Alan Henning in retribution for the UK's bombing of IS positions. US citizen Peter Kassig is named as the next potential victim by IS.

14 October   IS captures the city of Hit, Iraq, after it was abandoned by the local Iraqi army garrison.

20 October   Martin Rouleau-Couture drives his car into two soldiers, killing one, in Saint-Jean-sur-Richelieu, Quebec, Canada. Rouleau-Couture had expressed support for IS online.

22 October   Michael Bibeau shoots and kills a soldier at the Canadian Parliament in Ottawa, Canada. Bibeau pledged his allegiance to IS in a video posted online.

29 October   IS executes 300 members of the Abu Nimr tribe in al Anbar province, Iraq.

31 October   The UN releases a report stating that 15,000 foreign fighters from 80 countries have travelled to Iraq and Syria to join IS.

8 November   US President Obama orders an additional 1,500 troops to Iraq in order to support and train Iraqi government soldiers fighting IS.

10 November   IS media outlets release five audio and text statements from groups of IS supporters in Libya, Saudi Arabia and Yemen, as well as from Junud al Khilafa in Algeria and Ansar Beit al Maqdis, a radical Islamist militant group based in the Sinai peninsula, Egypt. Each group pledges allegiance to IS and to Abu Bakr al Baghdadi as their Caliph.

13 November   Abu Bakr al Baghdadi issues an online audio statement stating that IS has created new *wilayat* (provinces) in Egypt, Saudi Arabia, Libya, Algeria and Yemen. He also

acknowledges support from IS followers in Tunisia, the Philippines, Indonesia and Nigeria, and promises to establish *wilayat* shortly in those territories.

16 November IS releases a video showing the decapitated body of Peter Kassig, killed in revenge for the US bombing of IS in Syria and Iraq.

15 December Man Haron Monis, an Australian Iranian, takes 18 people hostage for 16 hours in a café in Sydney, Australia. Monis had previously pledged allegiance to IS. He kills one hostage and he and another hostage die in the police raid.

20 December The *Financial Times* reports that IS military police executed 100 foreign fighters who attempted to leave its capital in Raqqa, Syria.

24 December IS fighters capture Jordanian pilot Muath al Kasasbeh outside of Raqqa, Syria, whose F-16 fighter aircraft crashed during a bombing sortie against IS targets.

2015

7 January Said Kouachi and Chérif Kouachi storm the offices of the magazine *Charlie Hebdo* in Paris, France and kill twelve people, injuring eleven others. They declare that they 'have avenged the Prophet', following a series of satirical cartoons on Islam published by the magazine since 2006. They escape and are killed by French police two days later at an industrial-site printing office near Paris, where they hid to escape a large-scale manhunt. Chérif Kouachi tells the news television channel BFM, on a telephone call that morning, that he had been sent by AQAP.

8–9 January Amedy Coulibaly shoots and kills a police officer in Montrouge district, Paris, France. Coulibaly subsequently takes 19 people hostage at a Kosher supermarket in Porte de Vincennes, Paris for several hours and kills four hostages before being shot dead during an assault conducted by French police. On 11 January, a video of Coulibaly is posted online in which he is seen pledging allegiance to IS and indicating that he was an acquaintance of the *Charlie Hebdo* attackers, Said and Chérif Kouachi.

9 January IS publishes an audio message praising the *Charlie Hebdo* magazine attacks in Paris.

20 January IS releases a video showing kidnapped Japanese hostages Kenji Goto and Haruna Yukawa and demand a US$200 million ransom within 72 hours from the Japanese government to secure their release.

24 January	IS publishes an image of Kenji Goto holding the decapitated head of Haruna Yukawa. IS demands the release of the arrested female Iraqi militant Sajida al Rishawi, detained in Jordan, in exchange for Kenji Goto.
26 January	Abu Mohammed al 'Adnani releases an audio statement announcing the creation of a new IS *wilaya* in Khorasan, a region historically incorporating parts of Afghanistan and Pakistan.
27 January	Kurdish People's Protection Units (YPGs) and the Free Syrian Army regain control of Kobani from IS.
31 January	IS releases a video showing the beheading of Kenji Goto.
3 February	IS's Al Furqan Media releases a video showing Jordanian pilot Muath al Kasasbeh being burned alive in a cage. The video also shows the names and addresses of other Jordanian pilots that participated in air strikes and places a US$2,000 bounty on their heads.
4 February	Jordan executes two AQI prisoners, including Sajida al Rishawi, in retaliation for the killing of Muath al Kasasbeh. King Abdullah of Jordan promises a 'relentless war' on IS and orders airstrikes against IS in Iraq.
14–15 February	Omar Abdel Hamid El-Hussein fires on three locations in Copenhagen, including the Great Synagogue and a public forum with the Prophet Mohammad cartoonist Lars Vilks in attendance, killing two people. El-Hussein pledged allegiance to al Baghdadi in a video posted on his Facebook page.
16 February	Egypt begins bombing IS targets in Derna and Sirte, Libya, in retaliation for the beheading of 21 Egyptian Coptic Christian workers by IS in Libya.
2 March	30,000 Iraqi government forces begin an operation to retake Tikrit from IS.
12 March	IS accepts the pledge of allegiance from Boko Haram, a militant group operating in Nigeria, and renames the group the West Africa *wilaya*.
18 March	Three IS gunmen attack the Bardo National Museum, Tunis, in a siege lasting more than three hours. Twenty-three people die in the attack, including 20 foreign tourists, and 36 people are injured.
20 March	Four IS suicide bombers detonate themselves in the al Badr and al Hashoosh Houthi Shi'a-affiliated mosques in Sana'a,

Yemen at midday prayers; 142 people die in the attack and over 350 are injured.

9 April   Hackers claiming allegiance to IS cut transmission to eleven channels belonging to the French television international network TV5 Monde and take control of its websites and social media accounts for several hours. The hackers publish pro-ISIS propaganda and the details of the family members of French soldiers.

12 April   IS publishes a video showing its militants bulldozing and destroying monuments in the ancient Assyrian city of Nimrud, Iraq, because of their 'un-Islamic nature'.

3 May   In Garland, Texas in the United States, Elton Simpson and Nadir Soofi fire on the entrance to an exhibition featuring cartoons of the Prophet Mohammad, injuring a police officer. Simpson and Soofi pledged their support online to IS.

15 May   IS militants take full control of Ramadi, the capital of the Anbar province, following the withdrawal of all Iraqi government troops. IS releases an audio speech by Abu Bakr al Baghdadi, after six months of silence and continued rumours about his death.

22 May   An IS suicide bomber detonates himself during Friday prayers at the Shi'a Imam Ali ibn Abi Talib Mosque in Qatif, Saudi Arabia. The attack kills 21 people and is the first IS operation in Saudi Arabia.

24 May   Following an eleven-day offensive, IS captures Palmyra, Syria, a UNESCO World Heritage Site, and its surrounding towns and villages. IS also seizes control of the Tanf Iraqi-Syrian border crossing and two gas fields.

23 June   Abu Muhammad al 'Adnani announces the establishment of a new IS *wilaya* in the North Caucasus region of Russia.

23 June   IS begins a campaign to take control of Al Hasakah city, Syria, by detonating four suicide bombers at Syrian government checkpoints.

26 June   Seifeddine Rezgui, an IS militant, attacks the Riu Imperial Marhaba tourist beach and hotel resort in Port El Kantaoui, Sousse, Tunisia with an AK-47 assault rifle. Thirty-nine people die during the mass shooting, including Rezgui – 30 of the victims are from the United Kingdom.

26 June   Abu Suleiman al Muwahhid, an Islamic State suicide bomber, detonates himself during Friday prayers at the Shi'a

al Sadiq mosque in Kuwait City. Twenty-seven people die in the attack.

16 July · IS militants in the Sinai hit an Egyptian Navy frigate with an anti-tank missile off the coast of Rafah, Sinai.

20 July · A Kurdish IS suicide bomber detonates himself outside the Amara culture centre, Suruç, Turkey. Thirty-three people die in the attack.

1 August · The Syrian army and Kurdish YPG announce that all IS militants have been pushed out from Al Hasakah following 36 days of fighting.

7 August · IS militants executes around 300 members of the Mosul Electoral Commission.

18 August · IS publically beheads Khaled al Assad, the head of antiquities in Palmyra.

20 August · IS claims responsibility for a car bomb attack on the national security agency in north Cairo, Egypt. Twenty-nine people die in the attack, including six policemen.

21 August · Passengers on a train travelling from Amsterdam to Paris subdue Ayoub El Khazzani, a Moroccan national living in Belgium with IS sympathies, who was armed with two guns, a knife and gasoline.

29 August · Turkey conducts its first joint airstrikes against IS positions after joining the international US-led coalition.

30 September · Russia begins launching airstrikes against IS and other opposition groups in Syria, from its base at Hmeimim airport, Lattakia, in response to the Syrian government's request for assistance.

5 October · IS launches a failed assault on the capital of the Deir Ezzor governorate in Syria. The operation is rebuffed by Russian airstrikes and the Syrian army who kill over 150 IS militants.

7 October · In Aleppo, Syria, IS militants kill Hossein Hamedani, the leader of the Iranian Quds Force in Syria.

10 October · The Turkish government blames IS for two suicide bomb attacks outside Ankara Central Train Station that kill 103 people. IS does not claim responsibility for the operation.

31 October · IS in Sinai, Egypt, smuggles a one-kilogram TNT bomb on to Russian Metrojet Flight 9268 travelling from Sharm el Sheikh to St Petersburg, Russia. The plane crashes in North Sinai killing all 224 people on board.

12 November US and UK drones kill Mohammed Emwazi ('Jihadi John') in an airstrike on Raqqa, Syria. Two IS suicide bombers detonate explosives at a commercial district in Bourj el-Barajneh, a Shi'a district in Beirut, Lebanon. Forty-three people die in the attacks.

13 November At 9.16 pm, nine IS attackers, working in three teams, begin a series of coordinated mass shooting and suicide bombings in Paris, France. Three suicide bombers detonate themselves outside the Stade de France during a football match between France and Germany, attended by President Hollande. Between 9.25 pm and 9.40 pm, three different assailants fire on three different restaurants and one detonates himself at the Comptoir Voltaire café in the eleventh arrondissement. At 9.40 pm, the final group of militants enters the Bataclan theatre during a concert by the US band Eagles of Death Metal and fires on concert-goers for 20 minutes, with machine guns and hand grenades. The militants take up to 100 concert-goers hostage for two hours before an intervention by the French police. In total, 137 people die in the attacks, including seven IS militants. Two escape.

14 November President Hollande orders a state of emergency in France, temporarily shuts France's borders and mobilises an additional 1,500 soldiers following the Paris attacks.

21 November The Belgian government begins an unprecedented four-day security lockdown of the whole city of Brussels following information that IS militants were planning a Paris-style attack and that Salah Abdeslam, one of the perpetrators of the attack in Paris, was hiding in Brussels.

24 November An IS suicide bomber in Tunis detonates himself next to a bus carrying members of the Tunisian Presidential Security guard. Twelve guards are killed in the attack.

2 December The UK Parliament votes to extend its airstrike campaign against IS to Syria.

2 December Syed Farook and Tashfeen Malik, a married couple living in Redlands, California, shoot and kill 14 people at the San Bernardino County Health Department Christmas party. FBI officers shoot and kill Farook and Malik four hours after the attack; both Farook and Malik were described as supporters of IS.

24 December	Two hundred members of the Somali Al Shabaab militant group split and declare their allegiance to IS and Abu Bakr al Baghdadi.
28 December	Iraqi government forces announce that they have captured Ramadi from IS following a two-month operation. Prime Minister Haider al Abadi declares 30 December to be a national holiday in celebration of the victory.

2016

7 January	IS militants detonate a truck bomb at a police training camp in Zliten, Libya. Sixty police officers are killed in the attack and over 200 are injured.
8 January	Edward Archer shoots and wounds a police officer in Philadelphia in the United States. Archer pledges his allegiance to IS when taken into custody.
12 January	A Syrian IS suicide bomber detonates himself near the Blue Mosque in Istanbul, Turkey. Thirteen foreign tourists are killed in the attack.
31 January	IS hits the Shi'a-revered Zaynab mosque in the southern suburbs of Damascus, Syria with two car bombs and a suicide bomb. Seventy-one people are killed in the attack.
21 February	The Syrian government recaptures IS-controlled villages in the Al Safira plain outside of Aleppo.
18 March	Belgian police arrest Salah Abdeslam and four other suspected IS militants in a series of raids on apartments in the Molenbeek district, Brussels.
22 March	IS conducts an attack on two sites in Brussels, Belgium, killing 32 people and wounding 300. At 7.58 am, two bombs are detonated at the opposite ends of the check-in hall (level 3) of the main terminal of Zaventem International Airport. An hour later, at 9.11 am, an explosion hits the middle of a three-carriage train at the Maelbeek metro station in the city centre, close to several European Union institutions. Two brothers, Khalid and Brahim el-Bakraoui, and a third participant, Najim Laachraoui, conduct the operation and are killed during it.
25 March	United States Defence Secretary Ashton Carter announces that the US has killed the alleged IS second-in-command, Iraqi-born Abdul Rahman Mustafa al Qaduli, in an airstrike. IS releases two videos – respectively entitled *An Appropriate Recompense* and *They Are Suffering As You Are*

Suffering – in which it claims the 22 March operations on targets in Brussels, Belgium.

26 March	The Syrian army recaptures the city of Palmyra from IS.
18 May	The Iraqi army recaptures Rutbah city, Anbar province, from IS.
22 May	Iraqi Prime Minister Haider al Abadi announces the beginning of an operation to retake control of Fallujah from IS.
12 June	Omar Mateen shoots and kills 49 people at the Pulse gay nightclub in Orlando, Florida. Mateen took nightclubbers hostage before eventually being killed by the police. Mateen swore allegiance to IS in a telephone call to the police during the shooting.
13 June	Larossi Abbala, a French national claiming allegiance to IS, stabs to death Jean-Baptiste Salvaing, a French police commander, outside his house and kills his wife, Jessica Schneider, in Magnanville, north-west of Paris. Abballa films himself live on Facebook during the situation.
26 June	The Iraqi army announces that Fallujah is under its control.
28 June	Two IS militants throw a hand grenade into a bar in Kuala Lumpur, Malaysia. Eight people are injured in the attack.
28 June	The Turkish government blames IS for an attack by three militants on Istanbul's Atatürk Airport that killed 45 people. IS does not claim responsibility for the attack.
1 July	Five IS militants attack the Holy Artisan Bakery with firearms and explosives in Dhaka, Bangladesh and take people hostage. Twenty-nine people, including the five perpetrators, die in the attack.
13 July	IS confirms that Omar al Shishani, the group's military commander in Syria, was killed in Mosul, Iraq.
14 July	Mohamed Lahouaij Bouhlel drives a truck through crowds celebrating Bastille Day on the Promenade des Anglais in Nice, France. Eighty-six people are killed in the attack and IS claimed that Bouhlel was one of its soldiers.
19 July	Muhammad Riyad attacks and injures five people on a train in Wuerzburg, Germany, with an axe. IS publishes a video of Riyad pledging his allegiance to ISIS.
24 July	Mohammed Daleel, a Syrian refugee suicide bomber, detonates himself outside a bar in Ansbach, Germany, injuring 15 people. Daleel had previously recorded a video of himself pledging allegiance to IS.

26 July	Two IS supporters, Abdelmalik Petitjean and Adel Kermiche, take a priest, three nuns and two parishioners hostage in a Catholic church in Saint-Étienne-du-Rouvray, Normandy, France. The two militants filmed themselves killing the priest at the church's altar before being eventually killed by the police.
13 August	Kurdish forces capture Manbij city, Syria, from IS fighters.
20 August	A suicide bomber detonates himself at a wedding ceremony in Gaziantep, Turkey, killing 57 people.
30 August	A US airstrike kills Abu Mohammed al 'Adnani in Aleppo, Syria.
17 September	Dahir Adan stabs and injures ten people in a knife attack at the Crossroads Centre shopping mall in St Cloud, Minnesota, United States. IS claims responsibility for the attack and states that Adan was a soldier of the Caliphate.
17 September	Ahmad Khan Rahami detonates three bombs and plants several others in New York and New Jersey, United States, injuring 29 people. Rahami had cited IS and Abu Mohammed al 'Adnani in his personal journal.
5 October	Hicham Diop attacks police officers in Brussels, Belgium, with a machete, injuring two people. Diop had been in contact with IS operatives in Syria.
16 October	Syrian opposition fighters announce they have taken control of Dabiq, Syria, from IS.
19 October	Iraqi Prime Minister Haider al Abadi announces the launch of an operation to retake Mosul from IS.
24 October	Three ISIS militants attack a police training college in Quetta, Baluchistan, Pakistan. Sixty-two people die in the attack.
31 October	Amina al Almaniyya attacks police officers in Mulheim, Germany, with a knife, injuring two. An IS flag is found in Almaniyya's belongings.
1 November	Iraqi forces enter Mosul city for the first time and begin operations to retake the city from IS by launching an assault on Mosul's eastern bank.
7 November	Kurdish Peshmerga forces announce they have gained control of the IS-held city of Bashiqa, Iraq.
24 November	An IS truck bomb detonates at a gas station filled with Shi'a pilgrims in Hillah, Iraq, killing 125 people.
28 November	Abdul Razak Ali Artan drives a car into and stabs pedestrians at Ohio State University, Ohio, United States.

Thirteen people are injured in the attack, which is claimed by IS.

10 December IS suicide bombers attack a military base in Aden, Yemen, killing 50 soldiers.

11 December IS regains control of Palmyra, Syria, following a three-day battle with the Syrian army. An IS suicide bomber detonates himself at St Peters and St Paul's Church in Cairo, Egypt, killing 29 people.

18 December IS fighters conduct a series of mass shootings in Al Kerak, Jordan, before seeking refuge in an ancient Crusader castle. Thirteen people die in the combined attacks.

19 December Anin Amri drives a truck into a Christmas market on Breitsheidplatz in Berlin, Germany. Twelve people die in the attack and IS publishes a video showing Amri pledging allegiance to Abu Bakr al Baghdadi.

2017

1 January Abdulkadir Masharipov fires on nightclubbers at the Reina nightclub in Istanbul, Turkey. Thirty-six people die in the attack and IS releases a statement claiming responsibility.

2 January Three IS car bombs detonate in a Shi'a district of Sadr City, Iraq, killing 56 people.

24 January Iraqi Prime Minister Haider al Abadi announces that Iraqi forces have captured the eastern bank of Mosul from IS and will begin a new phase to retake the IS-held western bank.

3 February Abdallah el-Hamahmy attacks and injures a guard with a machete at the Louvre Museum, Paris, France. El-Hamahmy pledges his allegiance to IS on Twitter immediately prior to the attack.

16 February An IS suicide bomber detonates himself during a Sufi ritual at the Shrine of Lal Shabaz Qalandar in Sehwan, Pakistan. Ninety people die in the attack.

23 February Syrian opposition forces announce that they have taken full control of Al Bab, Syria, from IS.

4 March The Syrian army retakes control of Palmyra from IS.

22 March Khalid Masood drives a car into pedestrians in front of the Palace of Westminster and fatally stabs a police officer. Five people die in the attack, which IS later claims responsibility for.

3 April Akbarzhon Jalilov detonates an explosive device on the subway in St Petersburg, Russia, killing 15 people. Jalilov had reportedly trained with IS militants in Syria in 2014.

7 April	Rakhmat Alikov drives a truck into a department store in Stockholm, Sweden, killing four people. Alikov pledged his support to IS and had allegedly attempted to travel to Syria in 2015.
9 April	Two IS suicide bombers detonate themselves at two Coptic Christian churches in Alexandria and Tanta, Egypt, during services celebrating Palm Sunday. Forty-five people die in the attacks.
18 April	Kori Ali Mohammad kills three people in a series of shootings in four different locations in Fresno, California shouting 'Allahu Akbar' and his 'hatred for white people', before being apprehended by Fresno police officers.
20 April	Karim Cheurfi fires on a police bus parked on the Avenue des Champs-Élysées in Paris, France. One police officer is killed and IS claims responsibility for the attack.
24 May	The 22-year-old Salman Abedi detonates a suicide bomb at a music concert by singer Ariana Grande in Manchester, England, killing 22 people, including several children, and injuring 59.
3 June	In London, three men drive a van into pedestrians on London Bridge, then run into Borough Market and stab people sitting at restaurants, killing seven and wounding 48. IS claims the attack.
16 June	The Russian Defence Ministry releases a statement in which they announce that air strikes their forces conducted over Raqqa, Syria on 28 May might have killed Abu Bakr al Baghdadi.
19 June	In London, 47-year-old Darren Osborn drives a van into a crowd near the Finsbury Mosque, killing one person and injuring eleven.
21 June	In Brussels, 36-year-old Oussama Zariouh is caught attempting an attack with explosives in the Central Station.
22 June	The Iraqi authorities circulate video footage showing the destruction of the Great Mosque of Mosul, which they blame on IS. IS accuses the United States of destroying the mosque, a claim denied by the US.

Notes

Introduction

1. Salman Sayyid, *Recalling the Caliphate: Decolonisation and World Order*, London: Hurst and Company, 2014, p. 2.
2. Eugene Scott, 'Duffy: "There's a Difference" on White Terror and Muslim Terror', *CNN*, 8 February 2017; and Katie Mettler and Derek Hawkins, 'What's Largely and Glaringly Missing from Trump's List of Terrorist Attacks: Non-Western Victims', *Washington Post*, 7 February 2017.
3. Michael V. Bhatia, 'Fighting Words: Naming Terrorists, Bandits, Rebels and Other Violent Actors', *Third World Quarterly*, 26, 1, 2005, p. 7, emphasis added.
4. The name of the group has been the subject of debate and disagreement. Initially known officially in Arabic as Al Dawla al Islamiya fil Iraq wal Shaam (Islamic State in Iraq and the Shaam/Syria/Levant) since April 2013, the group redubbed itself, on 29 June 2014, Al Dawla al Islamiya (Islamic State). It was subsequently referred to by governments, media and experts as 'ISIS', 'ISIL' or IS using English-language acronyms. An acronym derived from the original Arabic name Al Dawla al Islamiya fil Iraq wal Shaam was coined on social media and rendered as the neologism 'Daesh'. However, acronyms do not exist in Arabic and Daesh refers to an Islamic State in Iraq and the Shaam which, as noted, was replaced simply by IS in June 2014. Some media outlets in the Arab world, notably Al Jazeera, refer to the group as 'Tandhim al Dawla' (the organisation of the state). That is, however, incomplete and does not give an indication of what kind of organisation and what type of state. Arab governments, for their part, and some of their international partners argued against calling the organisation al Dawla al Islamiya (the Islamic State) as, they noted, such an appellation reflected negatively on the religion of Islam. However, calling any group by its self-identified name does not carry an endorsement of that name's ideological or political referent (as the history of terrorist groups illustrates). The present work will refer to the entity using the name it gave itself, namely al Dawla al Islamiya or Islamic State (IS).
5. Anne L. Clunan and Harold A. Trinkunas provide a useful definition of globalisation in this context as 'the speed, quantity and especially cheapness of global flows of labour, capital, production, knowledge and ideas, for which the politically-critical corollary is the diffusion of authority over people, ideas, knowledge and technologies, capital, production processes (whether of services or goods) and their respective transportation networks'. See Anne L. Clunan and Harold A. Trinkunas, 'Conceptualising Ungoverned

Spaces', in Anne L. Clunan and Harold A. Trinkunas, eds, *Ungoverned Spaces: Alternatives to State Authority in an Era of Softened Sovereignty*, Stanford, California: Stanford University Press, 2010, p. 31.

6. For an illustration of this final line of thinking, see Sam Harris and Maajid Nawaz, *Islam and the Future of Tolerance: A Dialogue*, Cambridge, Massachusetts: Harvard University Press, 2015; or Glenn Beck, *It Is About Islam: Exposing the Truth about ISIS, Al Qaeda, Iran and the Caliphate*, New York: Threshold Editions, 2015.

7. William Atkinson notes, in this regard, that 'An archeologist is always careful to preserve the immediate context of an artifact in order to establish how it was used by its makers; once we place the artifact in a collection we are using it for purposes of our own.' See his 'Bound in *Blackwood's*: The Imperialism of the "The Heart of Darkness" in Its Immediate Context', *Twentieth Century Literature*, 50, 4, Winter 2004, pp. 368–93.

8. 'The group's apocalyptic religious ideology is the key to understanding its strategy', argues Graeme Wood in 'What ISIS Really Wants', *The Atlantic*, 315, 2, March 2015, pp. 78–94, denouncing 'a well-intentioned but dishonest campaign to deny the Islamic State's medieval religious nature.'

9. On the problematic absence of such a framework, see Frank Furedi, *Invitation to Terror: The Expanding Empire of the Unknown*, London: Continuum, 2007.

10. See Branwen Gruffydd-Jones, ed., *Decolonising International Relations*, London: Rowman and Littlefield Publishers, Inc., 2006; and Tarak Barkawi, 'Decolonising War', *European Journal of International Security*, 1, 22, July 2016, pp. 199–214.

11. Isabel V. Hull, *Absolute Destruction: Military Culture and the Practices of War in Imperial Germany*, Ithaca, New York: Cornell University Press, 2005.

12. In the English language, these include: Loretta Napoleoni, *The Islamist Phoenix*, New York: Seven Stories Press, 2014; Daniel Byman, *Al Qaeda, the Islamic State and the Global Jihadist Movement: What Everyone Needs to Know*, Oxford University Press, 2014; Patrick Cockburn, *The Rise of Islamic State*, London: Verso, 2015; Jason Burke, *The New Threat: From Islamic Militancy*, London: The Bodley Head, 2015; Jessica Stern and J.M. Berger, *ISIS: The State of Terror*, New York: HarperCollins, 2015; Benjamin Hall, *Inside ISIS: The Brutal Rise of a Terrorist Army*, New York: Centre Street/Hachette Book Group, 2015; Charles R. Lister, *The Syrian Jihad: Al Qaeda, the Islamic State and the Evolution of an Insurgency*, London: Hurst & Company, 2015; William McCants, *The ISIS Apocalypse: The History, Strategy and Doomsday Vision of the Islamic State*, New York: St Martin's Press, 2015; Jay Sekulow, *Rise of ISIS: A Threat We Can't Ignore*, New York: Howard Books, 2015; Joby Warrick, *Black Flags: The Rise of ISIS*, London: Bantam Press, 2015; Michael Weiss and Hassan Hassan, *ISIS: Inside the Army of Terror*, New York: Regan Arts, 2015; Fawaz A. Gerges, *ISIS: A History*, Princeton, New Jersey: Princeton University Press, 2016; Andre Hosken, *Empire of Fear: Inside the Islamic State*, London: Oneworld, 2016; Malcolm Nance, *Defeating ISIS: Who They Are, How They Fight, What They Believe*, New York: Skyhorse Publications, 2016; Michael Morell and Bill Harlow, *The*

Great War of Our Time: The CIA's Fight against Terrorism – From Al Qaida to ISIS, New York: Hachette Book Group, 2016; Lawrence Wright, *The Terror Years: From Al Qaeda to the Islamic State*, New York: Alfred A. Knopf, 2016; Patrick Cockburn, *The Age of Jihad: Islamic State and the Great War for the Middle East*, London: Verso, 2016; Graeme Wood, *The Way of the Strangers: Encounters with the Islamic State*, New York: Random House, 2016; Zaina Karam, *Life and Death in ISIS: How the Islamic StateBuilds its Caliphate*, New York: AP Editions, 2016; and Ahmed S. Hashim, *The Caliphate at War: The Ideological, Organisational and Military Innovations of Islamic State*, London: Hurst, 2017.

13. The veracity of these documents is also seldom questioned. See Adam Taylor, 'Leaked Documents May Reveal the Inner Workings of the Islamic State: But What if They Are Fake?', *Washington Post*, 30 December 2015.

14. Irfan Ahmad, 'On the State of the (Im)possible: Notes on Wael Hallaq's Thesis', *Journal of Religious and Political Practice*, 1, 97, 2015, p. 104. Also see Iza R. Hussin, *The Politics of Islamic Law: Local Elites, Colonial Authority and the Making of the Muslim State*, Chicago: University of Chicago Press, 2016.

15. In a review of Pankaj Mishra's insightful *Age of Anger: A History of the Present* (2017), Michael Ignatieff displays these traits of paternalistic, Eurocentric intellectual intolerance. Delimiting what he sees as the acceptable and proper way of making sense of the anger of radical Islamism, he reprimands Mishra thus: 'Mishra doesn't bother with such distinctions, it seems, because he sympathises with the anger of the jihadists and believes it has some justification … *Never*, so far as I know, has a free and freedom-loving intellectual handed a gang of killers such a lofty worldview.' See Michael Ignatieff, 'Where Are We Going?', *New York Review of Books*, 64, 6, 6–19 April 2017, p. 4, emphasis added.

16. See, among many such examples, Irshad Manji, *The Trouble with Islam Today: A Muslim's Call for Reform in Her Faith*, Canada: Random House, 2003; or Timur Kuran, *The Long Divergence: How Islamic Law Held Back the Middle East*, Princeton, New Jersey: Princeton University Press, 2011.

17. The *Real Time* host was reminded by actor Ben Affleck that: America 'killed more Muslims than they've killed us by an awful lot … and somehow we're exempt from these things because they're not really a reflection of what we believe in. We did it by accident.' The show aired on the US cable channel HBO on 3 October 2014.

18. Lisa Stampnitzky, *Disciplining Terror: How Experts Invented 'Terrorism'*, Cambridge: Cambridge University Press, 2013. Building on James Ferguson's notion of 'anti-knowledge' (developed in his *The Anti-Politics Machine: 'Development', 'Depoliticisation' and Bureaucratic Power in Lesotho*, Minneapolis: University of Minnesota Press, 1994), Stampnitzky defines such a phenomenon as 'an active refusal of explanation itself', p. 187. She goes on to explain that: '[I]n the situation of anti-knowledge, knowledge and inquiry that entail knowing the terrorist are proscribed. It is as though the language of evil creates a "black box" around the terrorist, which creates

its own explanation: terrorists commit terrorism because they are evil. Any further attempt to pursue alternative explanations, thereby seeking to break the black box of "evil", is seen as a profanation, even a sacrilege. The roots of the politics of anti-knowledge is hence that, if terrorists are evil and irrational, then one cannot – and indeed *should not* – know them' (p. 189, italics in original).

19. After his takeover in Egypt in 2013, General Abdelfattah al Sisi had the Muslim Brotherhood (which had officially renounced violence in 1971) declared a 'terrorist group', and violently clamped down on them. In the United States, following attacks on policemen in 2016 (following repeated shootings of unarmed African Americans), a petition was signed to label the anti-racism group Black Lives Matter a 'terror group'. See CBS News, 'White House Responds to Petition to Label Black Lives Matter a "Terror" Group', 18 July 2016.

20. Rukmini Callimachi, 'Enslaving Young Girls, the Islamic State Builds a Vast System of Rape', *New York Times*, 14 August 2015, p. A1.

21. Chris Hedges, *Empire of Illusion: The End of Literacy and the Triumph of Spectacle*, New York: Nation Books, 2009; and Philip Roth Interview with Cynthia Haven, *Stanford News*, Stanford University, 3 February 2014.

22. Glenn Greenwald, 'The "War on Terror" – by Design – Can Never End', *Guardian*, 4 January 2013.

23. Des Freedman, 'The Terror News Cycle', *London Review of Books*, 24 May 2017.

24. See, for instance, Amitav Acharya, 'The Periphery as the Core: The Third World and Security Studies', in Keith Krause and Michael C. Williams, eds, *Critical Security Studies*, London: UCL Press, 1997, pp. 299–328.

25. Discussing the identity of their abductors during a bank heist, one of the hostages in the Spike Lee film *Inside Man* (2006) matter-of-factly says to another, 'maybe it's Al Qaeda'.

26. Bathia, 'Fighting Words', p. 5.

27. See Keith Lowe, *Savage Continent: Europe in the Aftermath of World War II*, London: Penguin Books, 2012. As Lowe's work notes: '[T]he claim that the postwar years were an era of unbroken peace seems hopelessly overstated … In the aftermath of the war, waves of vengeance and retribution washed over every sphere of European life … The story of Europe in the immediate postwar period … is firstly a story of the descent into anarchy', p. xv.

28. Hamid Dabashi, *Brown Skin, White Masks*, London: Pluto Press, 2011, p. 125.

29. On this question, see Virginia Held, 'Legitimate Authority in Non-State Groups using Violence', *Journal of Social Philosophy*, 36, 2, 2005, pp. 175–193; Richard W. Miller, 'Terrorism and Legitimacy: A Response to Virginia Held', *Journal of Social Philosophy*, 36, 2, 2005, pp. 194–201; and Eric W. Schoon, 'The Asymmetry of Legitimacy: Analysing the Legitimation of Violence in 30 Cases of Insurgent Revolution', *Social Forces*, 93, 2, December 2014, pp. 779–801.

30. See Pinar Bilgin, 'The "Western-Centrism" of Security Studies: "Blind Spot" or Constitutive Practice?', *Security Dialogue*, 41, 6, 2010, pp. 615–22.

31. On this point, see the discussion by Salman Sayyid, 'Empire, Islam and the Postcolonial', in Graham Huggan, ed., *Oxford Handbook of Postcolonial Studies*, Oxford: Oxford University Press, 2013, pp. 127–41.

32. See Robert Vitalis, *White World Order, Black Power Politics: The Birth of American International Relations*, Ithaca, New York: Cornell University Press, 2015. Vitalis notes: 'The problem is the current understanding of turn-of-the-century place of race in the thought of social scientists of the era. The strand that still resonates in our time about empire, states and the like is considered to be the real scientific or theoretical core of the scholar's work, while the strand that involves now-repudiated racial constructs is treated instead as mere "language", "metaphors" and "prejudices" of the era', p. 26.

33. To use the term of L.H.M. Ling in 'Cultural Chauvinism and the Liberal International Order: "West versus Rest" in Asia's Financial Crisis', in Geeta Chowdhury and Sheila Nair, eds, *Power in a Postcolonial World: Race, Gender and Class in International Relations*, London: Routledge, 2002, pp. 115–41.

34. Tarak Barkawi, 'Decolonising War', *European Journal of International Security*, 1, 2, July 2016, p. 200, original emphasis. Also see Patrick Porter, *Military Orientalism: Eastern War through Western Eyes*, New York: Columbia University Press, 2009; and Montgomery McFate, *Military Anthropology: Soldiers, Scholars and Subjects at the Margins of Empire*, London: Hurst, 2017. Porter writes: 'Westerners have debated about themselves, their own societies and policies, through visions of the Orient. The history of "military Orientalism" … is also a history of Western anxieties, ranging from fear to envy […] *Warfare has a reciprocal dynamic*. Rather than being the by-product of separate and discrete autonomous cultures, *it is shaped also by the reactive processes of competition, imitation and globalisation*', pp. 18–19, emphasis added.

35. See, for instance, the discussion by Vaugh Rasberry in his *Race and the Totalitarian Century: Geopolitics in the Black Literary Imagination*, Cambridge, Massachusetts: Harvard University Press, 2016.

36. On this issue, see Lisa Anderson, *Pursuing Truth, Exercising Power: Social Science and Public Policy in the 21st Century*, New York: Columbia University Press, 2005.

37. Philip K. Lawrence, *Modernity and War: The Creed of Absolute Violence*, London: Macmillan, 1997, p. 3, emphasis added.

38. Karma Nabulsi, 'Traditions of Justice in War: The Modern Debate in Historical Perspective', in Stathis N. Kalyvas, Ian Shapiro and Tarek Massoud, eds, *Order, Conflict and Violence*, Cambridge: Cambridge University Press, 2008, p. 137.

39. Ondrej Ditrych, *Tracing the Discourses of Terrorism: Identity, Genealogy and the State*, London: Palgrave Macmillan, 2014, p. 1.

40. Emanuele Saccarelli and Latha Varadarajan, *Imperialism: Past and Present*, New York: Oxford University Press, 2015, p. 5.

41. As does Michael Ignatieff in 'The Challenges of American Imperial Power', *Naval War College Review*, 56, 2, Spring 2003, p. 56.

42. Erin Steuter and Deborah Wills, *At War with a Metaphor: Media, Propaganda and Racism in the War on Terror*, Lanham, Maryland: Lexington Books, 2008, p. 190.

43. Julian Saurin, 'International Relations as the Imperial Illusion; or the Need to Decolonise IR', Gruffydd-Jones, *Decolonising International Relations*, p. 25, emphasis added.

44. David Theo Goldberg, *Racist Culture: Philosophy and the Politics of Meaning*, Cambridge, Massachusetts: Blackwell, 1993, p. 1. As Jennifer Pitts demonstrated, many of the staple concepts of liberal political thought have been mobilised in favour of the European imperial enterprise, and European liberalism was forged alongside and deeply affected by imperial expansion. See her *A Turn to Empire: The Rise of Imperial Liberalism in Britain and France*, Princeton, New Jersey: Princeton University Press, 2006, p. 4.

45. See Paul Thomas Chamberlin's argument in his *The Global Offensive: The United States, the Palestine Liberation Organisation and the Making of the Post-Cold War Order*, New York: Oxford University Press, 2012.

46. Ayşe Zarakol, 'What Makes Terrorism Modern? Terrorism, Legitimacy and the International System', *Review of International Studies*, 37, 5, December 2011, pp. 23–36.

47. Andrew Philips considers these challenges (i.e. 'the threat of Islamist radicalism and transnational terrorism') as 'more transient and less profound than many have assumed'. See his Andrew Phillips, *War, Religion and Empire: The Transformation of International Orders*, Cambridge: Cambridge University Press, 2010, p. 12, and for a fuller discussion chapter 10, pp. 261–99.

48. Paul Johnson, 'The Answer to Terrorism? Colonialism', *The Wall Street Journal*, 9 October 2001. Johnson writes: 'America has no alternative but to wage war against states ... It could be that a new form of colony, the Western-administered former terrorist state, is only just over the horizon.'

49. See Bob Woodward, *Veil: The Secret Wars of the CIA, 1981–1987*, New York: Simon and Schuster, 1987; and Jeremy Scahill, *Dirty Wars: The World is a Battlefield*, New York: Nation Books, 2013.

50. See, for instance, Michael P. Scharf, 'How the War against ISIS Changed International Law', *Case Western Reserve Journal of International Law*, 48, 2016, pp. 1–54. The author argues that the 2015 attacks by the group ushered a 'Grotian moment' – namely 'an instance of rapid formation of a new rule of customary international law' – which in this case would 'recognis[e] the right of states to attack non-state actors when the territorial state is unable or unwilling to suppress the threat they pose'. He concludes that: 'The implication of this newly-accepted change in the international law of self-defence is that any state can now lawfully use force against non-state actors (terrorists, rebels, pirates, drug cartels, etc.) that are present in the territory of another state if the territorial state is unable or unwilling to suppress the threat posed by those non-state actors. The number of candidates for such action is quite large.'

51. Ramón Grosfoguel, 'Decolonising Post-Colonial Studies and Paradigms of Political Economy: Transmodernity, Decolonial Thinking and Global Coloniality', *Transmodernity*, 1, 1, 2011, p. 34.

52. Sayyid, *Recalling the Caliphate*, p. 47.

53. See Claudia Verhoeven, *The Odd Man Karakozov: Imperial Russia, Modernity and the Birth of Terrorism*, Ithaca, New York: Cornell University Press, 2009.

54. See, for instance, Michael Youssef, *Revolt against Modernity: Muslim Zealots and the West*, Leiden: Brill, 1985. As Talal Asad remarks, orthodox discourse is not so much opposed to change, rather it aspires to be authoritative. See the chapter 'The Limits of Religious Criticism in the Middle East: Notes on Islamic Public Arguments' in his *Genealogies of Religion: Discipline and Reasons of Power in Christianity and Islam*, Johns Hopkins University Press, Baltimore: 1993, pp. 200–36.

55. Achille Mbembe, 'Provisional Notes on the Postcolony', *Africa*, 62, 1, 1992, p. 3.

56. David E. Apter, 'Political Violence in Analytical Perspective', in David E. Apter, ed., *The Legitimisation of Violence*, London: Macmillan, 1997, p. 25, emphasis added.

57. The common 'Zawahiri' spelling in English is due to the use of an Egyptian colloquial mispronunciation of the Arabic letter 'dha' as 'za'. Al Dhawahiri is an Egyptian national.

58. For a proposed research agenda for the study of popular culture in international relations, see Kyle Grayson, Matt Davies and Simon Philpott, 'Pop Goes IR? Researching the Popular Culture-World Politics Continuum', *Politics*, 29, 3, 2009, pp. 155–63.

59. See the documentaries *Do Not Resist* (2016) by Craig Atkinson and *Peace Officer* (2015) by Scott Christopherson and Brad Barber.

60. Anthony Richards, *Conceptualising Terrorism*, Oxford: Oxford University Press, 2015.

Chapter 1

1. See, for instance, the memoirs (only published in French) of Palestinian Fatah senior operator Mohammad Daoud Odeh, known as Abu Daoud, in which he recounts the events leading up to the 5 September 1972 operation in Munich and the connections with European groups: Abou Daoud, *Palestine: De Jérusalem à Munich*, Paris: Anne Carrière, 1999. Also see on this period the documentary by Barbet Schroeder on the life of French lawyer and militant Jacques Vergès, *Terror's Advocate*, 2007.

2. Robert Keohane and Joseph S. Nye, Jr., *Transnational Relations and World Politics*, Cambridge, Massachusetts: Harvard University Press, 1972.

3. The story of an individual operator such as the Swiss businessman François Genoud, who facilitated many connections between Middle Eastern and European groups during the 1970s, is relevant in that regard. See Pierre Péan, *L'Extrémiste: François Genoud, De Hitler à Carlos*, Paris: Fayard, 2006.

4. S. Yaqub Ibrahim, 'Theory of the Rise of Al Qaeda', *Behavioural Sciences of Terrorism and Political Aggression*, April 2017, p. 18.
5. Osama Bin Laden, 'Message to the American People', 29 January 2004.
6. See Sheikh Abdullah 'Azzam, *Defence of the Muslim Lands: The First Obligation after Iman* [belief], 1984. Audio footage of 'Azzam making the same point was integrated in a 4 July 2007 message by Ayman al Dhawahiri. Also see Abu al Wali al Masri (Mustapha Hamid), 'The History of the Arab Afghans, from the Time of their Arrival in Afghanistan until their Departure with the Taliban', *Al Sharq Al Awsat* (London), series published on 8–14 December 2004.
7. On this period, see Camille Tawil, *Al Qa'eda wa Akhawaatuha: Qisat al Jihadiyun al 'Arab [Al Qaeda and its Sisters: The Story of the Arab Jihadists]*, London: Dar al Saqi, 2007.
8. See, for instance, Jack McDonald, *Enemies Known and Unknown: Targeted Killings and America's Transnational War*, London: Hurst, 2017.
9. Abdulla Anas interview with Tam Hussein, 'Jihad, Then and Now', *Majalla*, 8 February 2014.
10. When Iraq invaded Kuwait in August 1990 and was facing the prospect of a US military intervention, Osama Bin Laden offered to send an army of his fighters to help the Iraqis battle the American troops.
11. Bertrand Badie, *L'Impuissance de la Puissance*, Paris: Fayard, 2005.
12. Richard A. Clarke, 'Mission to Jeddah', The Middle East Institute, 7 August 2016.
13. Louise Richardson, 'Terrorists as Transnational Actors', *Terrorism and Political Violence*, 11, 4, 1999, p. 216.
14. James Rosenau, *Along the Domestic-Foreign Frontier: Exploring Governance in a Turbulent World*, Cambridge: Cambridge University Press, 1997, p. 350.
15. The full quote from Thomas Edward Lawrence's *Seven Pillars of Wisdom* (1922) is: 'All men dream, but not equally. Those who dream by night in the dusty recesses of their minds wake in the day to find that it was a vanity. But the dreamers of the day are dangerous men for they may act their dreams with open eyes to make it possible.'
16. Michael Rear, *Intervention, Ethnic Conflict and State-Building in Iraq: A Paradigm for the Post-Colonial State*, London: Routledge, 2008, p. 153.
17. Mairaj Syed, 'Jihad in Classical Legal and Moral Thought', in Jacob Neusner, Bruce D. Chilton and R.E. Tully, *Just War in Religion and Politics: Studies in Religion and the Social Order*, Lanham, Maryland: University Press of America, 2013, p. 152.
18. See Sebastiano Andreotti, 'The Ikhwan Movement and Its Role in Saudi Arabia's State-Building', in Kenneth Christie and Mohammad Masad, eds, *State Formation and Identity in the Middle East and Africa*, New York: Palgrave Macmillan, 2013, pp. 87–105.
19. See Yaroslav Trofimov, *The Siege of Mecca: The Forgotten Uprising in Islam's Holiest Shrine*, New York: Doubleday, 2007.
20. See Michael Bonner, *Aristocratic Violence and Holy War: Studies in the Jihad in Arab-Byzantine Frontier*, New Haven, Connecticut: American Oriental

Society, 1996. Also see Hamit Bozarslan, *Le Luxe et la Violence: Domination et Contestation chez Ibn Khaldûn*, Paris: CNRS, 2014. In discussing Ibn Khaldun's theory, Bozarslan notes that the self-legitimation of the 'noble' warrior builds, in its 'performative speech-acts', on the glory of past wars (p. 30). One can see Bin Laden doing precisely that in many of his latter-day speeches in 2003–4.

21. For a historical background to this notion in Islam, see Bonner, *Aristocratic Violence*, chapter 1, pp. 11–42.

22. Mahmood Mamdani, *Good Muslim, Bad Muslim: America, the Cold War and the Roots of Terror*, New York: Random House, 2004, p. 33.

23. Roger Scruton, *The West and the Rest: Globalisation and the Terrorist Threat*, London: Continuum, 2002, pp. 131–2.

24. Robert Snyder, 'Hating America: Bin Laden as a Civilisational Revolutionary', *Review of Politics*, 65, 4, Fall 2003, pp. 325–49.

25. Ayşe Zarakol, 'What Makes Terrorism Modern? Terrorism, Legitimacy and the International System', *Review of International Studies*, 37, 5, December 2011, pp. 23–36, emphasis added.

26. See Terry McDermott, *Perfect Soldiers: The Hijackers: Who They Were, Why They Did It*, New York: HarperCollins, 2005.

27. See Neamattolah Nojumi, *The Rise of the Taliban in Afghanistan: Mass Mobilisation, Civil War and the Future of the Region*, New York: 2002; and Syed Saleem Shahzad, *Inside Al Qaeda and the Taliban: Beyond Bin Laden and 9/11*, London: Pluto Press, 2011.

28. See Martin A. Miller, *The Foundations of Modern Terrorism: States, Society and the Dynamics of Political Violence*, Cambridge: Cambridge University Press, 2013, p. 245.

29. On this aspect, see Simon Staffell and Akil Awan, eds, *Jihadism Transformed: Al Qaeda and Islamic State's Global Battle of Ideas*, London: Hurst, 2016.

30. Slavoj Žižek, 'ISIS is a Disgrace to True Fundamentalism', *New York Times*, 3 September 2014, emphasis added. The analysis originally appeared in his book, *Violence: Six Sideways Reflections*, New York: Picador, 2008.

31. For an English translation of the interview, see David N. Gibbs, 'Afghanistan: The Soviet Invasion in Retrospect', *International Politics*, 37, June 2000, pp. 241–2.

32. Cable News Network (CNN), 'Pakistani Man Executed for CIA Killings', 15 November 2002.

33. See Diego Gambetta and Steffen Hertog, *Engineers of Jihad: The Curious Connection between Violent Extremism and Education*, Princeton, New Jersey: Princeton University Press, 2015.

34. See Peter Lance, *Triple Cross: How Bin Laden's Master Spy Penetrated the CIA, the Green Berets and the FBI*, New York: HarperCollins, 2009.

35. See Bryanjar Lia, *Architect of Global Jihad: The Life of Al Qaeda Strategist Abu Mus'ab al-Suri*, London: Hurst, 2009.

36. On the US thinking, see Sean T. Lawson, *Nonlinear Science and Warfare: Chaos, Complexity and the US Military in the Information Age*, London: Routledge, 2014; in particular chapter 6, 'From Fourth-Generation Warfare

to Global Insurgency: Complexity in the Wake of Operation Iraqi Freedom', pp. 130–51.

37. Hew Strachan, 'The Changing Character of War', in Karl Erik Haug and Ole Jørgen Maaø, eds, *Conceptualising Modern War*, London: Hurst and Company, 2011, p. 9.

38. Osama Bin Mohammad Bin Laden, 'An Open Letter to King Fahd on the Occasion of the Recent Cabinet Reshuffle', 3 August 1995.

39. Jane Mayer recounts one such incident where an alarm went off in the White House and there was suspicion of a nerve attack in which Vice President Dick Cheney was infected, which turned out to be erroneous: 'During the ten days after the Vice-President's scare, threats of mortal attack were nonetheless so frequent, and so terrifying, that on 29 October, Cheney quietly insisted upon absenting himself from the White House to what was described as a 'secure, undisclosed location'; 'No one in the Bush administration, including Cheney, had had the foresight or imagination to see Bin Laden's plot unfold.' See *The Dark Side: The Inside Story of How the War on Terror Turned into a War on American Ideals*, New York: Anchor Books, 2008, pp. 3–4 and 6.

40. On the magazine, see Julian Droogan and Shane Peattie, 'Reading Jihad: Mapping the Shifting Themes of *Inspire* Magazine', *Terrorism and Political Violence*, online, 30 August 2016, pp. 1–34.

41. David C. Hofmann, 'The Influence of Charismatic Authority on Operational Strategies and Attack Outcomes of Terrorist Groups', *Journal of Strategic Security*, 9, 2, 2016, p. 45.

42. On this aspect, see Anthony Vinci, 'Becoming the Enemy: Convergence in the American and Al Qaeda's Ways of Warfare', *Journal of Strategic Studies*, 31, 1, 2008, pp. 69–88.

43. Porter, *Military Orientalism*, p. 190.

44. See Stephen A. Harmon, *Terror and Insurgency in the Sahara-Sahel Region: Corruption, Contraband, Jihad and the Mali War of 2012–2013*, London: Ashgate, 2014; and Christopher S. Chivvis, *The French War on Al Qa'ida in Africa*, Cambridge: Cambridge University Press, 2016.

45. The conditions of the death of Bin Laden were murky, marred by ambiguities and spin which fed conspiracy theories. See Jonathan Mahler, 'What Do We Really Know About Osama Bin Laden's Death?', *New York Times Magazine*, 15 October 2015; and Seymour M. Hersh, *The Killing of Osama Bin Laden*, London: Verso, 2016.

Chapter 2

1. Jon Schwarz, 'Why Do So Many Americans Fear Muslims? Decades of Denial about America's Role in the World', *The Intercept*, 18 February 2017.

2. *The 9/11 Commission Report: Final Report of the National Commission on Terrorist Attacks Upon the United States*, New York: W.W. Norton, 2004, p. 393.

3. See Joy Gordon, *Invisible War: The United States and Iraq Sanctions*, Cambridge, Massachusetts: Harvard University Press, 2012; and H.C. Von

Sponeck, *A Different Kind of War: The UN Sanctions Regime in Iraq*, New York: Berghahn Books, 2006.

4. Paul Johnson, 'The Answer to Terrorism? Colonialism', *Wall Street Journal*, 9 October 2001.

5. Peter W. Galbraith, *The End of Iraq: How American Incompetence Created a War Without End*, New York: Simon and Schuster, 2006; Jonathan Steele, *Defeat: Why America and Britain Lost Iraq*, London: I.B.Tauris, 2007; Thomas E. Ricks, *Fiasco: The American Military Adventure in Iraq*, New York: Penguin, 2006; Emma Sky, *The Unraveling: High Hopes and Missed Opportunities in Iraq*, New York: PublicAffairs, 2015; Charles Ferguson, *No End in Sight: Iraq's Descent into Chaos*, New York: PublicAffairs, 2008; Michael Scheuer, *Marching Towards Hell: America and Islam after Iraq*, New York: The Free Press, 2008; and Eric Herring and Glen Rangwala, *Iraq in Fragments: The Occupation and its Legacy*, London: Hurst and Company, 2006.

6. The literature about the management of the war in Iraq is extensive. See, in particular, Rajiv Chandrasekaran, *Imperial Life in the Emerald City: Inside Iraq's Green Zone*, New York: Vintage, 2007.

7. For instance, Jim Frederick, *Black Hearts: One Platoon's Descent into Madness in Iraq's Triangle of Death*, New York: Broadway Books, 2011.

8. Michael Kaufman, 'What Does the Pentagon see in *The Battle of Algiers?*', *New York Times*, 7 September 2003.

9. For a criticism of post-9/11 counter-insurgency and its imperial nature, see Alex Marshall, 'Imperial Nostalgia, the Liberal Lie and the Perils of Postmodern Counter-insurgency', *Small Wars and Insurgencies*, 21, 2, June 2010, pp. 233–58. Marshall remarks: 'Counter-insurgency theory today may retain its own grammar, but nonetheless finds itself applied in scenarios where that grammar no longer corresponds to any wider political logic. Counter-insurgency doctrine in the West since September 11 has above all become an operational panacea for what continues to remain a dangerous strategic vacuum; a position all the more tenuous, given that counter-insurgency doctrine itself has now been retrospectively mythologised as having offered the key to "clear cut victories" in the past', p. 244.

10. James Risen, 'Iraqi Terror Hasn't Hit US in Years, CIA says', *New York Times*, 6 February 2002, p. 1; James Risen and Douglas Jehl, 'Arms Expert Says He Was Pressed to Distort Iraq Evidence', *New York Times*, 26 June 2003, p.1.

11. Dave Baiocchi, 'Measuring Army Deployments to Iraq and Afghanistan', Rand Corporation, 2013.

12. Ralph Wilde, 'Colonialism Redux? Territorial Administration by International Organisations, Colonial Echoes and the Legitimacy of the "International"', in Aidan Hehir and Neil Robinson, eds, *State-Building: Theory and Practice*, London: Routledge, 2007, p. 29, original emphasis.

13. Nir Rosen, *Aftermath: Following the Bloodshed of America's Wars in the Muslim World*, New York: Nation Books, 2010, p. 10. *Shaqi* has a second meaning in many parts of the Arab world, namely 'crazy'.

14. James Thui Gathii, 'Dispossession through International Law: Iraq in Historical and Comparative Context', in Brandwen Gruffydd-Jones, ed.,

Decolonising International Relations, Plymouth: Rowman and Littlefeld, 2005, p. 131. Gathii's discussion of the 'privatisation of Iraq' highlights the distorting of a norm whereby, as he notes, 'the peculiar nature of the international law applied towards non-European peoples is a reflection of a unique form of Western, American or European power rather than a direct translation of international law as such', p. 146.

15. Michael Hechter and Nika Kabiri, 'Attaining Social Order in Iraq', in Stathis N. Kalyvas, Ian Shapiro and Tarek Massoud, eds, *Order, Conflict and Violence*, Cambridge: Cambridge University Press, 2008, pp. 55–6.

16. Toby Dodge, *Iraq: From War to a New Authoritarianism*, London: International Institute for Strategic Studies, 2012, p. 120. The militarisation of Iraqi society was also echoing the militarisation of American society itself (see Chapter 4).

17. Patrick Cockburn and David Usborne, 'Burning with Anger: Iraqis Infuriated by New Flag that was Designed in London', *Independent*, 28 April 2004. The article notes: 'A further reason for popular anger is that many Iraqis are convinced that their new flag is modelled on the Israeli flag.'

18. Julian Go, *Patterns of Empire: The British and American Empires, 1688 to the Present*, Cambridge: Cambridge University Press, 2011, pp. 223–4.

19. Walter Russell Mead, 'The Revolutionary', *Esquire*, 1 November 2004.

20. Claudine Haroche, 'Le Sentiment d'Humiliation dans la Colonisation', in Séverine Kodjo-Grandvaux and Geneviève Koubi, eds, *Droit and Colonisation*, Brussels: Bruylant, 2007, p. 207. Author's translation. Also see Ann Laura Stoler, *Carnal Knowledge and Imperial Power: Race and the Intimate in Colonial Rule*, Oakland, California: University of California Press, 2002.

21. Nick Turse, *Kill Anything that Moves: The Real American War in Vietnam*, New York: Picador, 2014, p. 6.

22. Harlan Ullman, 'Outside View: America's Historical Amnesia', United Press International, 24 April 2013.

23. Mona Mahmood, Maggie O'Kane, Chavala Madlena and Teresa Smith, 'Revealed: Pentagon's to Iraqi Torture Centres', *Guardian*, 6 March 2013.

24. The phrases were coined by Nir Rosen as the titles of parts 1 and 2 of his *Aftermath*. As Libya, Egypt, Syria and other countries pushed forward into unexpected change after the revolts of 2011, they started displaying features some of their regional neighbours had at some point previously experienced. This gave the analogy-inclined observer a chance to take note of the '*asabyiasation* of Iraqi politics (back to *fitna* after nationalism), the Iraqisation of Libya (out of insecurity and anomie just as seen in Mesopotamia in the 2000s), the Lebanonisation of Syria (intrigue and geopolitics shifting from Beirut to Damascus) and the Pakistanisation of Egypt (army, religion, deep state and international clientelism).

25. Charles Tripp, *A History of Iraq*, Cambridge: Cambridge University Press, 2000, p. 1.

26. Riccardo Bocco and Jordi Tejel, 'Introduction', in Jordi Tejel, Peter Sluglett, Riccardo Bocco and Hamit Bozarslan, eds, *Writing the Modern History of*

Iraq: Historiographical and Political Challenges, London: World Scientific Publishing, 2012, p. xii.

27. Faleh A. Jabar, 'The War Generation in Iraq: A Case of Failed Etatist Nationalism', in Lawrence G. Potter and Gary S. Sick, eds, *Iran, Iraq and the Legacies of War*, New York: Palgrave Macmillan, 2004, p. 123.

28. See Nir Rosen's account, 'Anatomy of a Civil War: Iraq's Descent into Chaos', *Boston Review*, 31, 6, November/December 2006, pp. 7–21.

29. David Masciotra, 'America's Great Mistakes: Has Everyone Forgotten that the Vietnam and Iraq Wars were Unnecessary, Stupid and Destructive?', *Salon. com*, 7 August 2016.

30. Emanuele Saccarelli and Latha Varadarajan, *Imperialism Past and Present*, New York: Oxford University Press, 2015, p. 2.

31. As did others in the Arab world beyond Iraq. In Tunisia, in March 2016, soldiers took a selfie with the corpses of Islamist insurgents killed during a battle between the military and IS-supporting operators in the city of Ben Guerdane, and posted it online. The picture was subsequently 'liked' by the Tunisian Minister of Information, Neji Jalloul, on a live television programme.

32. Lawyers Committee for Human Rights, *A Year of Loss: Re-examining Civil Liberties since September 11*, New York, September 2002.

33. Jim Dwyer, 'Mourning after 9/11, Outrage Ever After', *New York Times*, 15 March 2008, p. A18. Revealing the impact and mimetic adoption of such official vengeful ways, the Jordanian military offered, in 2015, to do the same for the father of a man whose son had been burned alive by IS.

34. See the initial 2004–5 works of Seymour M. Hersh, *Chain of Command: The Road from 9/11 to Abu Ghraib*, New York: HarperCollins, 2004; Mark Danner, *Torture and Truth: America, Abu Ghraib and the War on Terror*, New York: New York Review of Books, 2004; and Karen J. Greenberg, Joshua L. Dratel and Anthony Lewis, eds, *The Torture Papers: The Road to Abu Ghraib*, Cambridge: Cambridge University Press, 2005; as well as Philip Gourevitch and Errol Morris, *The Ballad of Abu Ghraib: Standard Operating Procedure*, New York: Penguin Books, 2009; and Karen J. Greenberg, *Rogue Justice: The Making of the Security State*, New York: Penguin, 2016.

35. William Glaberson, 'Military Insider Becomes Critic of Hearings at Guantanamo', *New York Times*, 23 July 2007, p. A1 and p. A16. Also see Eric Fair, *Consequence: A Memoir*, New York: Henry Holt and Co., 2016; and Clive Stafford Smith, *Eight O'Clock Ferry to the Windward Side: Seeking Justice in Guantanamo Bay*, New York: Nation Books, 2007.

36. The memoranda are available at www.torturingdemocracy.org.

37. On how the legal definition of torture is reduced to technicalities, see David Luban, *Torture, Power and Law*, Cambridge: Cambridge University Press, 2014.

38. Seymour M. Hersh, 'The General's Report', *New Yorker*, 26 June 2007, pp. 58–69.

39. Neil A. Lewis, 'Red Cross Finds Detainee Abuse in Guantanamo', *New York Times*, 30 November 2004, pp. A1 and A4; and Thom Shanker and Andrea

Elliott, 'Rumsfeld Admits He Told Jailers to Keep Detainee in Iraq Out of Red Cross View', *New York Times*, 18 June 2004, p. A13.

40. Michael Keller, *Torture Central: Emails from Abu Ghraib*, Bloomington, Indiana: IUniverse, 2007.

41. Alissa Rubin, 'US Military Said to Utilize "Black Jail"', *International Herald Tribune*, 30 November 2009, p. 4.

42. Homicides allegedly took place in Guantánamo as well. See Scott Horton, 'The Guantánamo "Suicides": A Camp Delta Sergeant Blows the Whistle', *Harper's Magazine*, 320, 1918, March 2010, pp. 27–37.

43. 'Abu Ghraib Swept Under the Carpet', *New York Times*, 30 August 2007, p. A22. The editorial notes 'the remix of reality and denial of responsibility'.

44. Tara McKelvey, *Monstering: Inside America's Policy of Secret Interrogations and Torture in the Terror War*, New York: Carroll and Graf Publishers, 2007, pp. 128–9. Specifically, on this 'unimaginable and unspeakable' dimension, see Henry Giroux, *Hearts of Darkness: Torturing Children in the War on Terror*, London: Routledge, 2010.

45. As the spouse of a soldier declared to the cultural historian Morris Berman. See his *Dark Ages America: The Final Phase of Empire*, New York: W.W. Norton, 2011, p. 223.

46. Janina Struk, *Private Pictures: Soldiers' Inside View of War*, London: I.B.Tauris, 2011, p. 7. Also see Provance's testimonial in the documentary directed by Errol Morris, *Standing Operating Procedure*, Sony Pictures Classic, 2008.

47. Raymond Bonner, 'After 9/11, We Were All Judith Miller', *Politico*, 21 April 2015.

48. For instance, Lizzie Dearden, 'Four British Soldiers "Forced Iraqi Teenager Into River in Which He Drowned"', *Independent*, 16 September 2016.

49. Mark Danner interview with Hugh Eakin, 'Our New Politics of Torture', *New York Review of Books*, 30 December 2014.

50. Lisa Hajjar, 'The CIA Didn't Just Torture, It Experimented on Human Beings', *The Nation*, 5 January 2015.

51. Ed Vulliamy, 'Is Britain Guilty of Systemic Torture in Iraq?', *Guardian*, 19 January 2013. The accusations, documented by British civil rights lawyers, list: 'an orgy of sadism, outlawed interrogation methods and unlawful killings by soldiers and intelligence officers against Iraqi civilians and prisoners of war between 2003 and 2008. ... Civilians say they were subjected to hooding, beating, threats of rape and execution, forced nakedness and maintaining stress positions, violence against wives and children, ritual humiliation.' Also Agence France Press (AFP), 'UK Troops Deny Mutilating Iraq Insurgents', 3 September 2013.

52. Seymour S. Hersh, 'Annals of National Security: The Gray Zone: How a Secret Pentagon Programme Came to Abu Ghraib', *New Yorker*, 17 May 2004.

53. See Steven H. Miles, *Oath Betrayed: Torture, Medical Complicity and the War on Terror*, New York: Random House, 2006; and the documentary by Martha Davis, *Doctors of the Dark Side*, Shelter Island Productions, 2011. Two psychologists who allegedly helped the CIA develop said techniques were subsequently sued by victims, and the Trump administration attempted

to prevent testimony from CIA officers in that case. See James Risen, Sheri Fink and Charlie Savage, 'State Secrets Privilege Invoked to Block Testimony in CIA Torture Case', *New York Times*, 8 March 2017. Also see the report by Stephen Soldz, Nathaniel Raymond and Steven Reisner, *All the Presidents' Psychologists: The American Psychological Association's Secret Complicity with the White House and US Intelligence Community in Support of the CIA's 'Enhanced' Interrogation Programme*, April 2015.

54. Danner, 'Our New Politics of Torture'.
55. Jonathan Landay and Mark Hosenball, 'Trump May Reinstate Secret CIA "Black Site Prisons"': US Officials', Reuters, 25 January 2017.
56. Sexual humiliation of Arab terrorists by US law enforcement officials using photos was foreshadowed in the 1998 film *The Siege*, indeed in the aftermath of a terrorist bombing in New York depicted as a prelude to extensive securitisation. For an insightful history of the CIA's pre- and post-9/11 use of torture and its relationship with film, see Lisa Hajjar, 'From *The Manchurian Candidate* to *Zero Dark Thirty*: Reading the CIA's History of Torture through Hollywood's Thrillers', 2016, unpublished draft. Also see Alex Adams, *Political Torture in Popular Culture: The Role of Representations in the Post-9/11 Torture Debate*, London: Routledge, 2016.
57. Andrew Rosenthal, 'There is Silence in the Streets; Where Have All the Protesters Gone?', *New York Times*, 31 August 2006, p. A26.
58. See the 577-page report by the Constitution Project, *Detainee Treatment: Report of the Constitution's Project's Task Force*, 2013, http://detaineetaskforce.org/report/.
59. Douglas A. Johnson, Alberto Mora and Averell Schmidt, 'The Strategic Costs of Torture: How "Enhanced Interrogation" Hurt America', *Foreign Affairs*, 95, 5, September/October 2016, pp. 121.
60. Seymour Hersh recounts one such episode of the 'intimate' relationship between journalists and the US Army in a 21 May 2015 podcast with the *London Review of Books*; www.lrb.co.uk/v37/n10/seymour-m-hersh/the-killing-of-osama-bin-laden, from 22.00 onwards.
61. Bob Herbert, 'Abusing Iraqi Civilians', *New York Times*, 10 July 2007, p. A23; Also see Jameel Jaffer and Amrit Singh, *Administration of Torture: A Documentary Record from Washington to Abu Ghraib and Beyond*, New York: Columbia University Press, 2007.
62. By 2016, almost half the US population (46 per cent) would be in favour of torture, as documented in a report by the ICRC. See Kevin Sieff, 'More Americans Support Torture than Afghans, Iraqis and South Sudanese. Why?', *Washington Post*, 5 December 2016, p. A1.
63. See Chris Mackey and Greg Miller, *The Interrogators: Inside the Secret War against Al Qaeda*, New York: Little, Brown and Company, 2004.
64. Throughout the 2000s and 2010s, after each episode of 'retaking' a city previously held by rebels, the Iraqi authorities and the militias associated with them often engaged in repression and human rights violations. Such practices expanded to families of detainees, just as the US had done after 2003. See, for instance, Human Rights Watch, 'Iraq: Displacement, Detention

of Suspected "ISIS" families', 5 March 2017; and Ali Arkady, 'Nicht Helden, sondern Monster' [Not Heroes, but Monsters], *Der Spiegel*, 21 May 2017. The journalist Arkady reported how the Iraqi army unit treated him as part of their team, allowed him to film and photograph the abuses and invited him to join in the acts.

65. The battlefield ability of Western-sponsored regimes that came later in Iraq and Afghanistan was inferior to that of the fallen local authoritarian regimes. In fact, the robustness of the insurgencies came partly from the remnants of those defeated armies. For a discussion of this question, which reaches different conclusions, see Caitlin Talmadge, *The Dictator's Army: Battlefield Effectiveness in Authoritarian Regimes*, Ithaca, New York: Cornell University Press, 2015.

66. 'Man Who Oversaw Saddam Hussein's Hanging: "The Room was Full of Death"', Associated Press, 27 December 2013.

67. Michael Daly, 'ISIS Leader: "See You in New York"', *Daily Beast*, 6 June 2014.

Chapter 3

1. When, for example, in 2005, the former petty criminal-dominated Algerian Salafist Group for Predication and Combat (GSPC) sought to join Al Qaeda, to eventually become AQIM in January 2007, it did so through correspondence with al Zarqawi, whose brashness appealed more to the group's ways than Bin Laden's or al Dhawahiri's traditional conservatism. A letter to that effect was sent by GSPC leader Abu Mus'ab Abdel Wadoud to al Zarqawi on 29 April 2006.

2. Kyle W. Orton, 'How Saddam Hussein Gave Us ISIS', *New York Times*, 23 December 2015.

3. Charlie Winter, 'War by Suicide: A Statistical Analysis of the Islamic State's Martyrdom Industry', International Centre for Counter-Terrorism, The Hague, March 2017.

4. See Thomas Hegghammer, 'Saudis in Iraq: Patterns of Radicalisation and Recruitment', *Cultures & Conflicts*, July 2016.

5. See Joby Warrick, *The Triple Agent: The Al Qaeda Mole Who Infiltrated the CIA*, New York: Vintage Books, 2012. Reverse penetration of extremist Islamist circles took place as well, with a number of Western operators pretending to join the ranks of the radical groups only to spy on them. See, for instance, the case of Morten Storm recounted in his book *Agent Storm: My Life Inside Al Qaeda and the CIA*, New York: Grove Press, 2015.

6. See, for instance, Michel Moutot, 'A Year after Bin Laden Slain, Al Qaeda "in Ruins"', Agence France Presse, 29 April 2012; and Michael S. Schmidt and Eric Schmitt, 'Leaving Iraq, US Fears New Surge of Qaeda Terror', *New York Times*, 5 November 2011, p. A1. Schmidt and Schmitt offered that ISI was 'unlikely to regain its prior strength'.

7. See the two-part report by Jessica D. Lewis, *Al Qaeda in Iraq Resurgent: The Breaking the Walls Campaign*, part 1 (September 2013) and part 2 (October 2013), Washington, DC: Institute for the Study of War.

8. Adi Ophir, 'The Politics of Catastrophisation: Emergency and Exception', in Didier Fassin and Mariella Pandoff, eds, *Contemporary States of Emergency: The Politics of Military and Humanitarian Interventions*, Cambridge, Massachusetts: MIT Press, 2010, p. 61, emphasis added.

9. The social makeup of Iraq has long been conditioned by recurrent uprisings, notably in the 1920s against the British occupation. These memories of rebellion have lingered in the local polity, and their effect can be seen in recent episodes starting with the battle of Fallujah in 2004. On this issue, see, for instance, Montgomery McFate, 'The "Memory of War": Tribes and the Legitimate Use of Force in Iraq', in Jeffrey H. Norwitz, ed., *Armed Groups: Studies in National Security, Counterterrorism and Counterinsurgency*, Newport, Rhode Island: Naval War College, 2008, pp. 291–310.

10. On the wider, more politically anchored pursuit of a revamping of the Caliphate, see Reza Pankhurst, *The Inevitable Caliphate? A History of the Struggle for Global Islamic Union, 1924 to the Present*, London: Hurst, 2014.

11. Chris Good, 'Secret Service "Aware" of Apparent ISIS Flag Photo in Front of White House', *ABC News*, 14 August 2014.

12. Paul Staniland, *Networks of Rebellion: Explaining Insurgent Cohesion and Collapse*, Ithaca, New York: Cornell University Press, 2014, p. 217.

13. See Clunan and Trinkunas, *Ungoverned Spaces*.

14. T.E. Lawrence, 'The Evolution of a Revolt', *Army Quarterly and Defence Journal*, October 1920, p. 4.

15. See Hassan Abu Hanieyh and Mohammad Abu Rumman, *The Islamic State Organisation: The Sunni Crisis and the Struggle for Global Jihadism*, Amman: Friedrich Ebert Stiftung, 2014.

16. See Yezid Sayigh, 'Da'esh: Khilafa Islamiya 'Alamiya am Douaila Islamiya fil Iraq' (ISIS: Global Islamic Caliphate or Islamic Mini-State in Iraq?), *Al Hayat*, 24 July 2014.

17. Abdulkader Tayob, *Religion in Modern Islamic Discourse*, London: Hurst & Company, 2009, p. 101.

18. Tayob, *Religion in Modern Islamic Discourse*, p. 103.

19. Heather Rae, *State Identities and the Homogenisation of Peoples*, Cambridge: Cambridge University Press, 2002. Rae notes that 'understanding the construction of identities and interests is crucial to understanding political action, both domestic and international, and that culture and symbolism play important roles in this', p. 299.

20. Nazih Ayubi, 'The Theory and Practice of the Islamic State', in *Political Islam: Religion and Politics in the Arab World*, London: Routledge, 1991, pp. 2–3.

21. See Robert Jackson, *Quasi-States: Sovereignty, International Relations and the Third World*, Cambridge: Cambridge University Press, 1990, p. 21.

22. Christoph Günther and Tom Kaden, 'Beyond Mere Terrorism: The Islamic State's Authority as a Social Movement and as a Quasi-State', *Security and Peace*, 2, 2016, p. 134.

23. On this key period, see Paul Thomas Chamberlin, *The Global Offensive: The United States, the Palestine Liberation Organisation, and the Making of the Post-Cold War Order*, New York: Oxford University Press, 2012.

24. See, for instance, Alexander Meleagrou-Hitchens, 'Al Qaeda's Most Dangerous Franchise', *Wall Street Journal*, 10 May 2012, p. A1.

25. Omar Ashour, 'Complex Networks of Insurgency under Authoritarian Rule', *DGAP kompakt*, German Council on Foreign Relations, no. 15, August 2016, p. 4.

26. Frances Robles, 'Trying to Stanch Trinidad's Flow of Young Recruits to ISIS', *New York Times*, 21 February 2017; and Richard C. Paddock, 'In Indonesia and Philippines, Militants Find a Common Bond: ISIS', *New York Times*, 26 May 2017, p. A9.

27. See Rukmini Callimachi, 'How a Secretive Branch of ISIS Built a Global Network of Killers', *New York Times*, 3 August 2016, p. A1.

Chapter 4

1. On IS's use of technology, see Abdel Bari Atwan, *Islamic State: The Digital Caliphate*, London: Saqi, 2015.

2. Besides the videos, material has been released in Arabic, Azeri, Chinese, Dutch, English, French, German, Hebrew, Indonesian (Bahasa and Melayu), Italian, Japanese, Kurdish, Polish, Portuguese, Russian, Somali, Spanish and Turkish.

3. Episodes I, II and III had been released by Al Furqan respectively in June and August 2012 and January 2013, before Al Hayat Media Centre released the fourth instalment in May 2014 with a noticeable quality upgrade and English subtitles.

4. Craig Whiteside, 'New Masters of Revolutionary Warfare: The Islamic State Movement (2002–2016)', *Perspectives on Terrorism*, 10, 4, 2016, online.

5. Robert Pape et al., 'The American Face of ISIS: Analysis of ISIS-related Terrorism in the US', Chicago Project on Security and Threats and Australian Strategic Policy Institute, February 2017.

6. Jeremy Scahill, *Dirty Wars: The World is a Battlefield*, New York: Nation Books, 2013, p. 289.

7. An FBI translator, Daniela Greene, with top-secret security clearance was assigned to investigate Cusper, travelled to Syria in 2014 and ended up marrying him. She returned subsequently to the United States and cooperated with the US authorities. Sentenced to two years in prison, she was released in 2016.

8. Nabil Bulos and Patrick J. McDonnell, 'Meet Chechclearr, the Web-savvy Foreign Islamic Militant in Syria', *Los Angeles Times*, 4 February 2014.

9. Asawin Suebsaeng, 'US Turns to *Zero Dark Thirty* Writer for Anti-ISIS Propaganda', *Daily Beast*, 28 September 2015; and Rita Katz, 'The State Department's Twitter War with ISIS is Embarrassing', *Time*, 16 September 2014.

10. See Robert Verkaik, *Jihadi John: The Making of a Terrorist*, London: Oneworld, 2016.

11. 'Woolwich Attack: The Terrorist's Rant', *Telegraph*, 10 May 2017; and Jamie Grieson, 'Lee Rigby Murder: Michael Adebolajo Handed Witness a Note Attempting to Justify Actions', *Independent*, 19 December 2013.

12. Lori Hinnant, 'IS Trains 400 Fighters to Attack Europe in Wave of Bloodshed', Associated Press, 23 March 2016.

13. Hishaam D. Aidi, 'Jihadis in the Hood: Race, Urban Islam and the War on Terror', in Manning Marable and Hishaam D. Aidi, eds, *Black Routes to Islam*, New York: Palgrave Macmillan, 2009.

14. On this aspect, see Judith Butler and Athena Athanasiou, *Dispossession: The Performative in the Political*, London: Polity, 2013.

15. Diane E. Davis, 'Non-State Armed Actors, New Imagined Communities and the Shifting Patterns of Sovereignty and Insecurity in the Modern World', *Contemporary Security Policy*, 30, 2, August 2009, p. 227.

16. Michael North, *Novelty: A History of the New*, Chicago: Chicago University Press, 2013, p. 3, emphasis added.

17. Dominic Thomas, *Africa and France: Postcolonial Cultures, Migration and Racism*, Indianapolis: Indiana University Press, 2013, p. 4; Laurent Dubois, 'La République Métissée: Citizenship, Colonialism and the Borders of French History', in Stephen Howe, ed., *The New Imperial History Reader*, London: Routledge, 2010, p. 424.

18. Farhad Khosrokhavar, 'Jihad and the French Exception', *New York Times*, 19 July 2016.

19. Cornel West, 'Black Postmodernist Practices: Interview with Anders Stephanson', in *The Cornel West Reader*, New York: Civitas, p. 288.

20. See, for instance, Elvire Camus, 'Marine, Convertie à l'Islam: "Je Suis Toujours la Même, en Mieux"', *Le Monde*, Paris, 19 March 2016. Pre-IS cases include Alexandre D. (last name withheld), a convert to Islam, arrested in May 2013 in Paris for stabbing a French soldier; and David Drugeon, a 24-year-old from Brittany accused of joining the Al Qaeda-affiliated group Jund al Khilafa in Pakistan in 2012 and, subsequently, travelling to Syria to join the rebellion against Assad.

21. See, as well, the film *Pour l'Amour de Dieu* (2006). The appeal of rebellion on the part of individuals from the metropolis joining battlefronts of southern operators has a long history. In French-occupied Algeria, for instance, a number of Frenchmen and Frenchwomen helped the National Liberation Front struggle. See Natalya Vince, 'Transgressing Boundaries: Gender, Race, Religion and "Françaises Musulmanes" during the Algerian War of Independence', *French Historical Studies*, 33, 3, Summer 2010, pp. 445–75.

22. See, in the American context of the late 1960s and early 1970s, James A. Tyner, 'Defend the Ghetto: Space and the Urban Politics of the Black Panther Party', *Annals of the Association of American Geographers*, 96, 1, 2006, pp. 105–18.

23. Tarak Barkawi, 'Decolonising War', p. 212.

24. Tarak Barkawi, 'On the Pedagogy of Small Wars' *International Affairs*, 80, 1, 2004, p. 20, emphasis added.

25. Chris Hedges, *Empire of Illusion*, p. 16.

26. Joseph A. Massad, *Islam in Liberalism*, Chicago: University of Chicago Press, 2015, p. 313.

27. Chris Hedges, *Wages of Rebellion: The Moral Imperative of Rebellion*, New York: Nation Books, 2015, p. 20.

28. Christopher Coker, 'Metrowars: The Shape of Future Wars', in Caroline Holmqvist-Jonsäter and Christopher Coker, eds, *The Character of War in the 21st Century*, London: Routledge, 2010, p. 121.

29. Aziz al Azmeh, *Islam and Modernities*, London: Verso, 1993, p. 2.

30. David Theo Goldberg, *Racist Culture: Philosophy and the Politics of Meaning*, Cambridge, Massachusetts: Blackwell, 1993, pp. 6–7, original emphasis.

31. Talal Asad, *Genealogies of Religion: Discipline and Reasons of Power in Christianity and Islam*, Baltimore: Johns Hopkins University Press, 1993, p. 13, emphasis added.

32. Patrick Simon, 'Race, Ethnicisation et Discriminations: Une Répétition de l'Histoire ou une Singularité Postcoloniale?', in Nicolas Bancel et al., *Ruptures Postcoloniales: Les Nouveaux Visages de la Société Française*, Paris: La Découverte, 2010, p. 360, author's translation.

33. See Laurent Obertone, *La France Orange Mécanique*, Paris: Ring, 2013. Borrowing the societal violence imagery of Stanley Kubrick's film *A Clockwork Orange*, the book is both an indication of the nature of that drift in French society and a compendium of the rampant disorder building up in recent years in the country.

34. See Éric Zemmour, *Un Quinquennat pour Rien*, Paris: Albin Michel, 2016. Also see Hacène Belmessous, *Opérations Banlieues: Comment l'État Prépare la Guerre Urbaine dans les Cités Françaises*, Paris: La Découverte, 2011; and, more generally, David A. Bell, *Shadows of Revolution: Reflections on France, Past and Present*. New York: Oxford University Press, 2016.

35. See Bryan Burrough, *Days of Rage: America's Radical Underground, the FBI and the Forgotten Age of Revolutionary Violence*, New York: Penguin, 2015; and the review article by James Lardner, 'The Years of Rage', *New York Review of Books*, 62, 14, 24 September 2015, pp. 60–3.

36. See Chamberlin, *The Global Offensive*; and, for an early conceptualisation, Riyad Najib Al-Rayyis, *Guerrillas for Palestine*, New York: Palgrave, 1976.

37. As Bryan Burrough remarks in his study of this period: 'Imagine if this happened today: Hundreds of young Americans – white, black and Hispanic – disappear from their everyday lives and secretly form urban guerrilla groups. Dedicated to confronting the government and righting society's wrongs, they smuggle bombs into skyscrapers and federal buildings and detonate them from coast to coast. They strike inside the Pentagon, inside the US Capitol, at a courthouse in Boston, at dozens of multinational corporations, at a Wall Street restaurant packed with lunchtime diners. People die. They rob banks, dozens of them, launch raids on National Guard arsenals and assassinate policemen, in New York, in San Francisco, in Atlanta … This was a slice of America during the tumultuous 1970s.' See *Days of Rage*, p. 3. Also see Christopher Hewitt, *Political Violence and Terrorism in Modern America*, Westport, Connecticut: Praeger Security International, 2005; Rob Kirkpatrick, *1969: The Year Everything Changed*, New York: Skyhorse, 2009; and Andreas Killen, *1973 Nervous Breakdown: Watergate, Warhol and the Birth of Post-Sixties America*, New York: Bloomsbury, 2006.

38. Cited in Burrough, *Days of Rage*, p. 4. Also see, for similar accounts of a war-like experience, John Bryan, *This Soldier Still at War*, New York: Harcourt Brace Jovanovich, 1975; and Ahmad Muhammad, *We Will Return in the Whirlwind: Black Radical Organisations, 1960–1975*, Chicago: Charles H. Kerr Publishing Company, 2007.

39. Philip Jenkins, *Decade of Nightmares: The End of the Sixties and the Making of Eighties America*, New York: Oxford University Press, 2006, p. 5.

40. Examples include Jeffrey Toobin, *American Heiress: The Wild Saga of the Kidnapping, Crimes and Trial of Patty Hearst*, New York: Doubleday, 2016; and Brendan I. Koerner, *The Skies Belong to Us: Love and Terror in the Golden Age of Hijacking*, New York: Broadway Books, 2014.

41. See Carol Anderson, *White Rage: The Unspoken Truth of Our Racial Divide*, New York: Bloomsbury, 2016.

42. Pape et al., 'The American Face of ISIS'.

43. *New York Times*, 3 October 1962, p. A30.

44. On the under-studied geopolitical thinking of Malcolm X, see James A. Tyner and Robert J. Kruse II, 'The Geopolitics of Malcolm X', *Antipode*, 36, 1, January 2004, pp. 24–42; and Saladin Ambar, *Malcolm X at Oxford: Racial Politics in a Global Era*. New York: Oxford University Press, 2014.

45. Sohail Daulatzai, *Black Star, Crescent Moon: The Muslim International and Black Freedom beyond America*, Minneapolis, Minnesota: University of Minnesota Press, 2012.

46. Sam Greenlee, *Baghdad Blues: The Revolution that Brought Saddam Hussein to Power*, New York: Bantam Books, 1976. The book was reprinted in 1991 after the invasion of Iraq.

47. https://mappingpoliceviolence.org/.

48. Andrea F. Siegel, 'Malvo Sketches Depicted "Jihad"', *Baltimore Sun*, 4 December 2003.

49. As Ronald N. Jacobs remarks: 'If ever a case can be made for the existence of separate public spheres, *from the beginning*, African-American history provides it' (original emphasis); in his *Race, Media and the Crisis of Civil Society: From Watts to Rodney King*, Cambridge: Cambridge University Press, 2000, p. 20.

50. Spencer Ackerman, 'Guantánamo Torturer Led Brutal Chicago Regime of Shackling and Confession' and 'Bad Lieutenant: American Police Brutality, Exported from Chicago to Guantánamo', *Guardian*, both on 18 February 2015.

51. Su'ad Abdul Khabeer, 'Islam on Trial: Response', *Boston Review*, February 2017.

52. Comments in *The 13th*, documentary directed by Ava DuVernay, Netflix, 2017, emphasis added. Also see Rebecca C. Hetey and Jennifer L. Eberhardt, 'Racial Disparities in Incarceration Increase Acceptance of Punitive Policies', *Psychological Science*, 25, 10, 2014, pp. 1949–54.

53. 'It's a Scary Time for the World, Says Martin Scorsese', *Belfast Telegraph*, 24 February 2017.

54. Lorenzo Vidino, Seth Harrison and Clarissa Spada, 'ISIS and Al Shabaab in Minnesota's Twin Cities: The American Hotbed', in Arturo Varvelli, ed., *Jihadist Hotbeds: Understanding Local Radicalisation Processes*, Milan: ISPI, 2016, p. 48.

55. As Radley Balko notes: 'Pop culture has always had a big influence on police culture, sometimes reflecting prevailing sentiment and sometimes driving it.' See his *Rise of the Warrior Cop: The Militarisation of America's Police Forces*, New York: Public Affairs, 2013, p. 304.

56. See Steve Herbert, *Policing Space: Territoriality and the Los Angeles Police Department*, Minneapolis, Minnesota: University of Minnesota Press, 1994. More generally, David Storey, *Territory: The Claiming of Space*, London: Prentice-Hall, 2001.

57. Matt Apuzzo, 'War Gear Flows to Police Departments', *New York Times*, 8 June 2014. Generally on this issue, see the work of Professor Pete Kraska at the School of Justice Studies at Eastern Kentucky University.

58. Dana Priest and William M. Arkin, *Top Secret America: The Rise of the New American Security State*, New York: Little, Brown and Company, 2011, p. 262; and Frank Donner, *Protectors of Privilege: Red Squads and Police Repression in Urban America*, Berkeley, California: University of California Press, 1990.

Conclusion

1. See, for instance, Anonymous, 'The Mystery of ISIS', *New York Review of Books*, 13 August 2015. The author argues that 'nothing since the triumph of the Vandals in Roman North Africa has seemed so sudden, incomprehensible and difficult to reverse as the rise of ISIS ... None of our analysts, soldiers, diplomats, intelligence officers, politicians or journalists has yet produced an explanation rich enough – even in hindsight – to have predicted the movement's rise ... the clearest evidence that we do not understand this phenomenon is our consistent inability to predict ... these developments', that 'much of what ISIS has done clearly contradicts the moral intuitions and principles of many of its supporters' and that 'the thinkers, tacticians and leaders of the movement we know as ISIS are not great strategists'. In fact, the rise of IS followed logically from the insistent post-9/11 sequence, its actions were in sync with its militants' variegated dispositions and its senior and mid-level management operated strategically. For a critique of that article, see Costantino Pischedda, 'A Provocative Article Says the Islamic State is a Mystery: Here is Why That's Wrong', *Washington Post*, 27 August 2015.

2. Walter Mignolo, 'Yes We Can', Foreword to Hamid Dabashi, *Can Non-Europeans Think?*, London: Zed Books, 2015, p. x.

3. Marwan M. Kraidy, 'Terror, Territoriality, Temporality: Hypermedia Events in the Age of the Islamic State', *Television and News Media*, March 2017, p. 2.

4. As Kalpana Seshadri-Crooks notes, 'the notion of the margin as a site of struggle for the outermost limit ... is fetishized and reified as the ... authoritative critical position', in 'At the Margins of Postcolonial Studies', *Ariel*, 26, 3, July 1995, p. 66.

5. David E. Apter, 'Political Violence in Analytical Perspective', in David E. Apter, ed., *The Legitimisation of Violence*, London: MacMillan, 1997, p. 24.

6. Frank Furedi, *The Silent War: Imperialism and the Changing Perception of Race*, London, Pluto Press, 1998.

7. See Caroline Elkins, *Imperial Reckoning: The Untold Story of Britain's Gulag in Kenya*, New York: Henry Holt and Company, 2005; and David Anderson, *Histories of the Hanged: Britain's Dirty War in Kenya and the End of Empire*, London: Weidenfeld & Nicolson, 2013.

8. See Bill Kelleher, 'Ambivalence, Modernity and the State of Terror in Northern Ireland', *Political and Legal Anthropology Review*, 17, 1, 1994, pp. 31–40; Geraint Hugues, 'Militias in Internal Warfare: From the Colonial Era to the Contemporary Middle East', *Small Wars and Insurgencies*, 27, 2, 2016, pp. 196–225; and Frank Foley, *Countering Terrorism in Britain and France: Institutions, Norms and the Shadow of the Past*, Cambridge: Cambridge University Press, 2015.

9. Thomas E. Ricks, 'Are US Immigration Centres the Next Abu Ghraib?', *New York Times*, 27 February 2017.

10. Fanon writes: '[T]he colonial context is characterised by the dichotomy which it imposes upon the whole people', in *The Wretched of the Earth*, New York: Grove Press, 1968, p. 45.

11. See Catherine Hall and Sonya Rose, eds, *At Home with Empire: Metropolitan Culture and the Imperial World*, Cambridge: Cambridge University Press, 2006. On the materialisation of these dynamics, also see Sandip Hazareesingh, *The Colonial City and the Challenge of Modernity: Urban Hegemonies and Civic Contestations in Bombay, 1900–1925*, Hyderabad: Orient Longman, 2007. Herfried Münkler remarks that the new forms of imperial domination are 'not to be confused with rehabilitation of the old colonial empires'. They are not, in a literal sense, but the logic of dominion, control, dispossession, representation and violence is quite the same. See his *Empires: The Logic of World Domination from Ancient Rome to the United States*, London: Polity, 2007, p. ix.

12. Eric Fair, 'I Can't Be Forgiven for Abu Ghraib', *International New York Times*, 11 December 2014, p. 6.

13. Archibald Paton Thornton, *The Imperial Idea and its Enemies: A Study on British Power*, London: Macmillan, 1959; and Niall Ferguson, *Empire: The Rise and Demise of British World Order and the Lessons for Global Power*, London: Allen Lane, 2002. As Jennifer Pitts noted: 'the emergence of support for the violent conquest and despotic rule of non-Europeans in the mid-nineteenth century, among thinkers normally celebrated not only for their respect for human equality and liberty but also for their pluralism, implicates the liberal tradition, at this moment in its history, in an inegalitarian and decidedly non-humanitarian international politics', Pitts, *A Turn to Empire*, p. 240.

14. Paul Johnson, 'Colonialism's Back and Not a Moment Too Soon', *New York Times Magazine*, 18 April 1993; Robert D. Kaplan, 'It's Time to Bring Imperialism Back to the Middle East', *Foreign Affairs*, 25 May 2015.

15. Elizabeth A. Povinelli, 'The Governance of the Prior', *Interventions*, 13, 1, 2011, p. 16, emphasis added.

16. Stephen M. Walt, 'What Should We Do if the Islamic State Wins? Live With It', *Foreign Policy*, 10 June 2015. Vadim Nikitim, 'Why It's Time to Grant ISIS Diplomatic Recognition', *Independent*, 15 December 2015.

17. David Remnick, 'Going the Distance: On and Off the Road with Barack Obama', *New Yorker*, 27 January 2014. In a 7 September 2014 interview with NBC's *Meet the Press*, President Obama said later that he 'was not specifically referring to [IS]'.

18. Paul Rogers, *Irregular War: ISIS and the New Threat from the Margins*, London: I.B.Tauris, 2016, p. 152, emphasis added.

19. In Germany, in particular, this presence traces its roots back to the post-World War II period. See Ian Johnson, *A Mosque in Munich: Nazis, the CIA and the Rise of the Muslim Brotherhood in the West*, New York: Mariner Books, 2010.

20. See Mevliyar Er, 'Abd-el-Krim al-Khattabi: The Unknown Mentor of Che Guevara', *Terrorism and Political Violence*, 29, 2017, pp. 137–59.

21. Sean Mills, *The Empire Within: Postcolonial Thought and Political Activism in Sixties Montreal*, Montreal: McGill-Queen's University Press, 2010, pp. 19–20.

22. US Department of Homeland Security, 'Right-Wing Extremism: Current Economic and Political Climate Fueling Resurgence in Radicalisation and Recruitment', Office of Intelligence Analysis Assessment, 7 April 2009, p. 7.

23. Stephen Graham, *Cities Under Siege: The New Military Urbanism*, London: Verso, 2010, pp. xiii–xiv, emphasis added. Within 'a seemingly neutral and impartial acceleration of life – the unprecedented speed of life and social change implying the loss of memory and moral amnesia – … a citizen becomes a consumer and value-neutrality hides the fact of disengagement'; see Zygmunt Bauman and Leonidas Donskis, *Liquid Evil*, London: Polity, 2016, p. 3.

24. Stephen Graham, 'When Life Itself is War: On the Urbanisation of Military and Security Doctrine', *International Journal of Urban and Regional Research*, 36, 1, 2012, p. 149. Also see James Risen, *Pay Any Price: Greed, Power and Endless War*, New York: Mariner Books, 2015.

25. See Lars Dittmer, *New Evil: The Joker in 'The Dark Knight' as a Prototype of the Post-September 11 Villain*, Norderstedt, Germany: GRIN, 2009. Generally, Hollywood films 'played a vital role in imagining the universe and in shaping the vocabulary; defining the images, metaphors and tropes; and establishing the mental maps, archetypes, mind-sets and emotional framework through which most Americans came to think about themselves, their country and national security'; see Dan O'Meara, Alex Macleod, Frédérick Gagnon and David Grondin, *Movies, Myth and the National Security State*, Boulder, Colorado: Lynne Rienner, 2016, p. 4.

26. Michael Pesek, 'The Colonial Order Upside Down? British and Germans in East African Prisoner-of-War Camps During World War I', in Ulrike Lindner, Maren Mohring, Mark Stein and Silke Stroh, eds, *Hybrid Cultures,*

Nervous States: Britain and Germany in a (Post)Colonial World, Amsterdam: Rodopi, 2010, p. 25.

27. See Douglas Kellner, 'Media Spectacle and Domestic Terrorism: The Case of the Batman/Joker Cinema Massacre', *Review of Education, Pedagogy and Cultural Studies*, 35, 3, 2013, pp. 157–77.

28. Nick Turse, *The Complex: Mapping America's Military-Industrial-Technological-Entertainment-Academic-Media-Corporate Matrix*, New York: Metropolitan Books, 2008. Also see Andrew J. Bacevich, *The New American Militarism: How Americans are Seduced by War*, New York: Oxford University Press, 2005.

29. Karen Dawisha, 'Imperialism, Dependency and Autocolonialism in the Eurasian Space', in Ken Booth, ed., *Statecraft and Security: The Cold War and Beyond*, Cambridge: Cambridge University Press, 1998, p. 166.

30. This is the term used by Lisa Stampnitzky in her *Disciplining Terror: How Experts Invented 'Terrorism'* Cambridge: Cambridge University Press, 2013, p. 109.

31. Rodolfo Kusch, *Pensamiento Indigena y Popular en América*, Buenos Aires: Puebla, José M. Cajica, Jr., 1970; Walter Mignolo, 'Introduction: Immigrant Consciousness', in Rodolfo Kusch, *Indigenous and Popular Thinking in America*, trans. María Lugones and Joshua M. Price, Durham, North Carolina: Duke University Press, 2010, pp. xiii–liv.

32. Hamid Dabashi, *Can Non-Europeans Think?*, London: Verso, 2015, p. 11.

33. Matt McDonald, 'Emancipation and Critical Terrorism Studies', in Richard Jackson, Marie Breen Smyth and Jeroen Gunning, eds, *Critical Terrorism Studies: A New Research Agenda*, London: Routledge, 2009, p. 111.

34. See Siba Grovogui, 'Time, Technology and the Imperial Eye', in Anna M. Agathangelou and Kyle D. Killian, eds, *Time, Temporality and Violence: (De)fatalising the Present, Forging Radical Alternatives*, London: Routledge, 2016, pp. 45–60.

35. See Pamela L. Bunker, Lisa J. Campbell and Robert Bunker, 'Torture, Beheading and Narcocultos', *Small Wars and Insurgencies*, 21, 1, 2010, pp. 145–78; Shawn T. Flanigan, 'Terrorists Next Door? A Comparison of Mexican Drug Cartels and Middle Eastern Terrorist Organisations', *Terrorism and Political Violence*, 24, 2, 2012, pp. 279–94; and Eric Alda and Joseph L. Sala, 'Links between Terrorism, Organised Crime and Crime: The Case of the Sahel Region', *Stability: International Journal of Security and Development*, 3, 1, 27, 2014, pp. 1–9. Also see the 2015 film *Sicario* by Denis Villeneuve.

36. See Makau Mutua, *Human Rights: A Political and Cultural Critique*, Philadelphia: University of Pennsylvania Press, 2002; and Frédéric Megret, 'From "Savages" to "Unlawful Combatants": A Post-Colonial Look at International Law's Other', in Anne Orford, ed., *International Law and its Others*, Cambridge: Cambridge University Press, 2006, pp. 265–317.

37. See Henry A. Giroux, *The Violence of Organised Forgetting: Thinking Beyond America's Disimagination Machine*, San Francisco: City Lights Books, 2014.

Index